Advance praise for *Two Minutes for God*

"Reverend Peter Panagore's charming, humorous, and profound stories support our relationship with God by connecting us to our own selves and to each other. It is because of Panagore's compassion for the human experience that we gain a deeper understanding of life and how to live it. This is the art of storytelling at its best!"

—SUSAN DEY, ACTRESS

TOUCHSTONE

FAITH

Two Minutes

for God

QUICK FIXES FOR THE SPIRIT

REVEREND PETER B. PANAGORE

A Touchstone Faith Book
Published by Simon & Schuster
New York   London   Toronto   Sydney

Touchstone Faith
A Division of Simon & Schuster, Inc.
1230 Avenue of the Americas
New York, NY 10020

First Touchstone Faith paperback edition December 2007

TOUCHSTONE FAITH and colophon are registered trademarks of Simon & Schuster, Inc.

For information about special discounts for bulk purchases, please contact Simon & Schuster Special Sales at 1-800-456-6798 or business@simonandschuster.com.

Designed by Mary Austin Speaker

Manufactured in the United States of America

10   9   8   7   6   5   4   3   2   1

Library of Congress Cataloging-in-Publication Data
Panagore, Peter Baldwin.
    Two minutes for God: quick fixes for the spirit / by Peter Baldwin Panagore
        p. cm.
    "A Touchstone Faith book."
1. Fasts and feasts—Meditations. 2. Holidays—Meditations. I.Title.
    BL590.P36 2008
    204'.32—dc22   2007033458

ISBN-13: 978-1-4165-3826-4
ISBN-10:   1-4165-3826-7

Contents

Introduction

People ask me, "Are your stories true?" I reply, "Yes, absolutely they are—except for the parts that aren't, and I won't tell you which parts."

This collection of devotional stories comes from real life. They are tales about me, my neighbors, my friends, my family, people I know, and people I don't know. Stories come from paintings and films I've seen, and from poems, essays, and books I've read. There might even be a yarn about you. Folks in the harbor town where I live are always trying to figure out which story is about them or me (and I keep them guessing about that). The stories in this book were originally written for broadcast on a TV program called *Daily Devotions,* which is seen during the morning news on the two NBC affiliates in Maine every day. *Daily Devotions,* aka the First Radio Parish Church of America, has been on radio since 1926 and on TV since 1954. You can also find us at www.dailydevotions.org.

Why stories? Human beings have been telling stories to one another since we discovered language, because we reveal ourselves through stories and because the Teacher told stories. I quote the Teacher frequently, often paraphrasing his remarks to capture a subtle meaning, to ease reading, or to fit with my conversational style of writing. No matter how simple my stories may seem, I hope they illuminate a tiny piece of the sacred that exists inside the secular. It seems to be working because one day while shopping for boots at the L.L. Bean store in Freeport, Maine, a salesclerk told me that the *Daily Devotions* stories he watches on TV are like shiny little nuggets he carries with him in his pocket all day. It was kind of him to say so, but it's not for me to say exactly what the stories are or aren't to those who hear or read them.

The notes provided for many entries correspond to Scripture, but the message is God's job, not mine. I'm just a storyteller winding my way through life on my way home.

The Teacher said heaven was his home—I think it is mine and yours, too.

My prayer for you is this: may this book help lead you home, and, in the meantime, may God be with you every day in every way.

Two Minutes

Every Day

*P*eople ask, "Why did *you* [usually said with some measure of disbelief] become a minister?" It's selfish. I want God. I went into ministry thinking it's the perfect public cover for a private spiritual life of seeking God. What other job is there where I get paid cash to pray? (It's never much cash, but . . .) Prayer looks so much like . . . doing nothing . . . that it's a wonder I've gotten away with it for as long as I have. As often as I can, I stop whatever I am doing and sit still. I close my eyes, and from the outside it looks worse than my doing nothing in the middle of a workday. It looks like I'm sleeping. Truthfully, sometimes I do fall asleep, but it's rare, and when that happens, it's no longer prayer, it's a power nap!

Prayer can feel like doing nothing. Prayer sometimes appears so unproductive. At the end of a long, hot, hard day of prayer, what do I have to show for it? Sore knees? That's the strange thing about prayer. It looks like it's unproductive, yet in my own life, prayer remains the basis of my connection to God. When I take time to pray, God blesses my days; when I don't take time to pray, I excel at making a fine mess.

Let's Pray:

God help us find time to pray, if not now, then when? Amen.

Today's Thought Is: Seek heaven first;
everything else comes after that.[1]

Spying a flock of herring gulls standing on the low-tide beach, the dog would sprint right at them, his paws coming down hard on the packed wet sand, water and foam splashing, his tail flying straight out behind him like a banner of honor. They'd wait for him, watching his approach, talking among themselves, laughing really, and joking as herring gulls noisily do. They'd linger until the last moment and, then, leap together skyward, twirl once above his head, and finally fly off a distance, land in the sand, and wait for him to charge again. He'd chase all day, but never, not once, in ten years of trying, did he ever catch a single gull. Was he smart enough to understand the game? Every time he chased a flock, did he believe that, this time, he'd catch one? Whatever he thought, at the end of each exhausting run, he'd come home, his tail relaxed and wagging, with a smile on his snout. Chasing gulls made him happy. Maybe catching them never mattered to him. Maybe he just loved the process.

In the practice of the spiritual life, there is no catching heaven. It's always just out of reach. All we ever do is pursue it, learn to love the chase, and enjoy the quest.

Let's Pray:

Dear God, we ask that at the end of each day, our spiritual journey leaves us optimistic and wanting more. Keep us tantalized. Amen.

Today's Thought Is: "Aim at Heaven and you will get Earth 'thrown in'; aim at Earth and you will get neither."[2]

*L*ong ago two brothers owned a house on the eastern side of Linekin Bay. They decided to move it to the western side. Small-minded folk scoffed. One cold winter the bay froze deep and solid. The brothers jacked up the house, put it on skids, and dragged it by oxen to the bay's edge. Each day they'd walk a couple dozen yards from the house, auger a hole in the ice, place in an anchor, and, using a block and tackle, would winch it and inch it westward. At day's end they'd hike home, eat dinner, and go to bed. The next day they'd rise with the winter sun, then repeat the process.

All winter the house sat and slid and sat and slid across the bay. Each day they hauled it closer to their goal. Before spring, they'd placed it on its new foundation. These men had faith—in God, themselves, and the weather. They had a goal. They worked hard for their success and no doubt celebrated when they were done.

What's worth having is worth working toward. It may take daring. It may include risk. It certainly requires vision and hard work. No one succeeds without taking a chance. It may even look as foolish as working a house across a frozen bay seemed to many. Keeping faith in God is like this. It takes risk and work. It takes challenging cultural convention and being willing to be scoffed at, having a goal, being determined, and seeing what others can't.

Let's Pray.

God, keep us up to the challenge. Give us grace to stick to our faith and be stubborn enough to reach our goal. Amen.

Today's Thought Is: **Keep your eye on the prize.**

*I*t's not a killer outfit. The Barbie clothes kept this lobster alive since September. A blue Barbie blouse, a red-and-white-checkered skirt, and pink spike heels isn't normal autumn wear for a lobster living in the channel off Mount Desert Island, Maine. "You try squeezing Barbie shoes on a lobster," one lobsterman said. As a joke a couple of lobstermen drove over to Ellsworth, bought a Barbie outfit, later hauled up a friend's trap, dressed up a pound-and-a-half lobster, put the fancy "bug" back in the trap, and then reset it. Barbie Lobster was caught ten times but was always set free because of her sense of style. The last time she was caught she was a bit disheveled, with just her pink spike heels hanging on. If she survives the winter, local lobsterman have got her spring fashions ready to go.[3]

Certainly, nobody mistook this crustacean for a real Barbie doll. (I probably didn't need to point that out.) However, sometimes the clothes or the coverings charlatans wear fool us all. We might be taken in by slick talk, apparent wealth, good looks, or our own dreams and weaknesses. The good Rabbi warns us about people purposefully disguising their true intentions while hoping to gobble us whole. Maybe they're after our savings account, maybe they want our virtue, maybe they want our minds and souls to control. He warns us to beware those false spiritual types who come disguised and prettified as harmless, but who are really sharp-clawed predators capable of tearing us apart.

Let's Pray:

Dear God, keep us safe from manipulators and con artists who prey on the meager means of the elderly and the souls of the innocent. Amen.

Today's Thought Is: **A façade conceals intention.**[4]

*D*o you remember the cartoon when Daffy Duck crawls in a desert gasping, "Water, water"? He spies water in a pool. Gulps it down. Spits it out. It's sand. Mirages aren't only in cartoons, or deserts. On hot summer days there are mirages of pools shimmering on our black-topped roadways. In winter, when seawater is warmer than cold air, we may see mirages of real islands suddenly floating above the ocean on cushions of sky. Deep-sea sailors tell tales of mirages, too. There are towering cities hovering on the horizon, always just out of reach, and there are ships that seemingly sail upside down

A mirage is a trick of physics. It's the refracting—the bending—of light through layers of hot and cold air. Although we can photograph mirages, they are illusions. They are not there.

God may seem like an illusion, a figment of imagination. God can't be seen. God can't be photographed. God can seem to be always out there, somewhere, just beyond reach. But unlike mirages, God is not a trick of the light. For those who have been touched by God, no vision—no photo—is necessary. For doubters, only proof will convince them.

That's too bad. There is no proof—except ancient writings, millions of believers, and the human heart. It's in the heart, not the eye, where God is found. It's as the Teacher said, "Search, and you will find. Knock, and the door will be opened."[5]

Let's Pray:

Dear God, sometimes we need a reminder of your living presence; sometimes just hint of your existence would help. Give us a chance, God; touch our hearts with your light, that only hearts can see. Amen.

Today's Thought Is: God is Light.

A duck walks into a post office and asks the mistress, "Do you have any grapes?"

She says, "No."

The next day the duck walks into the post office and asks, "Do you have any grapes?"

She says, "You asked yesterday. No grapes!"

The next day the duck walks in and asks, "Do you have any grapes?"

She says, "No. If you come back asking that question, I'm going to nail you to this wall."

The next day the duck comes back and asks, "Do you have any nails?"

She says, "No. I don't have nails."

"Good," says the duck. "Do you have any grapes?"

Persistence. It's a trait we like in ourselves but aren't thrilled to see in others—in ducks, for instance.

A woman had a problem a judge could solve. After work, she'd drive over to the judge's house, knock on his door, and demand justice. This particular judge didn't bother to answer his door. Every night this woman drove across town to knock on the judge's door. Eventually she smartened up. She went over late one night after everybody was asleep, and she pounded on the door until she woke him up. Then pounded more until he finally said to himself, "By glory, if I don't go down and give this woman justice, she's gonna wear me out."

God also responds to persistence. Whatever it is, don't give up.

Lord, when we feel like quitting, when we feel like giving up, don't let us. Give us the persistence we need when we are trying to deepen our spiritual lives.

Amen.

Today's Thought Is: Persistence is a necessary spiritual virtue.

One spring, when I was a boy, my neighbor Mrs. Porter found a fluffy duckling. She took him home and named him Hamilton. Hamilton lived on her screen porch in a wooden box padded with rags. After school, I'd visit Hamilton. Hamilton learned to eat from my hand, played hide-and-seek among the chair legs, quacked hello when I arrived, and quacked good-bye when I left. In the summer, as Hamilton grew larger, I'd walk him on a leash on the sidewalk.

"Funny-looking dog," another neighbor said every time I walked that duck.

In September, I'd run a mile home from school, say a quick hello to my mom, then off I'd go to visit Hamilton. One October day I met Mrs. Porter on her front steps. A flock of mallards quacked in flight over head. We looked up.

She said, "I've been waiting for you, Peter. This morning Hamilton started quacking and hasn't stopped."

I understood. Hamilton was leaving. We went out into her front yard. I held Hamilton in my arms. Mrs. Porter said, "Hamilton is a wild duck. He should be with other ducks. He will fly south with new friends." That said, I sadly tossed Hamilton into the air. Off he sped quacking, joining the ducks headed south.

Children go off to school—young ones to kindergarten and older ones to college. Some are off to a full-time job, others to marriage and their own households, others to the military. It's hard to let them go, but it's necessary and important. No matter how much we love our children, and need them near us, there comes a time when we must let go.

Let's Pray.

Dear God, protect our children, be they young or old. Let them know we love them no matter where they go. Amen.

Today's Thought Is: Teach children how they should live, and they will remember it all their lives.[6]

I wear a helmet when I ride my bicycle. My kids gave it to me. It's a yellow helmet with a black visor. Although it's lightweight, it's still hot, uncomfortable, and not all that attractive as hats go. Truthfully, I prefer the wind blowing through my hair (or through what I have left of my hair). Still, it's a wonderful helmet.

One day in Boston traffic a car in front of me suddenly stopped. I hit him with my bike, sliding halfway up his roof. No harm done: no dents, no damage. Didn't really need my helmet, but I'm glad I had it on.

Another day while biking in Maine, speeding down a hill, all crouched and quick, my wheels caught in a ditch that ended abruptly with a very small wall. I braked too late and slammed my front wheel into the wall. My bike flipped upside down; I went heels over helmet. I hit the ground with just enough time to tuck and roll. I landed on my feet, bruised and a bit torn but not broken. My helmet was my skull's salvation.

What if, instead of wearing my helmet, I had had it strapped on the back of my bike? It wouldn't have done me any good. Often by the time we need faith, we're already in trouble. Faith is like a bike helmet. It works better if we put it on before we need it, even if it is a bit uncomfortable or looks uncool.

Let's Pray:

God, give us the protection of faith today so we'll be ready just in case. Amen.

Today's Thought Is: **Faith works.**

One dark and foggy night I cut across the lawn coming home from church. Nearing our deck I heard an animal eating from the dog's bowl by the back door. Figuring it was my faithful pooch, I decided to see how good a watchdog he was. I snuck up, leapt over the railing, and landed next to his bowl. It was a skunk who proceeded to spray me point-blank. I can't say who was more surprised.

First thing I did was go inside to tell my wife, who immediately sniffed the trouble and yelled at me, "OUT, OUT, OUT!" Outside I took off my clothes and thankfully discovered the nasty stench never reached my skin. The next day I was set to burn, bury, or otherwise destroy my jeans, shirt, and jean jacket. The phone rang. It was an old church lady who, having heard about the big event, called to say, "Best thing to do is hang 'em in the fog for a month. They'll be clean, by and by." I did, and she was right. It turns out Maine fog brightens whites, as well.

Life can toss us an unpleasant surprise now and again. Generally speaking, older folks have seen it all and know a thing or two about dealing with trouble. Faith communities—like churches and synagogues—are some of the few places in our society where the young and the old can interact. They're fine places to learn things you never thought you needed to know.

Let's Pray:

God, we thank you for the wisdom of our elders and the chance to learn from them. Amen.

Today's Thought Is: Get to know someone of a different generation.

*T*he belt in our dryer broke when a wet sneaker got jammed in the drum. It took weeks to get to the store to buy a new belt, then there was finding the time actually to install it.

Cars break down. Lightbulbs burn out. Switches short. Pants tear. Buttons pop off. Dishes shatter. Things break. Most are things we can fix—we glue, nail, mend, repair, or replace.

But abused children get broken on the inside. The wound is hard to see, hard to name, hard to fix. Children are not as durable as they may seem. Their parts aren't replaceable and can't be repaired with glue. When a heart is broken, when trust is shattered, it takes a long, long time, and great amounts of love and care, to mend it. Forever there are scars.

Often abuse gets passed from parents to children down through the generations. In this case, the wounds of the parents get passed on to the children.

It doesn't have to be this way. If you, as an adult, are broken on the inside from what happened to you as a child, and you find yourself struggling, seek help. Children, if there is abuse in your family or among your friends, or you are a victim, talk to a minister, a doctor, or a teacher.

End the cycle.

Let's Pray:

God bless the children who are abused, and bless their parents, too.
Heal their hearts and let them find help in you. Amen.

Today's Thought Is: God heals broken people.

*T*he Alakai swamp on the island of Kauai is the rainiest spot on Earth, receiving more than four hundred inches of rain a year. It is a forest filled with amazing plants. There are ferns that top seven feet in height whose fiddleheads are as thick as my wrist.

It's beautiful, but it can be dangerous. One day a man, covered in mud up to his shoulders, missing a shoe, came stumbling out. He'd been backpacking in the swamp when heavy rains arrived. Hiking out on the path, he sank in mud like quicksand, which threatened to swallow him whole. During the night it swallowed his pack and his shoe. By morning he barely escaped with his life, and then only because strangers helped him.

Bliss and beauty can quickly turn to trouble when we get stuck in the mud of dangerous relationships. Domestic violence, like quicksand, threatens to swallow women whole. It's hard to get out. It may feel impossible. It's like darkness has descended, and there is no escape.

But there is escape. No woman, no man, deserves abuse—verbal, physical, emotional, or otherwise. It is not easy, but there is a way out.

The trained counselors at any domestic violence shelter are there to help you. Many women I know personally, and a few men, have been saved from domestic violence by calling their local shelter. Shelters provide a safe path out of the swamp and darkness of domestic violence. Call today. Dial 911 or phone the National Domestic Violence Hotline: 1-800-799-SAFE (7233). Don't wait.

Let's Pray:

God, be with the women and men who are fearful of their spouses.
Help them act to save themselves. Amen.

Today's Thought Is: There is no excuse for domestic violence.

*T*here is a young fellow who teaches kids to play championship basketball. He's unique. As far as I know, he's never shot a hoop in his life. Never dribbled a ball. Can't pass. Can't run. But he understands the game, and he teaches it well. The kids listen, learn, and win. I'm sure he'd say he gets more out of it than he puts into it. Beyond all that—this respected coach teaches b-ball while seated in his electric wheelchair.

His life's been hard, but he chooses to use his talents rather than be beaten by his so-called disadvantage. This guy's got grit. He's an actual inspiration. Many boys and girls—and adults—look up to him even while he's seated, which is all the time. Our kids need heroes like him. His players understand what the score is. They understand how hard it is to be him. Yet there he is, all the time, working hard for them. We might go looking in the sports pages for heroes. Maybe we'll find one or two there. Chances are, though, if we look closer to home we'll find heroes in our midst who are placed there by God to inspire us.

Take a look around—maybe God's put a hero in your life.

Let's Pray:

God, we thank you for the heroes in our lives, for people who overcome the odds, who live fully, who give what they are able and strive to be more than they appear. Amen.

Today's Thought Is: Heroes are plain folks who discover that, in giving, we receive.

ill was born hearing. As a baby, illness made him completely deaf. Over the years Bill learned to communicate through speech reading, American Sign Language, computers, and pen and paper. He earns his living as a professional mime around Philadelphia. He has what he calls an invisible disability.

Since no one's perfect, most of us have a least one disability, invisible or not. It may be minor, like needing to wear glasses, or it may be bigger, like having autism. Maybe you had polio when you were a child, or MS now. Maybe, no matter how hard you try, you can't walk. Maybe you have dyslexia, or ADHD. But maybe, like Bill, you have advantages, too. Bill has what's called "kinesthetic brilliance," meaning he's very good with his body, which is the reason he performs onstage as a mime. Maybe you'll never learn to multiply well, but instead you're able to fix anything that's broken. Pretty often when we live with an annoyance—like deafness, glasses, poor eyesight, dyslexia, or extreme shyness—we discover it comes with blessings, too.

We may have to look for that blessing, and then we may have to work to develop it, but it's rare for it not to be there. God builds us to succeed.

Let's Pray:

Creator God, help any of us who are weighted down by apparent or invisible disabilities. Give us the chance to discover and develop the talents you have placed inside our bodies and minds. Amen.

Today's Thought Is: God loves us no matter who we are.

One summer there appeared a small snapping turtle swimming with his head sticking up just above the surface of our pond. The next winter, when the frozen pond was thick enough for us to skate on it, we wondered aloud if, come the following springtime, our turtle, by then fondly named Burtle, would return. When summer came again, Burtle was spotted on sunny days, warming himself along the pond embankment all alone. Burtle was a single turtle we came to love. Snappers aren't cuddly. They never nip playfully. They don't climb up on your bed, or curl up warmly on your lap. Wild turtles are hard-shelled when it comes to returning affection.

Perhaps we've all known people who, like Burtle the turtle, are tender on the inside while hard-shelled and snappy on the outside. Maybe they seem unlovable. But the Scriptures teach us that we are each made in the image of God, and they teach that God is love. No matter how hard-shelled a human heart may be on the outside, each is capable of giving and receiving love. It's built into our souls.

If your heart is hard-shelled and lonely, turn to the maker of love, turn to God, who is able to free every heart from hardness.

Let's Pray:

God, if we live lonely lives, creating distance between ourselves and those we ought to love, preventing us from giving or receiving love, shine your powerful love inside us that we might be made free. Amen.

Today's Thought Is: **Walls cannot keep out God's love.**

he *Dolphin* is a forty-four-foot sailing yacht. One October, her owner and captain, Bob, invited me to help sail her up to a boatyard to get her hauled for the winter. The wind forecast was for twenty mph. We set our sails then tacked toward the bay. In the outer harbor, the wind jumped unexpectedly to sixty mph. Bob was on the foredeck. I was at the helm. He shouted, "Turn the bow directly into the wind; head into the wind!" Bob wanted to lower sails. As we sped closer to shore, I tried turning upwind, but the powerful blow wouldn't let us. In desperation, I spun the wheel very hard a second time. As the boat turned, the bow dove deeply under water. The stern rose high in the air. The boat was nearly perpendicular to the sea; Bob slipped and clung; I fell against the wheel. We pirouetted like dancers *en pointe* on the boat's bow as the *Dolphin* dove down deeper. When Bob and I both believed all was lost, the wind released us and we righted, astounded at our terror and our redemption.

At times it appears in life that all is lost. Misfortune is our fate. We're headed unavoidably to the bottom. Times of terror may last a moment, or a lifetime. There may not be a saving miracle, but, on the other side of our struggle, there is always redemption.

Let's Pray

Dear God of redemption, in the struggles that we face, in the terrors of our lives—be they temporary or enduring—we ask that you be with us, until we reach the other side. Amen.

Today's Thought Is: This, too, shall pass.

cores of children dread the start of school in September. It's not just because they have to sit inside for six hours while September continues with its sunshine and summery temperatures. Many kids dread school because of their learning disabilities, which are agonizing and embarrassing. How do I know? Because I'm dyslexic. For me, words on a page slip about, refusing to stay still; numbers flip and switch. You don't want me helping with your math homework. Spelling? Thank goodness for keyboards and spell check. There are advantages to having learning disabilities, though—like when you're married and you get to say, "Sorry, dear, but you're just better at doing the monthly bills." Learning disabilities help me think in creative ways. Teachers never knew what to make of me. Was I brainless, or was I smart? It was frustrating. Eventually an eighth-grade remedial teacher taught me to read.

A popular two-liner for dyslexics is: "What's a dyslexic atheist? A person who doesn't believe in dogs." I believe in dogs and God, even though I used to blame God for making me this way. Why does God make people with any disabilities? Who knows? It's easy to get mad at God about this. It's easy to criticize God for our problems. It's tougher to stay in school, find solutions, and work hard. Young or old, just because you have a disability is no reason to think you're not smart. Chances are you're clever in unusual ways. Find your strengths.

Let's Pray

God, thank you for our differences—our disadvantages and advantages. Bless learning-disabled children as they struggle in school. Help them figure out ways to love learning. Amen.

Today's Thought Is: **Every cloud has a silver lining.**[7]

In Honduras there is a deceptive theology—the Gospel of Prosperity. Basically—give your heart to Jesus and you'll get rich. If you're rich, said the preacher who was dressed in an expensive suit, then God loves you. If you're poor, then you don't love God enough. This is malarkey. Unfortunately many poor Hondurans believe the rich are God's chosen. They see themselves as not faithful enough.

It's funny, I've found the faith held by some poor Hondurans to be stronger than the faith held by the wealthy. Faith is necessary when you don't know if you'll be able to buy food for your children today.

The Teacher wasn't against the rich. He said, "It is easier for a camel to go through the eye of a needle than for the rich to enter heaven."[8] The needle was a low-topped entry gate into Jerusalem. This defensive gate forced camels loaded with merchandise to kneel then crawl through. Given the ornery nature of camels, it was difficult, but it happened all the time—camels crawled through the needle gate. The Teacher told the rich man to sell all he had, give money to the poor, and follow him. God doesn't choose the poor over the rich, or the rich over the poor. God doesn't see as we see. God sees the treasures stored in our hearts. It's what's inside that matters.

Let's Pray:

God, grant that the treasure of our hearts is you. Amen.

Today's Thought Is: What we give to the poor is what we carry into heaven.

*B*ob was a district judge who refereed semipro football in his spare time. At one game, there was a pass, a catch, and a run followed by a game-changing touchdown. When the cheering ended, Bob blew his whistle. A flag on the play—an offense foul. No touchdown. Five-yard penalty. The accused player swore at Bob, "There was no foul." So Bob added ten more yards for bad language. The man tried to hit Bob. So Bob added ten more yards, setting the line of scrimmage back twenty-five yards! As he was being dragged from the field by the police, the player kept shouting, "It's not fair! There is no foul!"

"Tell it to the judge," an officer replied.

Months passed. Bob forgot about the incident. One morning the player walked into Bob's courtroom for arraignment. The player was seated before he recognized Judge Bob, who was smiling down at him from the bench. "Oh no!" the player shouted.

Incidentally, the player had no criminal record and never actually touched Judge Bob, so all the charges were dismissed.

Imagine your accuser being your judge, too. It's a tough spot. Almost hopeless, actually. Our circumstance is similar. When we harm ourselves or others, intentionally or unintentionally, we offend God at the same time. Scriptures call this sin and promise judgment. Fortunately for us, the Creator knows that to be human is to make mistakes—even really huge ones. All it takes is sincere belief and a contrite heart.

Let's Pray:

Creator God, help us avoid offending you, harming others,
or hurting ourselves. But when we do, sweeten our lives with contrite hearts,
and, please, be merciful. Amen.

Today's Thought Is: **God is kindhearted.**

family arrived at an animal shelter to choose a puppy. After searching rows of cages, they settled on picking a puppy from a litter of spaniels. They were a charming, cheerful, lively lot. One pup had a strip of newspaper caught across his eyes, and, while trying to push it off, his right paw got wedged in his red collar. He then tried with his left paw to remove the strip of paper and that leg got stuck, too. The hobbled pup's yelp and silliness caught the kids' hearts. It was a tenderhearted choice. The kids convinced themselves that this pup was clever. Their parents were skeptical of a dog that couldn't even get a strip of paper off his own nose.

Two years later, a ferocious Saint Bernard cornered their mother outside a store. The spaniel was nearby in the car, with the window open only inches. Seeing the other dog, the small spaniel forced his way out the window, dropped to the ground, and ran to defend his owner from the Saint Bernard, saving her from fright or worse. The kids had picked an underdog who later proved to be a daring dog.

God picks underdogs, too, all the time. Moses, who stuttered, got to preach to the Pharaoh. David, a shepherd boy, got to be king. Jesus, a carpenter's boy, grew up to change the world. Even his friends were underdogs and outcasts.

Let's Pray:

Dear God, be with the underdog, the little guy, the struggling mom, the wayward soul. Guide them to whatever greatness or goodwill you have in store. Help underdogs be daring dogs. Amen.

Today's Thought Is: God often chooses and uses the underdog.

THE POET AND THE HONEY JAR:
AN OLD TALE RETOLD

Once there was a poet who wrote poems for a merchant, who paid the poor poet with a daily a piece of cake and a bowl of honey. The poet ate the cake but saved the honey in a jar, which he carried on his head. In those days, honey was valuable, and one day, while walking down the road with his walking stick, the poet realized that his jar was full.

He thought about the money he would get if he sold the honey. I'll sell my honey, and then I'll buy four sheep. In a year I'll have eight sheep, and eventually I'll have a thousand sheep. Then I'll buy a cow and a bull. The cow will have calves and give milk, and the bull will help me plow the land. In a few years I'll have a herd of cows, and I will own a farm and become wealthy and build a mansion, and then I'll marry the beautiful daughter of a wealthy merchant. We will have wonderful children, and should bad men who wish to steal what I have earned attack us, I will defend all I own with this stick.

In so saying, the poet raised his stick and swung it threateningly about his head, accidentally smashing his honey jar.[9]

Let's Pray

Dear God, it is fun to fantasize about what good may happen, and what we might do, but keep us from being so distracted by our dreams that we lose control over today, and damage our futures by not paying attention to what needs care now. Amen.

Today's Thought Is: Don't brag about tomorrow, since you don't know what today will bring.[10]

areening side to side on a two-lane highway south of Calgary, Canada, our Honda eventually came to a stop, wedged partway beneath a tractor trailer flatbed and crumpled against the rear wheels. The two passengers (the driver and myself) were unhurt. The car was totaled. We had little money and no way to get to our destination: Bozeman, Montana. After a bit of pleading, we were allowed to sleep in our sleeping bags on the floor of the town's hotel. By pooling our cash, we afforded a single bus ride back for one of us, Tim, along with our backcountry skis and some of our climbing gear.

I hitched, leaving under the rising dawn of a pink-skied March morning. I made it most of the 496 miles with ease. A driver left me on Highway 15 outside of Butte. I waited for hours for a single car to pass in that sparsely populated state. It did not stop. The sun set. When the next car came, half an hour later, feeling desperate, I marched into its path waving my arms, making it stop. After climbing into the car and stuffing my backpack in with me, I gushed out my story. I was flat broke, hungry, and alone. The car was wrecked, and so was I. The driver took me into Butte, bought me dinner at a diner, drove me to a bus station, and paid for my one-way ticket to Bozeman. He never told me his name.

Let's Pray:

God, give us the courage and compassion to help our neighbors on the highways and byways of life. Help us be true neighbors, even to strangers. Amen.

Today's Thought Is: To whom can I be a good neighbor?

*I*n any neighborhood, in any county, anywhere, everywhere, bullies bully the weak.

One teen was beaten black and blue—and terrorized—by two bullies. He simply took it. Tired from their dark exertion, the bullies started to leave the home where they had beaten the boy. In a final act, one grabbed an unloaded rifle, pointing at this harmless boy, made the motion of a rifle recoil, and said, "Bang." The terrorized boy later told his mom, "I did what you told me. 'Do not fight back.' They wanted me to fight back. They wanted an excuse to hurt me badly. I could tell."

Weeks later on a bus to a regional technical school another boy with character and a sense of self became the next target of the two bullies. On the bus, these two bullies bound this boy's hands, stuffed a dirty sock into his mouth, and then repeatedly punched him. Other kids watched, doing nothing, either out of fear or amusement. Both bullies pulled knives to cut their victim free. The boy said little. Two teen girls, at risk to themselves, told the principal when they arrived at school.

There are always bullies who believe they can act with impunity, with freedom, and that nobody will dare stop them. Bullies prey on the weak and the isolated, using fear as a tool, saying, "If any of you oppose me, you'll be next." Bullies gain power when good people stand apart and do nothing.

Let's Pray:

Dear God, we pray for the victims of bullies, for the weak, the peculiar, the outcast, the target. Surround them with love, support, and protection. Give them the voice they need to speak out. Amen.

Today's Thought Is: God stands by the weak; we should, too.

A fellow who had bought his home a couple of years before was hunched in his damp, dirt cellar monkeying around with his water-filtration system, which wasn't working—again. Exasperated, he leaned up against a metal column—one of many—that the previous owner had installed to hold up the sagging first floor. Next thing he knew, the post had let go and fallen over, and he was lying in damp mud. Being much closer to the problem, he saw for the first time that the column had been footed by a wet, rotting block of spruce. Using a concrete block for a footing, he temporarily reset that lolly column. With his suspicions aroused, he checked the other eleven columns, discovering each was as carelessly footed as the first. For the next five hours the fellow scrounged blocks and rocks and crawled in the mud, resetting each post so the sagging house would stay up through the winter. Come summertime, he'd fixed it the right way. The man's single-minded goal that cold, wet day was to keep the house from collapsing.

What posts support your flooring? What's under your feet? Friends, love, family, health, bonds, schooling, the arts, science, tools, or hard work? What foots the posts that hold up your life? What's solid, enduring, and strong enough to hold everything up? It better be God, because nothing else lasts.

Let's Pray:

God, get us into the cellars of hearts to see if our faith footings are firm enough to hold up in stressful times. If not, help us find a place of worship that'll help. Amen.

Today's Thought Is: What's under your posts?

*T*he eight orphans and their caretaker escaped a revolution in Sierra Leone and arrived in the United States with a ninth child, who was being adopted by a Boothbay Harbor, Maine, family. The Boothbay parents rallied their entire town to support the orphans. Suddenly crews were scrapping charred debris, cleaning, painting, installing new plumbing and wiring, and generally making a fire-damaged inn livable. Compassionate crews of hastily gathered hardworking people joined together to renovate the inn, which would provide the orphans with temporary lodging, and the new inn owners donated the space for as long as it was needed.

In addition, volunteers drove the orphans to doctors, nurses, dentists, and hygienists, all of whom donated their services. Shots were given, teeth were cleaned and fixed, parasites were treated, and clothing, food, and shoes were donated—all free of charge. It was an overwhelming display of kindness that endured daily for six long months.

The eight children, with Pinky as their caretaker, lived in the inn on the hill, wearing clean clothes, shoes, and smiles. But behind their eyes dwelled fear, heartache, and terrifying memories.

The Teacher said, "Then the just will answer him, 'When did we see you hungry and gave you food, or thirsty and gave you a drink? When were you a stranger and we welcomed you, or nearly naked and gave you clothing?' God answered them, 'When you did it to one of the weakest of my people you did it to me.'"

Let's Pray:

Dear God, tell our hearts that when we serve the weakest and most vulnerable of your people, we serve you. Amen.

Today's Thought Is: **Compassionate acts are works of beauty.**

It was painted on a little sign in her kitchen: "You never know how many friends you have until you have a cottage by the sea." This holds true for ski lodges, hunting lodges, backwoods cabins, cottages on lakes, city apartments, and pretty much any place folks want to visit. Hospitality is a custom we find throughout the Bible. Abram and Sarah hosted travelers inside their tent. Jethro hosted Moses and essentially took him in off the streets.

Years ago, we had a house guest—God rest his humble soul—a temporarily homeless monk, Brother Denys, who worked among the urban poor. Brother Denys came to stay with us for a week and remained for six months. Yikes.

These days, in my modest opinion, the best guests clean up after themselves, volunteer to help with cooking or dishwashing, do their own laundry, and are willing to go off on their own and be self-sufficient when the host is occupied with work or necessary family functions. The worst guests trash the place, complain about everything, are always in the way, and never, ever, take care of themselves. Being a gracious host by extending hospitality is an openhearted act of faith. Being a courteous guest by behaving in a civilized manner when visiting for an hour, a day, a week is to be grateful for kindness.

Let's Pray.

God, thanks for those folks who welcome us openheartedly. May we be faithful hosts and faithful guests. Amen.

Today's Thought Is: Hospitality is an act of faith.

Around the time of the Twin Towers disaster, I'd been visiting the Barbara Bush pediatrics floor at Maine Medical for several months to visit a sweet child who'd had complications after surgery. I got to know a nurse or two by name and some of the cleaning crew by sight. One afternoon, I chatted with the nurses about the terrorists who had passed through Portland's jetport. I then caught the elevator going down and was joined by one of the cleaning crew. We nodded our hellos. On the next floor we stopped. Two men got in—both bearded and very dark skinned. One was tall, skinny, and younger. The other was short, round, older, and white haired. Both wore long hair and were well dressed.

Their discussion was loud and animated, in a language I'd never heard before, perhaps Pakistani or Kashmiri. They were gesticulating wildly and arguing, their voices rising and falling. It was curious. As the elevator slowed to a stop, the older man emphatically shouted three words in English: "Helicopter torpedo ship!" The other hesitated, then said in English, "Yes." The doors opened. Both stepped off. The doors closed. My fellow rider and I stared at each other. "Do you think we ought to report this?" I asked. He was as unsure as I was since we had no idea what they had been talking about. We didn't report it, but I did track them down. They were off-duty doctors discussing war.

Given the tension in our nation at the time, we were suspicious. Our suspicions nearly made us jump to the wrong conclusion.

Let's Pray:

God, help us be cautious in our judgments about those who look different than we do. Amen.

Today's Thought Is: Ignorance is a poor foundation for suspicion.

Originally, God has an idea about water. With a word, a dome appears, separating the waters above the dome from the waters below the dome. Waters. God calls the dome sky. And it's good. Then comes dry land, flora, then stars, the sun and moon, and fauna. It's all good. A little later, God creates humankind, and that's a good day, too. Then the humans make a fatal error. God uncovers their mistake and kicks them out.

Murder arrives next. A long time later humankind isn't behaving as well as when first created; in the time of Noah, humankind was acting in a downright ugly fashion. God looks around, gets gloomy, and says, "Look at the mess they've made. I'm sorry I ever made them." Then God gets another idea, and with a word, the fountains of the deep and the windows of the heavens open wide. Water pours down and floods the Earth, and virtually every breathing creature drowns. Only those few animals and humans aboard an ark survive. As the story ends on dry land again, Noah lights a fire and burns an offering on an altar, and God, smelling the pleasing aroma, inwardly makes a heartfelt promise never again to destroy every breathing creature as had been done.

In those passages: God thinks, walks, makes choices, feels sorrow, has regrets, and makes covenants. Humans gain knowledge, lose innocence, learn murder, fill the Earth, mess up everything, get destroyed, and start all over again . . . all in the first eleven chapters of Genesis.

Let's Pray.

Dear God, humankind seems like such trouble.
Why do you bother with us? Amen.

Today's Thought Is: **A careful read of Genesis is revealing.**[11]

The morning after he was assaulted, a minister lay in bed with a swollen, fractured ankle. There was a knock on the island's parsonage door. In walked a young lobsterman, who, having grown up in the church, had also long since left it. The lobsterman said, "The boys down at the dock had a little talk. We like you. If you agree, we'll go grab that fella, that bully who stove up your leg, haul him down to the dock after dark tonight, and break his leg. That'll square it for ya."

It was a sympathetic and considerate offer based on the island way of doing things, which is a lot like the book of Leviticus: "Anyone who injures another person must be dealt with according to the injury inflicted—fracture for fracture, eye for eye, tooth for tooth. Whatever anyone does to hurt another person must be paid back in kind."[12]

The minister was dreadfully tempted, but the offer spoke to his feelings. After complicated consideration, he declined. Seeking revenge against bullies is so tempting, but it's not acceptable. The bone-for-a-bone law went out a long time ago. Do not try to get back at the bullies. Seeking revenge may make things worse.

Let's Pray:

Dear God, when we have feelings of revenge, help us remember the words of the Rabbi, who said, "Do unto others what you would have them do to you." Amen.

Today's Thought Is: Listen to the Rabbi.[13]

*W*hen our neighbors moved in, we befriended them. Every weekend their son was at our home for what seemed like every meal. Then toys started to get broken by the neighbor boy. At first it was okay; toys break. And then we realized he was *purposefully* breaking them. I called his mom and asked her to speak to him. She said, 'My son would never!' and hung up. Then the boy threw rocks at our son and my husband. Next, that boy hid in our yard and pointed his BB gun at my son. I saw him. I told his mother. She replied with swears and accusations. We told the police. There's a restraining order, but they still verbally harass us. We try to ignore them and turn the other cheek, but my son's been afraid to play in the front yard for five years. I don't even like to be outside."

Turning the other cheek doesn't mean to be meek milksop. The Scriptures say, "If your enemies are hungry, feed them; if they are thirsty, give them something to drink; for by doing this you will heap burning coals on their heads." In other words, the Scriptures say that treating your enemies with compassion and love might really tick them off.

Let's Pray:

Dear God, open the eyes and hearts of the wounded who act uncivilly. Amen.

Today's Thought Is: **Compassion is not weakness.**

TEACH ME

n ancient tale of unknown origin tells the story of a soldier, returning from a foreign war, who meets a monk by the side of the road:

The soldier says, "You, teach me about hell and heaven."

The monk looks him up and down then says, "You're a soldier? Your repulsive face looks like that of a coward, and you seem too stupid to teach."

These insults anger the soldier until he shakes with fury. Putting his hand to his sword, he begins to pull it out threateningly.

The monk says, "Ah, simple soldier, you have a sword, do you? It's probably dull and rusty, like you."

The enraged soldier yanks out his sword, ready to strike, when the monk says, "That is the gate of hell."

The soldier's hands shake, tears well in his eyes, his mind fills with understanding. He drops his sword, falls to his knees, and begs forgiveness. The monk says, "That is the gate of heaven."

Heaven is often held up as a pie-in-the-sky-when-you-die idea. While the Scriptures teach that there is eternal afterlife in heaven, they also teach that heaven starts here, in this life, right now, inside your spiritual heart. But the Rabbi warns us to be careful of the treasure we pile into our hearts. If our treasure is rage, bitterness, jealousy, or hatred, we may find we're living in a hell. If we store love, hope, faith, forgiveness, and charity, we may find ourselves to be living in heaven right now.

Let's Pray:

God, free us from any hell that may subsist inside us as we sincerely ask forgiveness. Grant us heaven. Touch our hearts with the beauty of your love. Let paradise, let heaven, live and enlarge within us today. Amen.

Today's Thought Is: Heaven begins within us.

*A*n ancient tale retold:

One day a Teacher of God, known for miracles, took his disciples for a mountain hike. At the trailhead the Teacher said, "Before we climb, everybody choose a rock to carry."

Asked why, he replied, "You'll find out when we get there." Andreas chose a hefty stone and heaved it on his shoulder. His brother, Petro, chose a pebble that fit neatly in his pocket. All the way up Petro teased his lumbering, sweating brother. When they reached the top, the Teacher sat them under a tree and said, "It's time for lunch. Put your stones on the ground. There is one rule—no sharing." As the Teacher prayed to God, the stones turned into bread. "Eat!" he said.

Andreas smiled and chewed. Petro finished his lunch in a meager mouthful.

When it was time to leave, the Teacher instructed them to choose another rock. Andreas picked a one-pound stone. Petro picked the heaviest he could lift. It was hot. Petro struggled. In the valley the Teacher stopped at the shore of a lake, instructing, "Throw your stones into the lake." As they did, he turned and walked away.

Petro shouted, "Hey, What's this? Where's my reward?"

The Teacher said, "You had your reward."

Big stone, little pebble—Petro chose each from selfishness, thinking only of himself.

Faith is not about "What's in it for me?"

Let's Pray:

Dear God, help follow you without expectation of reward. Let your love for us be reward enough. Take selfishness from our hearts. Amen.

Today's Thought Is: Seek God, not the gifts of God.

*B*eautiful Deer Isle, twelve miles by six miles, has a northern and southern end—North Deer Isle and South Deer Isle. The entire island is the size of Manhattan, except it has several fewer people and is a bit quicker to get around than New York City. Just after roads were built, few islanders could afford cars, and it was day's walk from the north end to the south end. Sadie's home was on North Deer. Sadie was old, modestly poor, hardworking, and much loved.

I asked her once, "Have you live here your whole life?"

"No, deah," Sadie said sincerely. "I'm not from heah. I moved heah in thirty-eight, aftah marrying my husband. I'm from South Deer Isle." It took a while for me to see such a subtle truth. To an outsider, the island seemed, at first, like one place. Actually, it's a collection of several villages, each with its own sense of identity. From the outside we might believe all congregations are the same. We sometimes refer to "the Church," or "Judaism," or "Islam," as if in each of these religions there is only one way of thinking and believing, as if each religion consists of only one culture. All congregations—even local ones—have histories that inform who they are and how they believe.

If you're seeking God and one congregation doesn't fit right, don't misjudge by thinking every one is the same. Try other churches or synagogues or mosques—let God lead you to your spiritual home.

God, lead us to the congregation that fits us best. Amen.

Today's Thought Is: **God is bigger than religion.**

One evening after visiting hours, a young male minister visited a parishioner at an urban hospital. Armed security guarded the doors. The minister sported a ponytail, gold earring, loose tank top, cut-offs, and Birkenstocks, and carried a bouquet of flowers. His official hospital badge was back home; his wallet was forgotten in the car; he carried no ID. Getting in the main door wasn't too difficult. Getting past the information desk clerk took persuasion.

"You're not a minister," she declared.

"I am. Call my parishioner in her room." A call was made, his name and a description skeptically related. The armed guard watched. Hesitant permission was granted. On the elevator a suspicious staff person asked: "Who are you? Where are you going? What are you doing here?"

"I'm a minister going to visit a parishioner."

"You're not a minister."

"Call the front desk."

In the room the parishioner was recovering. Conversation flowed. A nurse entered. Introductions were made. "Nurse, this is my minister." The nurse replied: "You're not a minister."

Maybe we have ideas about what clergy are supposed to look like—white haired, stodgy, out of shape, out of style, stuffed shirt, stiff, formal. Expectations may get in the way of believing what's happening right in front of us— God sends a visitor, a gift, grace, and we don't believe because the gift doesn't fit our idea. God is active in our lives. Maybe, because we have a limited view of God, we don't see how God touches us.

Let's Pray:

God, break down barriers of expectations or ideas that prevent us from seeing the ways you act in our lives. Give us eyes to see. Amen.

Today's Thought Is: Look for God in unexpected people.

A minister needed a car. One parishioner owned a dealership and sold him a used, two-liter, metallic-silver sports convertible with high-speed tires on aluminum rims. Not a minister's car. He began parking the car with the top down in the clergy spot at the church; he had a tendency to leap the closed door then zip off as the wheels chirped in three gears; finally, he got a speeding ticket, causing his name to appear in the local newspaper. This combination of events elicited numerous negative phone calls to his church.

But the real message came while he was cutting through an inner-city neighborhood, top down and with U2 blaring on the stereo, on his way to a meeting. At a red light a driver in the next car whistled. "Man, you must have sold a lot of cocaine for that car." Pulling a roll of bills from his jacket pocket, he added, "Here's ten thousand cash for it, right now." The minister considered—it was more than he paid for it—before replying sensibly, "If I sell you this car, do you think I'll make it out of this neighborhood alive with ten gees in my pocket?"

The driver laughed. "Not a chance."

The light changed. Temptations aren't worth the trouble, danger, or aggravation. God often points this out to us with an ever-increasing volume. Hearing the message before it's too late? That's another question.

God, when our lives or our relationships are in danger, when our ears can't hear your message, increase the volume before it's too late. Amen.

Today's Thought Is: What we want and what we need aren't always the same.

*L*awrence the footman lived in the thirteenth century. His nobleman died, so he entered a monastery. Fathers were educated monks doing intellectual work. The uneducated became brothers who labored to maintain and sustain the community. Brother Lawrence was a kitchen-pot washer. The abbot noticed his radiance, like a halo. Brother Lawrence communed with God.

His teaching was this: Act as if God is present with you, and eventually God will be. It's a simple prayer practice to remember that God is present in the here and now, and its long-term use will lead to your experiencing the presence of God. Prayer is not just kneeling before bedtime, during worship time in your congregation, or in times of desperation. Prayer is many things. Remembering God's presence at all times is one effective form. This is what the Apostle Paul encouraged us to do—pray ceaselessly. Practicing being mindful of the presence of God is a way to do just that. It's easy enough and doesn't take any extra time out of our lives. It requires a bit of willpower. When can we do this? Anytime. Anywhere. While taking a shower, when standing in a grocery line, while stopped at a red light, when petting the pooch, or while taking a walk. It's not thinking about who God is, or what God is like—that's fine, too. It's just remembering that God is present.

Let's Pray.

Today, help our minds turn to you, God. When we have a moment,
help us remember your presence. Amen.

Today's Thought Is: **Practice the presence of God.**[14]

This story originates from the Metropolitan Diary section of the *New York Times* online.[15] A bus stopped in front of the Brooklyn Hospital Center, and a young couple got on. The woman carried a stroller. The man carried a two-week-old baby swaddled in soft blue blankets. They were offered seats, one in front of the other. When the bus started moving again, the baby began to wail. The new father appeared befuddled and began to bounce the baby up and down, up and down. At a stop, passengers got off. As some space was cleared, an older, very majestic woman appeared and made her way toward the crying baby. Without a word she stretched out her arms, and without any hesitation the young father offered this stranger, this woman, his newborn. She held the child to her chest and slowly rubbed his back. "You must be gentle," she matter-of-factly advised. In a moment, the baby stopped crying. She handed the child to the father, thanked him for allowing her to hold him, and returned to her seat.

God doesn't always come to us in a way we might expect. Sometimes God shows up, says nothing, and offers only the comfort of outreached arms. Without hesitation, we are to offer God the most vulnerable, most tender, part of ourselves—our souls, our hearts, our lives.

Let's Pray:

Dear God, stretch your arms to me this day, offer wisdom and comfort, and I, for my part, will offer you my vulnerability. Amen.

Today's Thought Is: God wants nothing less of us than that to which we cling most dearly.

She came around the point, the little lobster boat, her unmuffled motor roaring, dark smoke pouring from her stack, white water churning astern her—while making little headway. It was a curious sight since there was no wind blowing to ripple the sea on that merry morning under a blue, blue sky. As we watched, a boat thrice her size, right in line, three lengths astern, came under tow behind her. It looked like a children's story gone to sea—a teeny tiny boat hauling a humongously large boat. The little boat's captain did what every sailor would do when finding a friend floundering—toss a line, give up a morning's work, haul the friend to shore, and take no pay for the trouble. There is a fast rule on the water among fishermen in Maine: even if it's your mortal enemy who's in trouble, you rescue him, for the next time it could be you in need. And if you are in trouble, your enemy will rescue you. That's a custom that's come ashore. Neighbors lend a hand around here.

The Teacher put it this way: When a soldier asks you to carry his gear for a mile, you carry it for two. We've shorthanded this saying: go the extra mile. As a result, a person who might never even have heard a sacred word during his whole life may be be closer in heart to God than a minister or a nun.

Let's Pray:

Dear God, you say that when we lend a hand to help those in need, it's you we serve. Let us serve you even if we struggle to know you. Amen.

Today's Thought Is: The extra mile's not far at all.

*T*here is a rural Maine custom of waving. The small-town wave has several forms. In a car or truck, there is the common Thank-You Wave, when one hand is raised briefly alongside the face. It's done as a courtesy after someone kindly let's you into traffic, which happens all the time here. There are variations of the wave used to say hello to a neighbor's car that's headed in the opposite direction. For the Regular Saying-Hello Wave, aka the Hand-Off-the-Wheel Wave, one quickly raises one hand about an inch off the steering wheel then drops it down again. For the Single-Finger-Salute-Off-the-Wheel (it's the index finger!) one keeps a grip on the wheel and simply raises one index finger. Every wave made assumes a wave in return. There's also the Walking-Along-the-Side-of-a-Road-Without-Sidewalks Wave. The pedestrian raises the hand about a foot off the thigh, angled at four o'clock with the right arm. It's used when a driver slows down or pulls way over so as not to hit you as you walk. Variations of this wave are also used by runners, cyclists, and in-line skaters. Then there's the Raised-Arm Wave that boaters, sailors, and fishermen use when boats pass. My favorite wave belonged to Captain Bob Campbell. When skippering his ferry, Bob waved widely across the horizon, making a long arc with his palm facing downward. Every one of these small-town waves has an idea in common: recognition that we form a community of neighbors. It says, "I see you as a person. I see you as a neighbor. I see that you are like me." The wave binds us as a community. It's almost a spiritual act; it's almost a prayer.

Let's Pray:

God, bind us as a people, even with all our differences. When we wave, help us recognize that inside one another there's a little bit of you. Amen.

Today's Thought Is: **Actions can be prayers.**

*n late summer hundreds of red dragonflies were zipping in the yard up, down, under, over, stopping, flying, moving, eating, landing. No one enjoys insects landing on us—especially black flies, mosquitoes, or deer flies. We don't like millipedes creeping across our bare toes in the bathroom or pincher bugs sleeping in our unmentionables. But dragonflies seem smart and even friendly. When several dragonflies got into the house, each one willingly attached itself to my outstretched finger, accepting a ride outside.

I'm not the St. Francis of Assisi of bugs. If I were, I wouldn't be so unkind to mosquitoes. Dragonflies just accept humans. They eat the insects that munch on us, and they treat us with, well, an insect form of respect.

It's as if God said, "Look, people, I had to make biting bugs. They're part of the ecosystem—they're necessary. But to make it up to you, I'll create a beautiful insect that's clever and colorful, with gossamer wings and superior skills, and it'll eat the bugs that eat you.

This world is full of affliction—insects that bite. In life we face struggles. Life hurts. But God's world is also full of goodness and blessings. We need only to pay attention, to stop for a moment, to see the beauty and balance of God's creations and remember we are loved.

Let's Pray:

Thank you, God, for biting insects, which feed the beauty of the dragonflies. We thank you for the small wonders in this world. Amen.

Today's Thought Is: Be fed by God—look for beauty.

nother ancient story retold: Long ago there was a prized diamond, as big as your fist, hidden in a cave. When four thieves heard about this precious stone, they devised a plan to steal it, and they succeeded. They agreed to sell it but also understood that if the four of them showed their faces in the city together they might be caught.

The first thief said, "Tonight I'll sneak alone into the city in disguise, with the diamond, find a buyer, sell it, and then return here tomorrow with the money."

"No way," said the second, with a smile on his lips and suspicion in his heart. "You stay here. I'll go to the city."

"No," shouted the third, who wanted to keep the diamond always in his sight. "I'll go."

"No," demanded the fourth. "I'm in charge. I decide. It stays here where no one may see it."

They argued until they reached an unlikely accord to divide the stone. Taking a hammer and a sharp blade they cut the diamond—utterly destroying it. Each thief ended his days with nothing but hatred, bitterness, and anger for company. Why is it that we destroy the very things we love dearest and value most? When deception, suspicion, jealousy, and control creep into our hearts, when they rule our thoughts and actions, we often end up destroying our most precious relationships.

Let's Pray:

God of love, free us from the demons—distrust, jealousy, and deception— who may rule our hearts. Amen.

Today's Thought Is: Give us peace.

*I*n South America private homes are protected by high concrete walls with thousands of shards of sharp broken glass embedded in the concrete along the tops. In Central America private guards armed with machine guns are a common sight at bank entrances, grocery stores, and even outside of seminaries. In New Mexico a store has a sign that reads: "Premises protected by owner with shotgun two days a week. You guess which two." We all have something to protect, even if it's a shopping cart piled with the plastic bags of homeless wealth. What we own comes to define who we are, which is one reason we're so ready to protect our possessions.

But to whom do you belong? Who possesses you? Your parents? Your spouse? Your children? Your job? These relationships and our assets are grounded in this transitory, temporary world. Ultimately, whose are you? The answer ought to be obvious—we belong to God. When we are done with this world, we leave everything that has come to define us and return to God, our Maker.

What do we take with us? Nothing physical that's come to define us. What we take with us is who we truly are—how we treated others and the love we shared with them. It's by love that we're measured, not by possessions.

Let's Pray.

God, prevent our possessions from possessing us. Teach us that who we are is not what we own but how we love. Amen.

Today's Thought Is: **Everything is left behind, except love.**

*E*very autumn I use our creaky old lawn tractor for mowing the lumpy damp lands where our poison ivy crop grows so richly. It's too bad poison ivy is not profitable. This year's crop was a tender ground cover a foot tall. If a scientist could figure out a use for poison ivy, many of us would be rolling in it—so to speak. I mow the poison ivy, but I never get rid of it. It just grows back.

Don, my childhood and college friend, has never gotten poison ivy. I once saw him reach out, pick a big lovely bouquet, and rub it vigorously on his face. It turns out that he's not allergic to it. Even indoors I get itchy just thinking about it. The more I struggle with not thinking about poison ivy, strangely, the more my skin itches, even if I don't have the rash.

It's curious—no matter how many times we mow down certain thoughts, they grow back with an itchy demand for attention. What obsessive thought has you in its itchy grip? One way to disrupt itchy and annoying thoughts is prayer. Choose a favorite prayer, or sentences from Scripture, or holy words—something short and concise. When rash thoughts or obsessive itchy ideas grip you, begin repeating your prayer over and over, aloud or in your mind. Say it ten thousand times. Focus your mind on your prayer. If your mind wanders, return to your prayer. Keep God in mind. Prayer scratches that itch.

Let's Pray.

God, there are often itches in our lives that we shouldn't scratch but sometimes do. Help us avoid the circumstances and thoughts that cause us harm. Teach us to pray daily. Amen.

Today's Thought Is: **Prayer soothes the mind.**

The boy has empathy with animals, and they seem to know it. Instinctually, they love him, and he loves them. Even when he was a toddler, Beanie Babies covered the foot of his bed—chipmunks, chickadees, red squirrels. Nightly he enjoys the antics of Buster Bear, Chatterer the Squirrel, and Reddy Fox. No matter where he goes, dogs, cats, even horses approach him. Here's the irony—he's allergic to animals. Even with allergy medication, he has a strong reaction if he gets too close. He dreams of being a veterinarian, but he can't even visit the vet's office. One wonders why God makes us this way—gives us a talent or a desire and then makes it impossible to fulfill.

There is a woman who desperately wants babies, and she would make a marvelous mother. But biologically, even after medical intervention, she can't have them. And circumstances prevent adoption from being an option for her. There is another women who never wanted children—still doesn't—but she has three. There is a man who attended a top prep school and an Ivy League university, has a trust fund, and yet he squanders his life in indecision, fear, and alcohol. There is another man born with drive, talent, and brains, but he never amounted to much in his own eyes because he couldn't afford an education. I don't have an answer to these ironies, to these unjust states of affairs, I have only a prayer.

Let's Pray:

God, whatever it is we dream to change about ourselves but can't, we pray that you show us the upside to this disappointment. We ask with all our hearts that you give us peace about it. Amen.

Today's Thought Is: Every wound comes with a blessing.

*W*hen his dad ran off, leaving his mom alone, Nicky's uncle Dickie was the only man in his life. No one in town had a single good word to say about Uncle Dickie. He'd dropped out of school early, he cut wood in the forest to make money, he smoked a lot of weed, he often spent nights in the county lockup, and he drank pretty often.

Over all, a disreputable guy to have as an uncle. At Skip's elementary school, the first assignment of fifth grade was to prepare to say a few words about the person you most respect.

When it was his turn, Nicky said, "I respect my uncle Dickie." Every kid in town knew Dickie by reputation, so everyone laughed. When the teacher quieted them, Nicky continued, "I respect my uncle Dickie because my dad never bothers with me. My uncle Dickie loves me. I know he does, 'cause he tells me so, and he spends a lot time with me. One night last week we stayed up 'til one in the mornin' fixin' my bicycle so I could ride to school."

We often think we know all about a person, especially in a small town, where everybody seems to know everything about everyone else. Much of the time, though, we don't really know what lives inside a heart.

Let's Pray:

Thank you, God, for the tough guys with the true hearts who live rough but love much, and for the boys and girls who need them. Amen.

Today's Thought Is: A rough reputation does not exclude
a loving heart.

We've seen media photographs of U.S. soldiers and marines in ancient places—places named in Genesis, 2 Kings, and Jonah. The city of Nineveh was once the center of the Assyrian Empire. Loathed in the Bible as enemies, it was the first international empire freely flowing with art, music, trade, and religion. In Babylon our marines walk where the exiles of Israel slaved for hundreds of years, singing sad songs of longing. In Ur, where Abraham once lived among the Chaldeans, American men and women fresh from our inner cities, suburbs, and rural towns walk on ancient roads, sleep next to four-thousand-year-old statues, and live in the midst of our earliest history. They awake in Mesopotamia, the Fertile Crescent, the birthplace of civilization and agriculture.

Our service people, for whom we pray, will return to us not only battle worn and longing for home, but with eyes that have seen the battlements of Nineveh, with hands that have touched sculptures carved when sculpture was young, and with feet that have walked over the broken shards of the ancient places of human civilization.

Seeing such sites may change their perspective of history. It may impact their understanding of human civilization and of their place in it. I pray that their faith will deepen, their hearts will open, and their minds will be enlivened by the civilizations that were once great.

Let's Pray.

God bless our servicemen and -women as they encounter your ancient world while facing modern warfare. Let their understanding grow. May their hearts be filled with you, and may they return safely to those who love them. Amen.

Today's Thought Is: **May killing end and peace last.**

At the Tegucigalpa airport, back when Honduras was under military rule, a group of researchers waited in a parked plane. They were returning from a Nicaraguan project examining what role, if any, Christianity had in the recent revolution, and to make a public record of what they found.

One researcher, an activist Christian, while glancing out of the airplane window noticed clearly marked international military aircraft that newspapers had proclaimed were never in Tegucigalpa. Wanting evidence, she disembarked down a long, movable stairway. As she began photographing the aircraft that "weren't there," she heard a single, distinctive, loud, metallic click. Slowly lowering her camera, and even more slowly turning around, she faced a dark-eyed, dark-haired teenager, perhaps fifteen years old, dressed in a military camouflage fatigues and wearing spit-polished black boots. He held an M16 with its muzzle an inch from her chest; his finger was on the trigger, and the safety was off.

"What are you doing," he demanded in Spanish

"Taking pictures," she said.

"Give me the film. Get back on the plane," he shouted.

She gave and went.

Sometimes we encounter unfriendly forces because of our faith. It may simply be taking an unpopular stance. It may be standing up for yourself. It may be telling the truth when keeping silent would be easier. Whatever it is, keep the faith.

Let's Pray.

God, when we know we should be but aren't strong, give us the fortitude to be gently faithful, even if we fail. Amen.

Today's Thought Is: **Live your faith.**

*arly one snowy morning a high school student pulled his father's VW convertible into a parking spot at a ski area near the lodge. The convertible was cool. He was cool. He had freestyle skis and a job with the National Ski Patrol. He looked impressive, or so he thought, dressed in his cropped official patroller's jacket with its large blue cross stitched on the back.

As he pulled his skis from inside the Bug, another car—filled with adorable high school girls—parked alongside. He smiled. They smiled back. He turned and, making sure the girls could see his "official jacket," lifted his ski boots off the front seat. In a casual movement quickly invented to impress these cuties with his savoir faire, he swung his heavy ski boots out and dropped them nonchalantly on top of the convertible roof. But his boots slammed through the roof and landed neatly on the front seat, while leaving a large hole in the roof and plenty of problems. The cuties erupted into hysterical laughter.

Humiliated, the boy stared at the hole in the roof, the falling snow, and wished to be invisible. He knew he had to work the slopes where the girls would be skiing. Then he remembered—it was his father's car.

Ego, pride, temptation, self-absorption—all can distract us, creating problems and turning us into fools before God, girls, and anybody else. Keep your focus. Ignore ego.

Let's Pray:

God, keep us from egoism and self-centered arrogance. Teach us where the holes are in our lives. Keep us from making new ones. Amen.

Today's Thought Is: **The bigger the ego, the bigger the trouble.**

*T*his man looked like he was made of mud and soil, born right out of earth. Black coffee hair, chocolate eyes, sun-browned skin, calluses on each hand. In summer he'd go barefoot; come winter he looked abominable—ice and snow covered him head to toe after a day's work. He never socialized, but he played his piano. Played anything you liked—Mozart, Monk, Hendrix, or Tim McGraw. He'd hear it once then play it by ear. He kept his music hidden. It wasn't *his* music, not really. He didn't work for it. It just came natural, like a seed in the soil springing to life by the grace of God.

One day the local preacher guy was passing the man's double-wide. The preacher heard the music and so knocked on the door, shouting, "Listen, I hear your heavenly playing. Our church piano player can't play in public anymore. She's too old. Please, go listen to her hymns then come play for us." The next Sunday there was music fit for angels' ears. As he did with the preacher, God has a way of putting us in the right spot at the right time so we can make good use of our gifts.

God, some folks seem to have all the talent, all the luck, all the grace. Please let me see the gifts you've given me, and let me have the chance to use them, or to help someone else use theirs. Amen.

Today's Thought Is: **When opportunity knocks, answer.**

The theater professor was roaring from atop of stilts, "Being short's a problem to solve. Strap on a pair of stilts, stand up, and become giants." Just the idea of getting up on a pair of four-foot-high, strap-on stilts gave Joe, one of his students, a nosebleed. Joe feared heights. The professor explained, "There is nothing to it. It's easier than it looks. Once you're up—just never stand still."

As Joe's turn came, the professor said, "If you're the type who's never liked bunk beds, or tree climbing, or looking out windows from second stories, then up on stilts you'll face your fear." As Joe stood up on the stilts, the professor whispered, "Trust me. I'm right here." An amazing thing happened: Joe stood. He stood even though he was frightened. Stilt walking is much easier than it looks and is mostly about facing fear.

Many of us have fears—of heights, of falling, of loss, of the dark, of old age, of loneliness, of death. God asks for our trust when we face our fears. We don't have to do it alone. There are teachers, preachers, social workers, or therapists with skills willing to help us face and overcome our fears. Putting our faith in God is a solid place to start facing the worries of real life.

Let's Pray:

God, help us face our fears and worries with faith in you and trust in our hearts that whatever happens, even if we fall, you are with us. Amen.

Today's Thought Is: Facing fears with God is easier
than it looks.

*I*n the play *Our Town*, set in 1903, a character says something like—"Automobiles are coming. Better stay back. I remember when a dog could sleep in the middle of Main Street all day and nothing would bother him."[16] I thought about this quote when I saw a photo from 1906. It's a picture of a shiny new Stanley Steamer driven by a young man wearing goggles, a starched collar and a tie, and driving gauntlets. Seated next to him is a begoggled older man. They are roaring down a gravel road at a wicked fast twenty miles per hour, with dust flying and gravel spraying out behind them. Lore has it that this was the first car in Wyoming County, Pennsylvania. The sentiment of the character in *Our Town* was right: watch out; cars are coming, and they will change everything forever.

Change comes roaring, unstoppable, and it is inevitable. We grow up and grow old. We watch our kids age. We see new roads cut, highways widened, new homes built where farms once stood. Mills and factories close. Today nearly every adult owns a car or a truck. It wasn't always that way. Change is the only constant in this world—except for God. God, too, is constant and unchanging. If you're looking for a footing or a handhold in this slippery world, then God's the one for you.

Unchanging God, ever constant in your love for us, bless this world of changes.
Be the granite ledge beneath our feet as we face whatever changes
this day brings. Amen.

Today's Thought Is: **Seek the One who is beyond change.**

*G*od said to Adam, "Get outta the garden. Don't come back. Now you're going to have to sweat to put bread on your table, a cell phone in your hand, and gas in your truck. You'll get one day off a week. I'll call it Sabbath. It means to take a break, take a nap, play with the kids. Work is good. You'll like it (most of the time). But rest is good, too. You'll need it."

Okay, so that's not a direct Bible quote. But very few of us actually take a real day off a week. God made it a rule to rest, have potlucks, have fun, stay home, watch the game, go to worship, or hang with friends. Sabbath is important. Not just for working stiffs like Adam, but for working gals like Eve.

Sabbath used to be enforced by law when everything was closed on Sundays. Of course, stores being closed on Sundays wasn't fair to Jews or Muslims, who prefer Saturdays or Fridays over Sundays for their Sabbath. But still it was a day when stores were closed and there was nowhere to go. Currently, for Muslims, Jews, and Christians, and everybody else of any faith, or of no faith, taking a Sabbath day, including going to worship, takes self-discipline—but it's so good for the body, the soul, and our relationships.

Let's Pray:

God, when we need a Sabbath, a time-out, let us know, gently, and help us to take one weekly with you and the people we love. Amen.

Today's Thought Is: Nowadays a Sabbath day can be any day.

On the first ski day of the winter season, while speeding off the top of a steep headwall and catching air on a black diamond trail (i.e., a most difficult trail), and then turning in midflight, an experienced skier landed on the only exposed rock on the mountain and ripped a three-centimeter-long and one-centimeter-deep bulge on the inside edge of one ski, but he didn't know he had damaged his ski and didn't stop to look. He had trouble skiing all day.

"I can't seem to hold an edge on the ice," he complained to his friend at the bottom of the trail. "It's all in your head," his friend rejoined. All day long, thinking that he'd lost his skills because he was growing old, he slowed to keep from slipping.

That night, under lamplight, he saw the truth: a bent unbroken edge. He hammered the ski edge to straightness. He filled back in the gouged bottom with melted black plastic, then sanded it smooth. The next day, the ski shop ground the metal edges back to true and smoothed the rough bottom, making the ski as sharp as the bite of the northwest wind.

Through our faults, or just through circumstances, we may lose our edge and make mistakes. Letting our lives be reshaped and sharpened by God, in partnership with our own hard work, will get us back on the right trail.

Let's Pray:

Dear God, when we lose our edge, when we slip and sin, forgive us,
and then remold us back into shape. Amen.

Today's Thought Is: "God helps those who help themselves."[17]

An American history professor, who was a retired Marine colonel, once said to me, "Laziness is a quality that, in the proper hands, can be put to effective use."

"You're telling me," I said, "that laziness can lead to success?"

He smiled, saying, "In World War II, I was the aide-de-camp for a general in the European theater. Do you know how I got the job?"

"I don't," I answered.

"The general looked around the battalion, found the laziest man, and figured he'd be the most efficient. I was that lazy man."

Lazy? He didn't seem lazy to me. He was an ex-colonel, well past retirement age and still working as a full professor at a midwestern university. He wasn't a lazy man. What he was was generous of mind and heart, and efficient in speech, action, and life. He wasn't a corner cutter. He had high standards. He just didn't like to do things the hard way when there was an efficient, easier way.

People go looking for God by often taking the hard way. They try every religion there is, and when it doesn't quite fit, they cast it off and try another one. They work hard at it but don't get anywhere. If you're trying to find God, don't make it harder than it is. Here's the effective and better way: just invite God into your heart, over and over again.

Let's Pray:

Dear God, come into my heart today. Make it easy. I'm lazy. Amen.

Today's Thought Is: **God is near to all who call.**[18]

n September 1998, a group of twenty-one youths from Maine planned a work trip for early 1999 to Via del Rio, Honduras, a riverside village on the outskirts of San Pedro. The trip was almost canceled because Hurricane Mitch slammed ashore, ravaging the country with pounding winds and flooding rains. The destruction was shocking. Entire village populations were washed away. In Via del Rio, six feet of mud had buried the village. By the time the youths arrived in 1999, the media spotlight was off. The teens painted a church. After they got home, they heard that their painting of the church wasn't as important as the hope they had brought with them; their optimism strengthened the villagers. It took three years to clean up most of the mess down there, and the job still isn't finished.

As bad as Hurricane Mitch was, Hurricane Katrina was much worse. It's going to take years of commitment, dedication, and optimism to fix what has been broken in Louisiana, Mississippi, and Alabama. Now that the TV cameras are focused elsewhere, it's going to be hard to remember that the job isn't done. Maximizing our efforts and our giving in the middle of a crisis matters. But remembering that, *after* the crisis, those who suffered will continue to need our optimism, hope, and help in the years to come matters just as much. We can help immediately. Later on, when they still need us, we should do the same.

Let's Pray:

Dear God, give crisis victims courage, hope, faith, and strength. Grant us the determination to help them in the long run. Amen.

Today's Thought Is: The job isn't finished when the cameras are turned off.

o stand in ancient lands can be dizzying—particularly if it's atop a 782-foot-long, three-span "cantilever arch" bridge, built in 1932 high above the French King Gorge on the Connecticut River in western Massachusetts. The bridge lifts and falls when heavy trucks rumble by, or when the wind blows against it. Torrential rain fell for days. Down the river, and up along its tributaries, flooding made families abandon houses; roads were washed out; dams broke. It was a rain like Noah knew.

Below the bridge, roiling muddy waters energetically burst and boiled above the French King Hole—a 125-foot-deep abyss that the river slowly cuts ever deeper into the granite riverbed. Geologists say that this abyss, this French King Hole, originally resulted during the separation of a nearby fault deep inside Earth's supercontinent, Pangaea. Pangaea was the single land of ancient Earth that broke apart to form the seven continents we have today.

It was near the French King Hole, along this ancient fault called the Eastern Border Fault of the Connecticut Valley, that Pangaea started to break up 200 million years ago. This breakup ceased midstream (so to speak), and instead cracked off along a great fault east of Boston, Massachusetts, and east of Maine. Otherwise, Maine and Boston might have been located in Africa.

Standing in ancient places and thinking about science adds perspective to our lives. We humans are so young on this planet.

Dear God, the Earth was here before I got here, and it will be here after I leave, and life will go on like water through the gorge until time ends. You are All; I am little. Amen.

Today's Thought Is: **Geologic time adds perspective to life.**

*R*eading takes our imaginations on adventures to places far away. There are many good stories. Some of the best are in that old standby, the Bible. In it, there are stories of adventure, challenge, survival, failure, love, deception, heroes, wars, betrayal, murder, miracles, sex, and even a talking donkey. It's just a collection of smaller books bound together as one.

If you've never read the Bible, you probably don't know what you're missing. Sure, it's a heavy book, and some parts are easier to read than others. But don't be put off by the challenge. You can choose an easy-reading, modern version like the New Living Translation, or a scholarly translation like the New Revised Standard Version.

Read it slowly. If you want romance, read Song of Songs. If you want high adventure, try 1 Kings. If you want wildness, read the beginning of Ezekiel. Read a bit. Put it down. Read more another day. You may discover something about yourself in the process. In the end, you'll be glad you read it, because the Bible is the foundation of Western civilization, culture, and art.

Let's Pray:

God, Author of all that is, guide us as we pick up your Good Book to read the beautiful and terrible stories of our ancestors in faith so that we might understand who we are and who you are. Amen.

Today's Thought Is: The Good Book is a good read that teaches us about ourselves and the world around us.

*T*his comes from the *Working Waterfront*, August 2003.

It was a beautiful June day. Wallace Cartwright and his sternman were in Point Aconi Cove. That was where he saw it—twenty-five feet long, with a body the diameter of a five-gallon bucket. It had three humps on its back. It must've weighed four hundred pounds, at least. Its head was a foot above the water, disproportionately small to its body and looking almost like the head of a sea turtle. It went under and hid in the sea-floor mud. Cartwright hung around looking for it and followed it back out to deep water—at three or four knots. Unfortunately, he didn't have his camera aboard.

The curator of zoology at the Nova Scotia Museum of Natural History talked with him about it. The curator believes Cartwright may have seen an oarfish, but he added that there are several deepwater fish that appear to be new species. In the absence of a specimen he can only speculate. Cartwright says, "I looked up oarfish on the Internet, and I'm here to tell you it was definitely not an oarfish. An oarfish looks like a ribbon and this was tube shaped. Oarfish swim vertically and this was swimming horizontally. My neighbors will tell you I have a reputation as credible man."[19]

Being believable makes a difference when what you say is implausible. As far as I know, folks believed Cartwright. Reputation matters. They add credibility or incredibility to what we say. The witnesses of the resurrection were credible men. On their word alone a faith was formed.

Let's Pray:

God, our reputations matter. Help us be honest in all our dealings
and truthful in all our words. Amen.

Today's Thought Is: **A trusted reputation is a treasure.**

*T*wo words bring dread and trembling to American hearts—tax season.

Years ago, at a time when the IRS wasn't kinder and gentler, a clergy friend of mine received a goodly and unexpected chunk of cash—about $3,500—back from the IRS. It was such a strange occurrence that he actually called the IRS office in Massachusetts and spoke to an agent about it. After the agent looked at the minister's tax return, the agent assured him it was correct and the pastor was entitled to the money. The minister used it to pay off his car.

Five years later a letter from the IRS arrived in the pastor's mailbox. In simple language the IRS stated, "We made a mistake when we sent you the $3,500 dollars back in 1994. You must pay it back immediately, including interest, or face prosecution and a fine or jail." The minister went to an accountant, who called the IRS. The IRS was firm. They replied, "You should not have cashed the check and spent it. Pay it back or else." They put it in writing.

Who would have thought that when the old-style IRS sent a check made out in your name, the hidden rule was, do not sign it, do not cash it, do not spend it.

The minister paid. These days, with the kinder and gentler IRS, we expect nothing of the sort to happen, do we?

Let's Pray:

Dear God, we take you at your word. When you say you love us and are merciful, we believe you. Amen.

Today's Thought Is: **In God we trust.**

From Anthony de Mello's book, *Taking Flight:*

In Ireland, a Catholic priest, a Protestant minister, and a Jewish rabbi engaged in a heated theological discussion.

Suddenly an angel appeared and said, "God sends you blessings. Make one wish for peace and your wish will be fulfilled."

The minister said, "Let every Catholic disappear from our lovely island. Then peace will reign supreme."

The priest said, "Let there not be a single Protestant left on our sacred Irish soil. That's sure to bring peace."

"And you, Rabbi?" said the angel. "Do you have a wish?"

"No," said the rabbi. "Just grant the wishes of these two men and I will be pleased."[20]

Many people pray for peace. But peace doesn't start out there somewhere in Iraq, or in the West Bank. Peace starts right inside your own heart. Is it any wonder that nations don't get along too well, when siblings under the same roof, or neighbors across fences, fight, squabble, argue, and sometimes do violence? The peace we seek for the world is not ever going to come until each of us has God's peace in our hearts. Yes, we should continue to pray for peace in troubled lands, but let us also pray that God's peace, the peace that passes all understanding, lives inside our souls.

Let's Pray:

God of Peace, bless our souls with your peace, which we cannot understand but can feel and know comes from you. Bring peace to the lands where war and fighting is common by bringing peace to the hearts of the people. Amen.

Today's Thought Is: **God's peace be upon you.**

*F*earing an attack during World War II, land mines were laid in Alaska's Aleutian Islands. In the 1970s many of those land mines remained live. Occasionally, navy sailors stationed nearby would hear a mine detonated because of a wayward bird or the pressure of a frost heave. The mined areas were fenced. Signs read: "Stay out. Land Mines. Danger."

Two sailors stationed there liked hikes. One morning two of them set off on a day hike along the shore. Seeing it was late, they took the shortest route back to base through a treeless tundra valley. Just as they neared the road they saw a rusted barbed-wire fence heading left and right as far as they could see. After climbing over the fence, they read the fence sign that faced the road. In bold letters it read: "Warning. Danger. Do Not Cross. Land Mines in this valley." Clueless of this danger, they had hiked miles and miles through the Valley of the Shadow of Death safely.

Sometimes we are hapless, clueless fools wandering through the Valley of the Shadow of Death, or Danger, or Darkness. It's only later when we're safely looking back that we may see signs of danger where we walked. What got the two sailors safely through? What gets us through? In the words of one of those sailors, "By Jesus, we made it through." I think he meant it as a prayer of thanks.[21]

Let's Pray:

God, guide our feet this day as we wander through the minefields of home, of work, of school, of life. Bless us with your grace for safety. Amen.

Today's Thought Is: God guides the footsteps of the fortunate, the faithful, and the fool.

*A*n autumn storm comes howling with gusts up to seventy mph. Trees bend. Inches of rain fall mixed with maple leaves. Our lights flicker. We hear a beeping microwave; we see clocks blinking the wrong time. Lights dim down, off, then on, and then dim again, warning of a failure to come. How often do we feel as if the power or the light in our lives is flickering, dimmed, disconnected, or disrupted? How often does it look like God's light is off?

Saint John of the Cross wrote of terrible times when he was in spiritual darkness, lonely and alone. He says: When we feel most alone, we are not. When life is darkest, when we are frightened and feel unaccompanied—that is when God is most with us. It's then that God's presence with us is so brilliant with true light that we are blinded into seeming darkness. We're never alone. The storming darkness of our lives when we feel most alone is when we are not alone. The darkness is merely what our human eyes misperceive because of God's dazzling illumination.

Let's Pray:

God, if we feel alone, or lonely, or desperate in darkness, caught in a raging storm of life, give us a glimpse of your presence, a little light, so we don't feel so alone. Amen.

Today's Thought Is: **Always there.**

*I*n 1 Samuel, there's a conflict. God admits aloud that he regrets that he made Saul the king.

God comes up with a plan for the prophet Sam. "Even though Saul's not dead, I'll have you anoint a new king." This puts God's sidekick Sam in a tough spot. If Saul finds out about God's plan, Sam's a dead man. God says, "No problem, I've got an idea. Fill up your horn with oil, go find Jesse, and pretend you're going to sacrifice a cow. Trust me. I'll take care of everything. Just follow my lead. Among his kids, we'll find a king."

Sam goes. When he gets there, Sam says, "Jesse, come sacrifice this cow with me and bring along the boys." At the barbecue, Sam's getting ready for his big moment. When Jesse's son Eliab walks in, Sam says to himself, "Man, oh man, what a man! He's the eldest, tallest, best-looking, and strongest; he's got to be God's guy." God says, "Hold the horn. Don't be pouring any oil on him. He's not the one. You're seeing with the wrong eyes. Don't be looking at the outside. Look at the heart, like I do."

The other brothers parade past, and for each one Sam says, "This the one?"

"Nope. Nope. Nope," says God.

Sam asks Jesse, "You got another son?"

Jesse says, "Yah, the boy, he's watching my sheep." Turns out that the boy is God's man. Sam pours the oil on David, anointing him king.[22]

We see the stature of a person's body; God's sees the stature of a person's heart.

Let's Pray:

Dear God, we don't see the way you see, but we want to.
Give us eyes to see the heart. Amen.

Today's Thought Is: Seeing the heart isn't easy.

*E*ight hours across Montana were spent in the backseat of a big Buick next to a young Crow Indian whose right leg was freshly set in a plaster cast that he supported across our laps. His mother picked us up while we were hitching because her son needed to keep his leg elevated on the long ride to the end of the Crow Reservation. We got along so well that they drove right through their own town in Montana and brought us all the way to Sheridan, Wyoming, which isn't exactly next door. After ten minutes of hitchhiking while the sun was setting, we got our next ride in a Peterbilt eighteen-wheeler with a sleeping cab, driven by a Ph.D. in philosophy. We had an interesting talk through the long night, punctuated by catnaps in the onboard bunk.

At the bottom end of Wyoming, in Cheyenne, we stopped for breakfast at a truck stop. The driver bought. He was headed to Colorado; we were going to Boston. After breakfast we ambled past a long line of glum hitchhikers headed east. First guy said, "I've been here three days." The next guy said, "Been here four days," and it went on like that until we reached the end of the line, where our spirits were darker than diesel smoke. I held out the sign. The next car swerved over to us, stopped, and picked us up. Off we went.

Let's Pray:

Dear God, sometimes it seems that life is charmed. We don't know if we're living right, or whether you're just smiling at us, but whenever it happens, we're sure happy. Thanks. Amen.

Today's Thought Is: Thanks, God, for the blessing.

A young minister moved into the parsonage of a coastal church. The parsonage was an elegant affair set right on the picturesque harbor. This prime property ended at a seawall on the water's edge. The wall was built of crane-placed stone blocks, some twice the size of lobster crates. Once a day, the minister strolled down to the seawall stones to survey the scene. Winter came.

By early January, chunky sea ice had piled up in the parsonage cove, rising and falling with the twice-daily tide. One wintry afternoon the neophyte went down to stand upon the seawall stones to see the sea. What he saw was that one stone that weighed as much as a snowmobile had fallen into the cove, making a perfect step down to the low-tide beach. The next day he was stunned to see the stone back in its place on the wall, albeit turned a bit askew. This was puzzling.

Old Joe Percy, his next-door neighbor, happened to be outside just then. The preacher shouted to him, "What machine could have moved that stone?"

"By glory," Old Percy shouted back, "'twasn't a machine, must'a been the sea ice first droppin', then liftin' that stone on the tide."

The newbie was incredulous. "Ice couldn't have moved that stone. It's too heavy."

The old man replied, "If Jesus walked on wat'ah, then stones can ride on ice."

Let's Pray:

God, if your sea ice riding on tides can move stones, then please remove the stumbling blocks from our paths that cause us doubt and make us question your wisdom and wonders. Amen.

Today's Thought Is: **God makes stones float.**

A Mars Rover was roaming on Mars (surprised?), exploring the planet's surface. NASA's goal was to "search for and characterize a wide range of rocks and soils that hold clues to past water activity on Mars." The subplot: If there was water on Mars, could there have been microbial *life* on the Red Planet?

Perhaps no evidence of life will be found, no fossilized microorganisms discovered. *But,* what if there are? What if someday NASA finds indisputable evidence of life outside of Earth? It would be mind-boggling and faith bending. This is a theological question with implications perhaps as pertinent today as was Copernicus's discovery that the sun was the center of the solar system, not Earth. His heliocentric theory, which we know is fact, came to a head in Galileo's time (1633), when the Inquisition condemned the sun-centered solar system and sentenced Galileo to life imprisonment for publicly advocating it. It was too dangerous an idea and too radical a thought that human beings and our planet were not the center of God's universe and of everything in it. Vestiges of this view persist in the notion that, in all the universe (with its billions and billions of stars), Earth alone supports life.

If evidence of life is discovered on Mars, it would mean that the belief in the uniqueness of life on Earth is invalid. But it need not weaken anyone's faith, because God is big enough to do things of which we are as yet ignorant.

Let's Pray:

Dear God, you are inconceivably vast; you are greater than our imaginations can conceive. If life is discovered off Earth, help us celebrate your ingenuity and diversity. Amen.

Today's Thought Is: The Bible is a faith book, not a science book.

A trucker dropped the travelers in a valley after traversing a winding highway through the Ecuadorian mountains. The village was typical—carless dirt roads sided by cinder-block buildings fading in color, needing new paint, and surrounded by lush green jungle or fields of waving sugarcane, as well as a few toothless villagers of many ages.

A shiny and new Chevy Suburban stopped. It was completely out of place. The gentleman-driver called, "Care for a ride?" The travelers joined him as he promised a long ride to the city. "But first," he said, "let's stop for a cool cup of chocolate at my cattle ranch." Miles of bumpy lane led to a long paved roadway that wound past an orderly orchard of tall trees to reach his hacienda-style mansion.

They wandered in the cocoa orchard, sipping chocolate in elegant glasses beneath the ripening chocolate pods. Using his machete, he cut a pod off a tree trunk, sliced it, and handed each a piece of whitish pulp to eat. It was a magical day when time slows, when senses are overwhelmed by tropical strangeness—by jungle sights and tastes and sounds—a time when risks are unknowingly taken. One traveler allowed a most beautiful caterpillar to move up his arm. The caterpillar was inches long, with a bloodred fuzzy body and two-inch-long soft black spikes rising from its back.

The rancher suddenly struck the traveler's arm with enough force to bruise it, shouting, "If it bites you, you'll die!" There are risks to adventure, but there are rewards as well.

Let's Pray:

Dear God, may our spiritual lives, no matter what we do, even if we never leave our hometowns, be adventures guided and protected by you alone. Amen.

Today's Thought Is: A spiritual guide who is watchful is helpful.

*B*efore it was a homeless shelter, the brick mansion was a nuns' convent. Our church served dinners monthly to the eighty homeless folk who were guests. We cooked in the kitchen the nuns had used for a century. One day the health inspector came and said, "Update everything in the kitchen." Out went everything; in came stainless steel. The butcher-block cutting table, looking beyond repair, was thrown into the Dumpster. I saw it, asked permission, and took it home. The butcher-block cutting table would make a fine kitchen table.

In the wintertime, I worked on it inside our small barn. After I glued and clamped it, I sanded it down to bare wood. Then it was days and days of keeping the woodstove going in the barn and following a routine of varnish, dry, sand; varnish, dry, sand; varnish, dry, sand.

When it was doing its best work as a cutting table to feed prayerful nuns, and then for feeding homeless men and women, it wasn't pretty. Actually, it was beat-up looking, worn, all the worse for wear. But no matter how shiny it is today, back then it had more soul.

Let's Pray.

Dear God, your values are often different from ours. We often prize external beauty over depth of purpose and profundity of soul.
Teach us your values. Amen.

Today's Thought Is: Inner beauty radiates out the eyes and is gathered through giving ourselves away.

In the summer months—April 15 through October 15— we're connected to summer water, and our laundered whites come out white from the washing machine and shampoo actually rinses clean from our hair. The summer water is sweet drinking. Come winter—October 16 through April 14—we use our iron-rich well. Without a water-filtration system, our laundry in the winter comes out a uniform rust color, making it easier to match clothes in morning. The showerhead spits out abrasive micron-sized iron beads.

Unfiltered, straight from the tap, it's as murky as apple cider and not too good for drinking. Thank goodness for our well-water filtration system works, removes the rust, sweetens the water, and keeps our whites nearly bright, our hair manageable, and our drinking water drinkable. But the best drinking water comes from an old ground spring that never freezes. I haul bucketfuls to the house, sometimes using snowshoes when the snow is deep. We filter the spring for microbes, just to be cautious, and it's worth the effort. That's some delicious drinking water.

Everybody drinks water, maybe chlorinated right from the tap, or pumped from a well, or hauled, or bought. To live, we must have drinking water. One day Jesus met a woman at a well where she'd come to haul water. He said, If you drink my water you'll never thirst again. The water he offers isn't earthly. It's holy, it's spiritual, and it satisfies the soul and satiates the mind. We need only ask to drink.

Let's Pray:

God, give us a long drink of your sweet water so our souls never thirst again.
Satisfy our longing. Amen.

Today's Thought Is: Is your soul satisfied; is your mind satiated?

At one time I taught English for a rural GED program. We met once a week for three hours in a classroom at the island high school. My students were all women. Each had dropped out of school a decade before because of pregnancy. They each discovered life without a diploma was difficult and so worked hard both in class and at home. Written assignments included essays, poems, and stories. They wrote about themselves, about the pain and struggle of poverty. One or two dropped out. The dropouts always wrote about abuse. It was common for their husbands to force them to drop out. The men were scared that their wives might start thinking for themselves; the men were scared because they were losing control of their wives, their personal property; they were scared because the wives were learning new ideas and might soon come to understand that women aren't worthless.

Are men who act in such controlling ways abusive? As far as I recall, these women didn't suffer physical violence. They did suffer verbal violence, demeaning language, and issues of control in all aspects of their lives. And that's abuse. If you or someone you love or know needs help, if you believe you are in an abusive relationship, you can find help at our Web site —www .dailydevotions.org.

God loves you. You'll get through this.

God bless the women and men who live lives controlled and abused by those who profess to love them. Bless them and get them help. Amen.

Today's Thought Is: There is no excuse for abuse.

I never saw Mel Gibson's film *The Passion of Christ* because . . . well . . . I've read the book. Regarding who is to blame for Christ's death—we should blame God and Jesus, and nobody else. In the Gospels, God requires this death of Jesus.

On the eve of death, Jesus tries to squirm out of the deal in a heart-to-heart with God. In Matthew, it says, ". . . he threw himself on the ground and prayed, 'My Father, if it's possible, let this cup pass from me; yet not what I want but what you want.'"

In John, Pilate says, "Do you not know that I have power to release you, and power to crucify you?"

Jesus answers, "You would have no power over me unless it had been given you from above . . ." i.e., from God.[23]

According to the Gospel of John, Jesus knows it's going to happen, acts to let it happen, and lets it happen. He says, "'No one takes it [life] from me, but I lay it down of my own accord. I have power to lay it down, and I have power to take it up again. I have received this command from my Father.'"

It's not about blame. It's about choice. Jesus chooses. God chooses. The rest are just players on the stage.

Dear God, enough of centuries of blame, and fanning the flames of division and divisiveness. Heal us of our religious accusations, blame naming, and insensitivities. Amen.

Today's Thought Is: **God said it. Jesus did it.**

For the young among us, George Burns and Gracie Allen were a vaudeville comedy team and marital partners who also performed on radio and on television. Gracie, who was actually the brains, heart, and soul of the partnership, played a lovable airhead whose misunderstandings were laughable. At the end of their shows, George would say, "Say good night, Gracie." She'd say, "Good night, Gracie."

When she was dying, she feared for George. In the final love note she penned to him just before she died, she wrote, "Never place a period where God has placed a comma. . . ."

Lots of us, for all sorts of sincere reasons, have put periods where we ought to have commas:

God doesn't love me (period).

God is not there for me (period).

I do not believe in God (period).

God's too far away (period).

The thing is, God sincerely believes in us (period). God's still speaking to us, if only we would remove the periods and add a comma or two here and there.

Let's Pray:

Dear God, our own ideas sometimes get in your way. Sometimes we do all we can to block you out, by putting periods and no-trespassing signs all over our lives. How about lending us a comma? Amen.

Today's Thought Is: **God is still speaking.**[24]

*R*eporters are saying, Sunni this, and Shi'a that. What's the difference between them?

All Muslims share a belief in five basic pillars of faith: There is one God, and Muhammad is his Prophet. Pray five time daily: predawn, noon, afternoon, sunset, and evening. Fast from sunup to sundown during the thirty days of Ramadan. Perform a Hajj (a pilgrimage to Mecca) at least once in one's lifetime. And, give *zakāt*, or 2.5 percent of savings, each year to the poor.

Sunnis and Shi'is agree on these five. Their rift occurred long ago over the political and religious leadership issues regarding who should lead Islam after the Prophet's death. When Prophet Muhammad died in 632, a minority of followers wanted his son-in-law, Ali, to be the Imam, the new religious and political leader. This minority was called, "Shi'ati Ali," or the supporters of Ali. The Sunni majority decided to choose from among Islam's elders, and they elected an old friend of the Prophet's, Abu Bakr, as the first Caliph, a political and religious ruler. Basically, Sunnis believe they may approach God directly, while Shi'is believes they need a cleric's assistance.[25]

There is an institutional division between the two groups, and deep wounds on both sides. One could point to similar situations of shared basic beliefs and institutional divisions among Christians, or among Jews.

Let's Pray:

Dear God, help heal the divisions in our faith, and among your people, no matter their faith. Amen.

Today's Thought Is: **Ignorance prevents constructive dialogue.**

What would it mean if, in the years to come, the Red Sox had a couple of players who could repeatedly hit 650-yard home runs? I mean, besides Yankee fans crying in their seats? Sound athletically far-fetched? It's not, except maybe the Red Sox part in it, but we can hope. Batters hitting 650s—not crazy now that gene therapy for muscle enhancement is nearly here. It's being developed to relieve muscular dystrophy and to reverse the deterioration of muscle tissue in the elderly; and it has, of course, additional applications. A synthetic gene developed at the University of Pennsylvania prevents and reverses muscle wear and tear. It works in mice, and it looks good for humans. Athletes, naturally, have expressed interest in becoming genetically enhanced.[26]

Let's pretend that gene therapy is completely safe and healthy (maybe it will be someday), what then would be wrong with athletic genetic enhancement? What's wrong with a power-lifter at the Olympic Games lifting an SUV? Everybody has genes that are the luck of the draw. Not everybody can pitch in the big leagues. Our God-given genes have a lot to do with it. Certain athletes have genetic talents; others strive for athletic success. Is it morally wrong to change our bodies to suit desires? As we tinker with evolution, how do we make choices about what is right and what is wrong?

Let's Pray.

Dear God, we are changing your world faster than we can create structured ethical guidelines for our creations. We pray for guidance. Amen.

Today's Thought Is: What is human perfection?

Years ago a large out-of-state dragger was headed up Penobscot Bay with little regard for the local fishermen. One lobsterman was hauling his traps when that dragger hooked the trap he was hauling. The lobsterman radioed the dragger, asking her to cut her engines so he could free his trap. The dragger replied, "Cut your trap. We're not stopping."

Every islander on the bay knew that the out-of-state draggers were tearing up the bottom of the bay and smashing lobster traps as they went, so there wasn't a lot of goodwill around for those boats. A half-a-dozen other lobstermen working on the bay heard the radio exchange and came steaming fast. One, who intentionally crossed the bow of the dragger, was nearly hit trying to block the dragger's course. Angers flared. Lobstermen grabbed their rifles, which were hidden below deck. Somebody fired a warning shot across the dragger's bow. Aboard the dragger fishermen grabbed their rifles. Meanwhile, the original lobster boat was taking on water by the bucket load. Tensions grew. A shootout was about to begin when the Coast Guard came zooming over to stop what could have been death and disaster for many families. At the appearance of the Coast Guard, the weapons vanished and angers calmed. The dragger was stopped; the trap was disentangled.

Miraculous interventions can stop us in the nick of time from succumbing to anger or temptation. May God intervene in our lives with forces that prevent us from making terrible mistakes. May we have the courage and willpower to stop ourselves, as well.

Let's Pray:

God, if we encounter terrible temptations coming from strong emotions that might ruin our lives, our family life, or the lives of other families, stop us, or help us stop ourselves. Amen.

Today's Thought Is: "Whatever is begun in anger ends in shame."[27]

After weeks backpacking in the Gallatin National Forest, we needed a challenge. We left the wilderness trail to bushwhack through the mountains. We set up camp one evening at an alpine pond. It looked like nobody had been there in decades. Next morning at sunup I heard a noise. I unzipped the tent, opened it, and came nearly nose to nose with a curious moose. She didn't know what to make of us. Like many backpackers, I figured the nylon tent offered protection against the wilds, so I zipped it shut. When we awoke later, the moose was gone, the scenery was stunning, and the sky true blue.

If we hadn't left the trail, we'd never have seen the pond or the moose. But without our map we would have been lost. By reading the map, we knew where we stood and where to go. A map is necessary when traveling in places we've never been before. It keeps us on trail; or, if we wander, it shows us how to get back. On a map we can mark our destination and our intended route. The Holy Scriptures are a lot like a map. They show the lay of the spiritual land. They tell us how to get there from here, but we have to know how to read them, and we actually have to do the reading. Referring to the Scriptures keeps us on trail and helps us reach our ultimate destination.

Let's Pray.

God, wherever we wander in life, help us to find the way by using your written word as our map, leading to our ultimate home. Amen.

Today's Thought Is: **God gave us a map.**

O n *The Honeymooners,* Ralph Kramden used to say, "Ooh, Alice, one of these days: Bang! Zoom! Straight to the moon!" In 1961, President Kennedy officially launched our race to the moon, where we landed in 1969.

When the first humans stepped out of Africa millions of years ago, we began the long journey of our planetary exploration. Ever since, we've been wondering what's on the other side of the next hill, the next mountain, the next river, and next ocean. God gave us curiosity and a need to see what's around the next bend. When we learned to sail, we set out in ships to explore coastlines, and to search for the fabled lands beyond the horizon. Now curiosity takes us beyond the confines of our home planet.

Dear God, what is it we seek when we explore? What is it we want? Is it wealth, power, and glory, or do we have wanderlust because we seek you, and don't know it? Amen.

Today's Thought Is: **What do we seek?**

*T*he blizzard closed the school, doctor's office, dentist's office, market, and town government for the day. Still, she had to go to her office, so she drove the roads. A cautious driver on clear days, she took her time and was careful. The slick on the road was too much, though; her car slid, spun, and then struck a snowbank. She got out. No harm done, just stuck. It was bitter, blowy, and the snow was piling fast. Just as she began walking the mile toward the nearest house, the only pickup truck that was out slowed as it neared her. It was driven by a rough character—an avowed enemy of her husband—who was with two of his buddies. He had warned her husband, saying, "I'm going to get you! I know where you live! You watch out!" Locals advised her husband to "take the threat seriously," and the sheriff had suggested they get a gun.

Recognizing her, the man slowed and his truck crunched to a stop. The three men got out and walked toward her. There was nowhere to run and nobody to hear her should she scream. The men looked at her and her car. One rummaged in the truck's bed and returned with a chain. Saying nothing to her, or to the other men, he chained her car to the truck, put her transmission in neutral, put the truck in reverse, and hauled her out. They nodded to her and then left.

You might be surprised by what sort of person God chooses to use. It could be you.

Let's Pray:

God, clean our hearts. Link us to those in need. No matter what we've done, or who we are, we belong to you. Use us. Amen.

Today's Thought Is: **God uses both saints and scoundrels.**

*T*his motel was the only motel. If it wasn't for mold on the ceiling, the thin walls, and the noisy neighbors, then he wouldn't have minded the psychological torture of the rhythmic sound of rain dripping off the roof and onto the air conditioner next to his flat pillow. Twice during that night he got up to see if there was anything he could do to stop the dripping. Short of praying for a bolt of lightning to end his misery, there was nothing to be done, except await morning while enduring a fitful night of strange dreams. When morning came, he swallowed three cups of cold, stale coffee found in the motel office, and ate two half-thawed pastries—the Continental breakfast. Thus fortified, he sallied forth on that holiday to find that his spare tire—which he had put on the right front wheel the night before, while stopped on a hill, in the pouring rain—was nearly flat. Like a rum-sopped Subaru, he slopped his way on that soft tire into a gas station, found the pump, and rummaged for seventy-five cents to run it. Finding no change, he approached the attendant with a sawbuck. Seeing his car, the tire, the out-of-state plates, and the wild look of sleeplessness in his eyes, the attendant said, "Don't worry. No charge. I'll just turn it on." In that moment, her small act of kindness turned his day around.

Let's Pray:

Dear God, thank you for kind strangers who, with their small favors, live out what your Scriptures instruct. Amen.

Today's Thought Is: "And when was it that we saw you a stranger and welcomed you?"[28]

When a minister visited an old woman recovering from an agonizing surgery, the first thing she said was, "My son died in Vietnam." It wasn't patriotism that made her say this, but instead a pain deeper than any physical pain. It came from grief; she misses her son daily. Grief, like love, never ends. Eventually, if we live long enough, we all lose somebody we love. Humans share grief in common, although we always experience it alone. To feel grief is to be embraced by a profound and invisible loneliness. It's often isolating.

No one sees it but you. No one feels it but you. Everybody else seems to forget. Over the years this woman came to understand that she needed to speak about her grief. Grief demands acknowledgment because real grief defines us even when we're smiling, even when we're enjoying ourselves. It gives us depth, wisdom, and understanding about life, and, I hope, about our faith, too, if we believe in eternal life. Paul the Apostle says, "Love never ends." Neither does grief. You can't have one without risking the other. Grief is a measure of love lost. If we never loved, we would never grieve. Knowing this, I still choose to love. Do you?

Let's Pray:

God, we pray for those who mourn and ask that you grant them the strength and endurance to bear it and face another day. Bless them with joy. Bless them with a true smile. Bless them with hope. Amen.

Today's Thought Is: Love never ends.

As early dusk dropped, warm autumn rain and high winds were triggering minor havoc. The wind blew down an old spruce tree that was half blocking the only road on and off a narrow peninsula that juts out into the Gulf of Maine. The town manager, John, dressed in his yellow slicker, his slacks soaked to the skin from the rain, stood on the gravel shoulder directing traffic around the blown-down tree while calling the town road crew on his cell phone. A driver stopped his truck, got out, and asked John, "Do you think we can move it?"

"It's a little big for us, don't you think?" was his reply. The tree was seventeen feet long and two feet in diameter. It was heavy. Still, the young driver wanted to try. He grabbed hold of a thick branch, planted his feet, and heaved; but he failed to move it an inch. "Let's just wait for the crew, shall we?" said the town manager.

Sometimes it takes a whole crew of folks to get a job done. No matter how much heart or strength a person puts into a task, some jobs are just too big for one person. Effective faith is like that. The Epistles teach that Christianity is a group religion. It is not done well alone. If you've tried and tried on your own, maybe worked up a spiritual sweat and strained a muscle or two, but you still can't move along or find God, then maybe it's time you started working with a crew. Visit a house of faith.

Let's Pray.

God, lead those individuals who are pining for you, whose hearts are ready for you, into a community of faith. Amen.

Today's Thought Is: **Faith is a group effort.**

With furious flaming pillars reaching two hundred feet high, the menacing wildfires of California burned many homes to cinders. A reporter seeking to find the human angle of the story interviewed a school teacher who lost her house to the wildfire. For a while, the teacher said, it seemed that her neighborhood would be spared destruction, but then the wind changed direction. The teacher had only a few minutes to choose what she valued most among all her possessions before fleeing for her own life. She chose nothing of material value—no jewelry, no clothing, no electronic equipment, not even her favorite jacket. Escaping with only the clothes on her back, she carried with her a single folder containing her children's artwork. She hurried with their art to her school, placed the folder inside the pottery kiln, and hoped her treasure would survive the fire.

She had no time to plan, no time to think things through. She just reacted. She chose with her heart. She chose with love. Love was all she could carry. Love was all she could save. Ultimately, love is the only article we can carry with us into eternity. In a similar circumstance, may God forbid, what would you choose?

Let's Pray:

God, although we'll never know what we'll take with us in an emergency unless
we were forced to choose, we hope you'll always help us to pick love.
It weighs nothing, but it means everything. Amen.

Today's Thought Is: **Your heart is where your riches are.**[29]

One question I read in a journal while waiting in a doctor's office: "Do human beings need nature?"

My first thought in answering their question was, "Duh?! We need nature because we are nature, not above it, not outside it, just part of it." We aren't separate. We're creatures. We didn't make ourselves. We dominate on this planet, but we are part of it and need it to live. Try as we do, we're not in control.

Obviously we age and die, just like every living creature on the planet. There are bigger forces—ice storms, earth tremors, solar flares—which we can't control. On a molecular level, we're made of exactly the same matter as absolutely everything else in nature. What creates matter? The prophets, teachers, and the messiah say—God, our Creator. Everything else is created, is nature. Not outside, not above, just part of.

Let's Pray:

Creator, you made us different. You made us with opposable thumbs,
a reasoning brain, the abilities to speak, build, invent, and self-reflect.
We are nature. We seek you. We belong to you, God. Amen.

Today's Thought Is: We are nature capable of self-reflection.

A man told me about his hospitalized four-year-old grand-daughter, who had a baseball-sized tumor. The doctor had told him that "95 percent of tumors like this are cancerous. It's in a danger-ous place. It doesn't look good." The grandfather was ticked off at God and was loudly calling God some nasty names. When her biopsy came back, it showed that hers was in the narrow 5 percent that aren't cancerous and that she would be fine. She was okay. The grandfather apologized to God and said thanks, too. What struck me was the depth of the grandfather's faith and how comfortable he was—enough to be really angry.

Being angry with God is okay. God's tough. God can take it. People who are angry at God probably have more faith than they think they do. Some-times when folks are angry at God, they think they've lost their faith. When you get angry at your wife, or your husband, or your kids, does that mean you don't love them? It takes quite a bit of faith, not to mention moxie, to be gnashing your teeth at the Creator of the cosmos. If you're furious at God, then you almost certainly have faith in proportion to that fury.

Use it.

You might want to try channeling that anger, that faith, into prayer, by trying to discover what God wants from you rather than just blaming God for your predicament. This doesn't mean your troubles will vanish, but you might find some peace with your pain.

Let's Pray:

God, you allow us freedom to express ourselves to you. You know we might be angry. You know we might be hurting. Help us find peace. Amen.

Today's Thought Is: Being angry at God can be part of faith.

My grandfather had good morning habits. He said good habits make life easier. Every day, right out of bed, he'd make the bed he shared with my grandmother, and then shave his face, splash on Old Spice, wet his hair, brush it back, and get dressed before going downstairs for his coffee, with sugar and cream, and breakfast. In his seventies, he said he never wanted to get out of the habit of looking his very best for my grandmother, even first thing in the morning.

We all have habits. Some are healthy; some aren't. If you are reading this, then maybe you are in the habit of taking a couple minutes a day out of your life for God. This book might be part of your routine—part of your daily habit, like making your bed or brushing your teeth. Maybe you're in the habit of stopping for a moment to pray with me. Prayer is a healthy habit. It's easy, helpful, and quick.

Let's Pray:

God, help us keep up the routine of daily prayer so that if we ever really need you, we'll already be in the habit of talking with you. Amen.

Today's Thought Is: **Prayer is a healthy habit.**

Our theater troupe drove in from the Nevada desert, hurrying from our last performance to the next, hoping to arrive at our hotel in time to catch a few hours' sleep before we had to get on stage. Instead of riding in the fifteen-passenger van with the other performers, three of us sat in the back of our pickup truck, which was pulling a large trailer full of costumes, props, and equipment.

We three in the back of the truck were enjoying the sights and the hot sun of Las Vegas when we stopped at red light. A flatbed eighteen-wheeler rumbled to a stop next to us. It was heaped with beehives. Instantly we were enveloped by a thousand of bees. We froze as the cloud of bees buzzed our hair, near our noses, around our ears, elbows, knees, and toes. The light changed. Our driver floored it. We laughed until we reached the next light, when the bee truck idled next to us again. For seven city blocks we were surrounded by bees at each red light. There was no room in our truck's cab, our van was too far ahead, and the traffic was too heavy to stop. We endured those tickling bees and their chilling buzz. Eventually, we turned off the main drag.

Sometimes, through no fault of our own, we get stuck in dreadful situations. The best we can do sometimes is endure, be calm, and wait for it to end.

Let's Pray:

God, if we ever end up in alarming positions, help us to remain calm and patient, and encourage us to rely on you. Amen.

Today's Thought Is: Patience, calmness, endurance.

A self-admitted "old woman" was seated next to me at a Jackson Browne concert in the newly reopened Boothbay Opera House. It'd been closed for decades. She said, "When I was a girl, I roller-skated here. Town meetings were here, too. I remember back in the fifties, up in the balcony a bearded beatnik with an earring spoke his mind at those meetings, and then he'd swing over everybody's head on the post like an ape."

The night of the concert the house was packed. Looking up at the stage, halfway through the show, the old woman leaned over to me and shouted, "Who the hell is that singer anyway?" My face showed disbelief. Not at her language, but at the idea that she didn't know Jackson Browne. She said, "I bought tickets because it's a benefit for the opera house. I love this place!"

She applauded every song. At the end of the show I asked if she'd had a good time. She said, "I like him, but I don't care too much for his music. Did he write those songs? He did? Well, I'm glad I came. It's a great old building." This woman had loyalty. It didn't matter whether she liked the music of this particular famous singer or not. She was there for the cause.

All this reminds me of folks at church. Not everybody likes the minister, or what he or she has to say. But there are bigger issues than like or dislike, such as loyalty to God, to faith, to church, and to people.

Let's pray:

God, help us see beyond our likes and dislikes to the larger issues of life. If our fidelity is needed, help us remain steadfast. Amen.

Today's Thought Is: **Be loyal.**

*E*arly one morning Jesus was walking to a city. He had the morning munchies. Seeing a luscious fig tree, he approached it, anticipating mouthwatering, sweet, tender figs for breakfast. Maybe figs were out of season. Maybe the tree had been picked over. Maybe it was too young to bear fruit. Whatever the reason, this fig tree had no figs, just leaves. Jesus was ticked off. He said, "No more figs from this tree—ever!" Immediately, the tree shriveled down to a stick stuck in the ground.

"Unbelievable!" muttered the disciples as they rubbed their eyes, "Did you see that? A green tree! Now a brown stick! How did ya do that, Jesus?"

Jesus was nonchalant, saying, "It's nothing. If you have faith without doubt, you'll do more than little deeds like this. See that mountain over there. Well, for instance, if you tell it, 'Go jump in the lake,' it will jump."

Lots of faithful people put their belief into prayer by trying to move one mountain or another. Maybe it's for the Red Sox to win the World Series for a second time (which they finally did!), or for peace in the Middle East, or for the health of a very sick child, or for the life of a soldier, or for the money to pay for food or the rent, or for anything worthwhile and improbable. Yet somehow our prayer is not always answered—the mountain doesn't always move. Maybe the problem is not our faith or our doubts; maybe the problem is our desire. Maybe instead of praying, "My will be done," we'd be better off praying, "Your will be done, God."

Let's Pray:

God, align our hearts with your desires for us. May your will become our will, not the other way around. Amen.

Today's Thought Is: Pray like you mean it.

᷒nside a downtown Connecticut church for the well-to-do, the congregation was quite generous with charity. Checks were regularly and gladly written: the evening soup kitchens, the AIDS Awareness Project, Meals-on-Wheels, the needle exchange, and the local homeless shelter received support. Their giving was generous, important, and necessary, but it was done at arm's length.

One icy Sunday morning just as the good preacher began to preach, the double doors banged open. Stomping their feet and shushing one another loudly, three homeless men entered. Every head of silver twisted round to see, secretly hoping there'd be an empty pew anywhere but next to them. Week after week these same three men came, often late, often sipping coffee, often unbathed. They came and were ignored, avoided, and shunned.

Unable to endure it any longer, one Sunday morning, after the three took their seats in the far-back pew, a deacon of the church, well dressed and dignified in bearing, stood and moseyed along the center aisle. He gestured for the three homeless men to push in and make room for him, and then he sat. The following week two or three more joined those four, then ten, then many. It took a while for the church members to see human beings inside the street clothes. Only then did the church begin to learn about love.

Let's Pray:

Rich or poor, male or female, young or old, no matter our race—to you, God, no one is above or beneath the other. To you, God, we are equally loved. We thank you. Amen.

Today's Thought Is: **We are changed by faith in action.**

The phone rang late one night. It was an old friend in New York City. He said, "I'm at the hospital getting stitches. I need to get away. May I visit you tomorrow?"

"Sure," I said. "You coming alone?"

"Alone."

"What happened?"

"Tell you later."

A gauze bandage was taped across his forehead when he arrived. After dinner he spoke. He'd had a terrible and stupid argument with his significant other. She grabbed a leather belt. She whipped him—first with the strap and then the buckle. A buckle blow caught him and cut him as he struggled to escape their studio apartment. He caught a cab to the ER. A doctor put in eleven stitches. My friend slept in the waiting room that night. In the morning, when he knew she'd gone to work, he returned, packed, and left.

He revealed it wasn't the first time she'd hurt him badly enough to send him to the hospital. There been hitting, shoving, bruising, stitches, a broken bone, and abuse for years. It's not often you hear a man, especially a strong, athletic man like my friend, telling a story like this. Abuse is about dominance, control, and manipulation. Could he have "taken her"? Sure, he's sixty pounds bigger, but it's not about size. It's about control, humiliation, and violence.

Domestic violence doesn't occur only against women. Men can be battered, and so can children.

Let's Pray:

God, for those wounded—physically, psychologically, emotionally and spiritually—by abuse, give them hope, healing, and freedom from fear. Keep them safe. Amen.

Today's Thought Is: To find safety, call 800-799-7233 today.

THE WIFE WHO HAD NO SHADOW:
AN OLD TALE RETOLD

*L*ong ago there was a pastor's wife who was constantly afraid that they would never have enough money. One Monday, on her way to the bank to deliver the Sunday offering for the poor, she stole a little cash. Each week she did the same. She felt terrible, but she felt relief, too, for she was able to buy all her heart desired.

Months later, when she was walking with her husband in the churchyard under a full moon, the pastor suddenly noticed his wife did not have a shadow. This frightened him and he demanded that she confess all. She admitted what she'd done and he, on hearing her story, cursed her, saying, "Flowers will grow from the roof of the parsonage before God ever forgives you. Leave now and never return!"

Many years later, an old tattered woman knocked on the door of the parsonage asking for a meal. The housekeeper fed her and gave her a bed for the night. In the morning, the pastor discovered that the old woman had died in her sleep. On seeing her face, he recognized her immediately as his wife.

As he stood there contemplating the scene, the housekeeper, who had just arrived for the day, shouted, "Pastor! Come outside! It's a miracle!" Outside, the pastor saw that the parsonage roof was covered with beautiful flowers.

What humans curse and condemn, God forgives.

Dear God, whatever sins we hide, whatever dark shadows cover our hearts, we pray that, in your mercy, you'll forgive us. Amen.

Today's Thought Is: Our God of Light sees our shadows and loves us still.

A stranger appeared on the pier one day and sat down on the edge, with his legs dangling over the side, as he stared out to sea.

"He sure looks like he's waiting for something," mumbled the old captain as he sat on the dock repairing nets. The stranger showed up every morning, sat, and, with his legs dangling over the sea, just stared out at the water until nightfall. Curiosity overcame the captain when he noticed the stranger was growing thinner by the day.

"You waiting for something?" the captain asked.

"For my ship to come in," the stranger replied.

"*Your* ship?" the captain asked.

"It will be mine when it gets here," replied the stranger.

Pretty soon the stranger was near thin enough to slip through the captain's netting.

Finally, the stranger spoke first. "Captain, I'm getting hungry. Please feed me, and when my ship comes in, I'll make you wealthy."

"No, sir," said the captain, "but I'll give you work building my boat. If you work hard enough, eventually you might earn enough money to buy that boat from me."

"Why do I need a boat?" asked the stranger.

"So instead of sitting here wasting your time, you can go out there and meet that ship of yours halfway."

"Nope," the stranger replied, "if I work, I might miss my ship."

Let's Pray:

Dear God, while we're waiting for our ship to come in, help us to keep learning, keep trying, and keep living, so that we'll be able to meet our destiny halfway. Amen.

Today's Thought Is: **The lazy person wants but never gets.**[30]

A well-dressed couple arrives at a dinner party. In the entryway, the wife explains to their host, "The traffic was atrocious tonight; it was bumper to bumper. I hope you're not devastated because we're late."

Then she adds, "I did bring dessert, as promised, but I spilled the entire tray of my homemade baklava. It's a disastrous catastrophe!"

During dinner, the conversation turns to world news. Each couple reports that they donated money to an earthquake relief effort. "What happened over there," says the host, "was disastrous! A catastrophe! The loss of life, the destruction of property, was an overwhelming calamity."

Bumper-to-bumper traffic, a late arrival at a party, and a dropped dessert aren't equal to the enormous loss of life and to total destruction of property of an earthquake, yet often we use the same, or similar, words to describe both real devastation and spilled milk.

A wise teacher once said, "You don't wear Sunday-morning church clothes or Saturday-night fancy clothes to change the car oil. No, you wear your old clothes for car oil and set aside good clothes for elegant occasions. Words are the same. Certain words should be held back, not said, and not used, unless the occasion truly calls for them. Some words are too powerful; some words are too sacred, for common usage."

Let's Pray:

Dear God, words are like waves: they may be gentle or shocking; they may soothe us or destroy us. Help us to say what we mean, and to mean what we say. What meaningful or sacred word do you have for us today, God? Teach us to listen so that we might hear your words, and understand your meaning. Amen.

Today's Thought Is: **Are we cautious with words?**[31]

*S*cience points to the causations. Science doesn't ask about the purpose of a flood. Faith asks those question. Why is there suffering? What is the cosmic plan?

In the Gospels, Jesus is asked, "Whose sin was it who caused this man to be born blind?" The question means, Whose fault is it? Whom can we blame? Is it divine punishment? These questions are asked by Christians, Jews, Hindus, Muslims, and, if they happened to believe in God, Buddhists, too, when disaster strikes.

After the Twin Towers were destroyed, one TV preacher claimed that God let it happen because of America's immorality. The real question is: Is suffering punishment? We want to know: Is God vindictive? Those questions are as old as the book of Job.

After a disaster, pointing a finger and shouting "It's his fault!" or "It's her sin that caused this!" is at best speculative, and at worst inflammatory. One Sri Lankan Buddhist, whose deity statues miraculously survived the tsunami, claimed it was proof of God's judgment against Islam and the abandonment of traditional Buddhism. Certain Indian Hindu leaders, angered at the conversion of members of the lower castes to Christianity, blamed the flood on the Christians who were stealing Hindu souls. Zealous and ambitious minds always find ways to use tragedy to advance their private agendas.

Let's Pray.

Dear God, in times of disasters, personal or public, stop us from shaking our fists in anger, or pointing our fingers in blame. Instead, help us to find ways to live compassionately. Amen.

Today's Thought Is: **Suffering is an opportunity for serving.**[32]

A slight dripping sound of water was audible. A dozen times, I checked the pipes and found only dryness. Then on a Saturday morning—a holiday—with family visiting, I was on the sofa reading when my wife said, "Peter, come hear this."

The drips were drops, splashing my face, from the pipes that led from the downstairs bathroom to the upstairs bathroom. To discover the source, I peeled off the sopping wet drywall from the wooden ceiling above it. The heavy and soaked drywall fell, knocking apart a pipe connection. Upstairs I tore up my carefully laid ceramic tile floor, exposing a trapdoor opening that was too small for me to use to reach the leak. The saber saw fixed that. Too bad, though, that I didn't see the shower pipe, which I accidentally cut in two. First, a hidden leak between floors; then, a separated pipe connection downstairs; next, a cleanly cut third pipe upstairs. It all added up to no showers for guests, plus considerable deconstruction mess. I lost my humor.

In the midst of all this, while going to our small barn for supplies and tools, I pulled on the handle of the back door. It broke off in my hand.

I thought I had had a bad day until I heard about my neighbor's frozen and bursting septic system, which happened that same morning. She'd thought her septic troubles were bad until she heard about the tsunami.

Let's Pray:

Dear God, gently adjust our thinking, adjust our seeing, so that we may understand what truly matters. Amen.

Today's Thought Is: No matter how big our little troubles seem, proper perspective makes them smaller still.

y friend and colleague Reverend Fred Lyon sent this story to me:

"When my mother was a girl, her family had a habit of not removing the Christmas tree until her birthday, January 26. It was a habit that became a tradition. Throughout my own childhood, our family Christmas tree did not come down until a full month and one day after Christmas morning. Sometimes the tree remained standing in our living room beyond January. Mom's record for Yuletide endurance was the year our tree did not leave the house until Easter.

"I am not making this up.

"Valentine's hearts replaced Christmas decorations in February. Green and orange St. Patrick's Day shamrocks—for peace between Protestants and Catholics in Ireland—adorned the tree during March. Easter decorations hit the branches come April.

"My father shook his head, a lot. Our neighbors asked questions about when "that tree, there" inside our front window was coming down. Strangers stopped us in our yard and earnestly pointed out that the tree was still up, as if we had somehow managed to overlook six feet of Scots pine in our living room for several months.

"Even so, it was worth having the tree up. Instead of setting aside Christmas like one more present that soon bored us, the tree kept something of the Christmas spirit alive well into the new year."

Let's Pray:

Dear God, when we packed away the Christmas ornaments, did we pack away our faith as well? Renew us today with your spirit. Amen.

Today's Thought Is: Faith is for every day, not just for holidays.

*S*ri Lankan wildlife officials reported few animal deaths resulting from the Indian Ocean tsunami. The series of monstrous waves that washed up to two miles inland, destroying everything, surged into the island's biggest wildlife reserve. Yala National Park is home to elephants, deer, leopards, jackals, and crocodiles. When the waves struck, the animals were already gone.[33] How did they know?

Animals are more sensitive to their surroundings than humans are. It's well known that elephants and whales communicate over long distances using infrasound, a low frequency that humans can't hear. Dogs and wolves have ultrasound hearing well above the human range. Pigeons detect electromagnetic waves. Birds see ultraviolet light. When lions and tigers and bears sense something cataclysmic is creating unusual and dangerous vibrations, they run away. They don't have to understand it.

It doesn't take a sixth sense to know when it's time to get out of danger's path. A TV viewer of mine wrote to me about troubles in her extended family—multiple divorces, teenage depression, abuse, suicide attempts, hostile and threatening words, eruptions of anger, violence, miscommunication, betrayal, harassment, restraining orders, and frequent police visits. She wondered whether her decision to move to a nearby city was the correct choice. She wants a fresh start and the perspective of a healthy distance. Her friends think she's running away. It doesn't take a sixth sense to see she's sensibly gaining a little distance. We can't really run from our troubles, but we can get out of danger's way.

Let's Pray:

Dear God, you've given us the ability to sense danger, give us the wisdom to get out of the way. Amen.

Today's Thought Is: The clever see danger and hide; but the simple go on, and suffer for it.[34]

✧⁕✧

*I*t was a wickedly slick day on the slushy winter roads, and it became worse that night when roads were covered with ice. Our county sheriff's office fielded fifty wrecks, rollovers, totals, and fender benders.

Scott was wearing his seat belt that night, and so was his brother John, when John lost control of his jeep on the slick surface. For whatever reason, Scott says that he suddenly sensed God's presence with them, inside the jeep, which was odd because neither he nor his brother John are the "church-going" types, although both say they pray. They rolled over, landing in the woods unharmed. Their Cherokee was totaled. The officer at the scene said they were lucky to have been wearing seat belts; otherwise, they could have been seriously injured or killed.

Buckling up after the accident starts is too late. In order for the seat belt to work, we have to buckle up *before* trouble starts. The same can be said about inviting God into our lives. Why wait until trouble begins to form a relationship with God? You know trouble's coming, sooner or later. Better to put that belt on before trouble starts.

Let's Pray:

Dear God, feeling your love is good when life is tumbling out of control. Let that strong, undeniable feeling of your presence, that powerful connection, stay with us as long as possible; or at least allow that feeling to stay in our memories as a motivator for faith. Amen.

Today's Thought Is: Faith is the seat belt of life. Buckle up.

ver lunch, a friend mentioned that some of his friends had watched *Daily Devotions* on WCSH 6 TV in Maine. The friends wondered if my title, reverend, wasn't a bit stuffy, a bit off-putting for the reading/viewing audience. They have a point. Whenever I meet new people who hear I'm a reverend, they automatically make all sorts of assumptions about who I'm supposed to be . . . I leave that to your imagination.

Well, I've hit upon a possible solution for this. I've been looking into purchasing a new title, in fact, a royal title, normally $397, but now on sale for a mere $197 at a certain Web site whose physical address is in Las Vegas.

How does "Lord Panagore" sound? Too pretentious? "Duke Panagore"? "Sir Peter"? "Baron Panagore"? "Baron Panagore" has a ring to it, don't you think? Otherwise, I probably have to start using my middle name, which may go better with "lord," as in "Lord Baldwin." That sounds pretty good!

The seller of these legal royal titles promises that my life will change when I make hotel, restaurant, and airline reservations. People will fawn over me and do anything for me. He promises that I'll automatically gain entry into London's high society, be invited to the chicest parties, and be taken on exotic trips by my new well-heeled friends. He promises that merely by buying a title and putting it on my passport, car license, and credit cards, my popularity will skyrocket, and I'll gain new respect, escape the mundane, and enjoy unheard-of privileges.

And it'll be all because people will believe that I am something I am not.

Let's Pray:

Dear God, you see me for who I am. To you, image is nothing, and you love me anyway, for nothing is hidden from you. Amen.

Today's Thought Is: **Appear as you are, or be as you appear.**[35]

As he was tying his running shoes, Ramone stopped her walk on the indoor track to deliver her news—news that was matched by her gloomy look. "Do you drive a green VW?" Ramone asked.

"Yes," he said, with a sudden sense of doom.

"Well, I'm sorry I have to tell you this on such an icy, raw, nasty day, but your back left tire is flat."

Bearing bad news isn't sweet. The bearer, if she has empathy, feels the burden of the telling, even if it's only about a hole in a tire.

In his shorts, fleece top, and sneakers, he went out into the weather to change his tire. After switching it to the donut-sized spare, he drove over snow-slick roads to a nearby dealership. The helpful fellows behind the counter promised it'd be done by the time he finished his run. It was a nail. It wasn't tragic. Holes like that are easily fixed.

Other holes in our lives aren't so easily fixed, though. There are people who regularly bear bad news—doctors, lawyers, judges, stateside military officers, members of law enforcement, ministers, reporters, family members, and others who deal with life and death matters. It takes a heavy toll on people who must repeatedly present truly bad news to those who don't want to hear it.

Let's Pray.

Dear God, we pray for those who carry the burden of presenting bad news, and for those of us who must hear it. Give the bearers solace, and help the hearers love them still. Amen.

Today's Thought Is: "None love the messenger who brings bad news."[36]

*A*esop, according to Herodotus and others, was a freed slave in Greece who lived in the sixth century B.C. Various writings connect him with certain adventures and with such luminaries as King Croesus, who is reputed to have invented money. Maybe you've heard the phrase "as rich as Croesus." The fables attributed to Aesop may or may not have been written by him, but the fables themselves are old.

As a boy, when I prayed to God, or told my parents that I needed something, they'd say, "God helps those who help themselves." While I have found this to be true in life, I have not found it anywhere in the Bible, or in Christian literature. I have found it in *Aesop's Fables*, in the story titled "Hercules and the Wagoner." Here's how the story goes.

A Wagoner was once driving a heavy load along a very muddy way. Eventually, he came to a part of the road where the wheels sank halfway into the mire; the more the horses pulled, the deeper the wheels sank. So the Wagoner threw down his whip, knelt, and prayed to Hercules the Strong. "O Hercules, help me in this my hour of distress," quoth he. But Hercules appeared to him, and said, "Tut-tut, man, don't sprawl there. Get up and put your shoulder to the wheel. The gods help them that help themselves."[37]

This saying, when applied to our God and ourselves today, remains true. Have we called upon God to fix something in our lives that we could fix ourselves, if only we tried?

Let's Pray:

Dear God, don't let us use you as an excuse for not getting done what we should get done. Amen.

Today's Thought Is: **God helps those who help themselves.**

*T*rouble comes to all friendships sooner or later. The question is: Will the friendship survive? When a tragedy, misfortune, or illness happens, who sticks by you? "The Travelers and the Bear" is an old tale, attributed to Aesop, who wrote around the sixth century B.C. It goes as follows:

Two men were walking along together when a bear suddenly met them on their path. One of them quickly climbed up into a tree and hid himself in the branches. The other, seeing that he was about to be attacked, threw himself flat on the ground and, when the bear came up and felt him with his nose, and sniffed at him, the traveler held his breath and played dead. The bear soon left him, since it is said that a bear won't bother a dead body. When the bear was gone, the other traveler climbed down from the tree and jokingly asked his friend what it was the bear had whispered in his ear. "He gave me this advice," his companion answered. "Never travel with a friend who deserts you at the approach of danger."[38]

Misfortune tests the sincerity of friends. The Teacher used to say that the greatest love is shown when we lay down our lives for our friends. While that does occasionally happen, we don't actually have to die to prove our loyalty. All we need to do is be there when they really need us.

Let's Pray.

Dear God, when we're in trouble, let our true friends support us, and let us be true friends to those who need us. Amen.

Today's Thought Is: To give one's life for the sake of another is the greatest gift of all.[39]

*B*efore sunup, before I open my eyes in the comfort of my warm bed, the morning radio voice announces the nightly toll from the IEDs that exploded in Baghdad, Mosul, Fallujah, or other places in Iraq. As I linger over coffee in my kitchen, the war leads the news on TV, in the papers, and on the Web. The radio voice, the words in the paper, are all about WMDs, armor, or soldiers, generals, National Guard members, reservists, or neighbors, brothers, sisters, sons, daughters, mothers, and fathers.

One voice on the radio says we must stay. One face on the TV says we must leave. At home, we all feel it. We can't help but feel it, even when we're distracted for a moment, for an hour, for a time. The war sits like a jackal on our shoulders; it hangs in the air around us like thick cigarette smoke. We carry it, and we breathe it, because those men and women over there are people we know, people we love.

No matter where you stand—in support of the expansion of democracy, or as a decrier for peace—those women and men, those Americans, those neighbors and kin deserve our prayers of support. They deserve our thoughts, and our care, and our concern. Many of us know this already; some just need to be reminded.

Let's Pray.

Dear God, be with our armed forces at home and abroad as they struggle to survive, as they do their jobs. Bless the Iraqi and the Afghani people as well, and may they find justice and peace. Amen.

Today's Thought Is: Say a prayer for a soldier today.

A hard blow to the back of his head caused him to experience a temporary loss of vision in his left eye, but he could still see out of his right eye. The left eye was seeing black with lightning-type hot pink and brilliant orange flashes that arced across his vision field like a psychedelic laser show. As Tom came to, his doctor, who was leaning over him, told him how Muhammad Ali sustained brain damage from repeated blows to his head.

However, because the half-blind patient could still partly see, he insisted he could drive home. The doctor, being a man of brains and wisdom, and being the one without a head injury at the time, asked Tom if it wasn't possible that he might end up in a ditch somewhere, or worse—that he might end up causing an accident and forcing others into a ditch. The doctor insisted that Tom not drive. The doctor took Tom's keys.

Being able to see is an advantage when driving. The Teacher used to say that when the blind lead the blind, they both might fall into a ditch or, in this case, drive into one.

Let's Pray.

Dear God, blessed are those with spiritual insight whom you have chosen to lead us. Show us your path, lead us in light, and dispel our darkness. Amen.

Today's Thought Is: **Let those who can see lead.**

*T*he sand road ended abruptly at the grassy top of soft dunes that spilled down twenty feet to Silver Sands Beach. As the sun set, the children practiced flying. In order to fly, first the children had to run. A short sprint up the sand road, and then a high leap off the dune top, propelled the children skyward and outward, their arms spread wide, legs kicking the air ready for the landing, screams of delight issuing from their mouths. Hour after hour, the children leapt to flight, landing softly on the dune, getting sand everywhere—in ears and hair, up shirts, and down shorts.

It had to end. Dune jumping is now prohibited, protecting dunes from leaping children and other types of erosion. While it lasted, jumping off dune tops was a launching point for children's dreams. Believing one could fly, if only for a moment, empowered young imaginations to consider other dreams and other possibilities.

Let's Pray:

Dear God, bless us with imagination and vision so that, when we dream, we may see ourselves as more than we are, as perhaps what we might become; bless us with ambition and encouragement, and strengthen us to pursue our dreams. Amen.

Today's Thought Is: Gravity is reality, but so is flying.

*I*t's not mysterious to some folks, but to me the mysteries of modern cars are as impenetrable as the writing on ancient Sumerian clay tablets. Not long after I bought new tires and had the front end balanced, a *thump-thump* sound began up in the left front.

I made a fool of myself at my auto dealership by wondering aloud if one new tire had a defect. My mechanic told me, "It's probably a CV joint assembly." I acted as knowledgeable as the next guy.

I know enough to change the oil, to pump gas regularly, to jump a battery when it's dead, and to rotate the tires, but under that hood lays a landscape of rubber hoses, wires, cast aluminum, fuses, and computer chips that baffles me. It's okay not to know everything. There are things I understand and things I don't.

God has no such limitations. There's nothing too complicated for God, whether it's engine design, quantum mechanics, or life's troubles. If you have problems, if you feel broken, if you don't understand why, turn to God. It might not be as simple as fixing a CV joint—it might not be fixable at all—but sometimes just trusting God is the solution.

Let's Pray:

Dear God, this life is full of trouble. We don't understand how or why. Help us trust you. Amen.

Today's Thought Is: **In trouble? Trust in God.**

*S*cientific American titled it "Sponge-Nose Smarty Pants." The close-up photo showed a bottlenose dolphin wearing a sea sponge on her nose. Marine biologists working in Shark Bay saw that certain females wore sponges to protect their tender snouts when they were rooting for food on the seafloor. Not one male wore one, and neither did every female. The question was, Did the dolphins learn this, or was it instinct? Using DNA from 13 "spongers" and 172 "non-spongers," the biologists determined that all the spongers had a common ancestor, but they couldn't find a gene pattern that would cause the behavior. There was no wear-a-sponge-on-your-nose gene. Their conclusion? The dolphin mothers of a certain ancestral line teach it to their daughters.[40]

The role of a mother or a father is to protect a child from injury. We humans don't put sponges on the noses of our kids to protect them from harm, but we do make them wear bike helmets and help them to avoid injurious situations.

The last thing we want to do is intentionally inflict pain in our child's life, and yet sometimes it happens. In divorce, children are hurt. It may be best that the parents separate, but the pain to a child is real and lasting. Let's pray for the kids who can't be kept from emotional injury.

Let's Pray:

Dear God of soft places, give comfort to those children whose parents are divorcing. Guide them through this painful time, let them know that they are loved, and give them tools to cope. Amen.

Today's Thought Is: **Remind children that they are loved.**

At fifteen, with his first drink, Tommy saw his future as an alcoholic. He drank through high school and college. He destroyed his first marriage. His wife took their kids and ran. Being alone gave him more drinking time. He smashed cars regularly. He couldn't keep any job. Each morning, he'd start to drink until he passed out, then he'd wake up and start again.

I tried to get him to AA, but he wasn't ready. He wanted to quit but couldn't. In his last month of drinking, he swallowed twenty gallons of vodka. With a blood-alcohol level of .945, Tommy entered ten days of hell in a hospital ICU unit to detox, followed by six weeks in a recovery center.

When I bumped into him one day at the library, my first thought was, "Here's trouble," but looking at him carefully I could see that something had changed. He no longer weighed 130 pounds, no longer had rheumy eyes. He was at least 180 pounds, his eyes were clear, his speech sober. The day before had marked one year of sobriety for Tommy. I asked how he did it. He said, "I went to AA and asked God to lift my obsession, and God did."

Let's Pray.

Dear God, we give thanks for answered prayers, and letting us go low enough so that surrendering to you is our only chance. Bless those who need to surrender; help them to help themselves. Amen.

Today's Thought Is: AA and God make it possible to quit.

embers of one sailing crew learned their lessons. In their first year, they were consistent across the finish line—dead last. In their second year, they improved until they started capturing second-place finishes. Then a new a man joined the crew. He wasn't an experienced sailor, but even with the new guy the crew did pretty well.

Many things can go wrong quickly on a sailboat. After one race, while they were sailing toward home, the wind shifted quite suddenly, causing the mainsail to switch sides unexpectedly all on its own. When that happens, it's a fast danger.

Switching the mainsail is called jibing and is usually done under control. In either case, the captain shouts, "Jibe ho!" which means, "Duck quickly." This time the new guy didn't duck. The long aluminum tube at the bottom of the sail clunked the new guy hard on the head, nearly knocking him over the side, and flipped him literally heels over head. Other than an egg-shaped lump and a raging headache, he was okay. It's not likely he'll forget to duck next time. Me? It took two or three times of getting boomed for me to figure out it's best to duck.

Let's Pray.

Dear God, some lessons you teach us hurt; some are hard; some are hard to learn; some are all three. God, help us to not be hardheaded about it. Help us learn the first time. Amen.

Today's Thought Is: **Some lessons are learned over and over.**

A hard-nosed city cop who rose to the rank of sergeant, and was acting as the night-shift supervisor, was having trouble sleeping during the day. On his day off, Sarge went to see his doctor.

"Doc," Sarge said, "ever since I started working the night shift, I haven't been able to sleep. At home in the morning I pull down the room-darkening shades, I put in my earplugs, I lay down exhausted, but still I can't sleep. I haven't slept in weeks. It's not good when cops don't sleep. Besides this, I'm nervous all the time, and I get the twitchy shakes pretty often."

Doc proceeded with a regular examination. Afterward, the doc said, "I can't find anything wrong physically, but tell me, do you drink coffee?"

"Sure, down at headquarters, there's always a pot on. At night the station runs on coffee," said Sarge.

"How much coffee do you drink a night?" asked Doc.

"Not much," replied Sarge.

"One, two, three cups a night?" asked Doc.

"Ah, let me count one, two, three . . . maybe . . . fourteen or fifteen a night."

"Fourteen or fifteen? No wonder you can't sleep! Who could?"

Let's Pray:

Dear God, in order to treat our bodies like little temples of God, which is how you designed us, we need positive, healthy habits. Show us how to treat our bodies as holy places and help us feel your spirit within us. Amen.

Today's Thought Is: **Your body is God's temple.**[41]

nside the restaurant, as is proper, she set her cell phone to vibrate and then spent a productive and enjoyable business dinner with her colleagues. She wasn't worried about, and consequently didn't answer, a call from her eight-year-old daughter, who was home, she knew, with her responsible, nice-guy ex-husband. After dinner, she checked her voice mail. The first message was from an old friend who was checking up on her and making her laugh. The second message, which had been placed nearly an hour ago, made her nearly swerve off the road. In a panicked voice, her daughter was crying and asking, "Where's Daddy? He's supposed to be here! He isn't. Where are you? I think Daddy must be hurt or something 'cause he would never just leave me here alone!" She pulled over, guiltily accusing herself of being a horrid mother, and then, calming herself down, she called her ex's suburban home. Her son answered. All was well. Dad was okay. He'd had an unplanned drink with his colleagues on the way home, then suddenly remembered where he needed to be and had driven right over. She was glad everything was okay but was livid that her daughter had suffered those feelings of panic and abandonment. Fearing she'd speak irrationally because of her anger, she wisely decided to wait until the next evening, by which time she'd have calmed down, before she said anything to her ex.

Let's Pray:

Dear God, when insult, injustice, or injury causes anger to flash hot inside us, give us the wisdom to wait, and to speak only when reason has returned. Amen.

Today's Thought Is: A fool gives full vent to anger, but the wise person quietly waits.[42]

*O*r a hard-played friendly pickup game with its own rules: The infield is covered in the usual way, but the outfield may have as many as ten or twelve fielders covering it. Hit the ball into the woods to the right of the birch tree, and if nobody touches it before it goes in, it's a single; to the left of the birch tree, it's a double. Strikes are swings and misses, and there's no walking the batter.

In one game, an adult at shortstop convinced a twelve-year-old runner on third base that there were two outs when really there was only one. A fly ball was hit to center field, and, believing that there were two outs, the base runner ran home. The fly ball was caught in the air and tossed to the shortstop, who threw it to third, where the base was tagged for the last out. The boy would not have run on one out and a fly ball.

The boy had trusted his adult counterpart to be truthful. By manipulating the boy, the adult got the third out, but the boy learned to trust less those he thought he could trust the most.

Let's Pray:

Dear God, change the hearts of those who would intentionally mislead a child. Give children wisdom to detect manipulators, and the innocence to trust those who are trustworthy. Amen.

Today's Thought Is: The righteous walk in integrity—happy are the children who follow them![43]

There is a car that gets 12,666 miles per gallon. It was featured in the September 2005 issue of *Wired* magazine. If the engineers who built the ultrahigh-mileage car have their way, gas-guzzling will someday be a thing of the past—and, maybe, so will gasoline. This car runs on hydrogen, and at $58 per gallon, it's still a steal.

Designed at Zurich's Swiss Federal Institute of Technology, the Pac-Car II is slow, long, low, and lean. It's not a family car. It's knee high and narrow, and it looks more like a small, one-person submarine without a propeller than it does a car. The best driver for this "slow-ster" is a petite 100-pound mechanical-engineering student. Her lithe frame fits tightly inside this high-tech, three-wheeled, 62-pound, aerodynamic, banana-shaped vehicle. Instead of a 200-horsepower engine, it has two 150-watt motors. Yes, 150-watt motors. We use lightbulbs with more wattage.[44]

How can 300 continuous watts of energy provide the power to move 162 pounds 12,666 miles? One could ask a similar question of faith. How can something so small be so powerful in so many lives?

Let's Pray:

Dear God, we need a tiny wattage of faith, barely giving light, and we shall move the world. Amen.

Today's Thought Is: With a speck of faith, we can do the improbable.[45]

*I*n Appletown many independent apple orchards operated. Then one day, overseas apples washed ashore by the freighter full, and the price of apples fell like fruit in a hurricane. Most all the orchard owners gave up and sold out. Only one orchard remained. This old farmer loved apples; he loved apple trees and apple blossoms; he loved fresh cider, hard cider, applesauce, apple butter, baked apples, apple pie . . . but most of all he loved the pick-your-own apple pickers who came to pick.

It was hard times in the orchard during those years. The debt mounted, taxes grew, profits fell, but still the pick-your-own pickers came, and still the owner loved his apples. When the debt was worse than ever, the farmer faced a terrible choice: bankruptcy and lose everything, or sell out and pay the debt. He was land rich and cash poor. He didn't want to sell his land.

It looked like terrible trouble to the old man. Who was he if he wasn't an apple farmer? That's all he'd ever known. He had no use for being cash rich. The bank said, "Sell it all, or lose it all." Then he had an idea. He owned five hundred acres, and only fifty were in apples. Why not keep the orchard he treasured, sell off the rest, and pay the debt?

Let's Pray:

Dear God, show us how to love you and treasure you, and show us how to hang on to you, too. Amen.

Today's Thought Is: On finding a pearl of great price, he sold all that he had and bought it.[46]

*M*arcel Marceau, the famous French pantomime, often performed his renowned routine "The Mask Maker." In silence, he pretended he was playing with two masks—the mask of tragedy and the mask of comedy. He'd mime picking up one of these invisible masks and putting it on, and he'd be sad; and then he'd mime switching it for the happy mask. Back and forth, he switched his face, as quickly as he could. Suddenly the comic face was stuck. He couldn't get if off. He tried prying and pulling with all his strength. It would not budge. As the performance continued, his body expressed determination, desperation, anger, fear, tragedy, and sadness, and all the while on face was the comic smile. Eventually, he removed the mask, but not before the audience came to understand that we all wear masks.

On Halloween, children will wear masks to disguise their identities as they walk from door to door filling their bags with candy. It is the one time each year when we, as a society, allow ourselves and one another to be who we aren't, to look like we don't, and to be someone other than ourselves.

No matter the masks we wear, no matter what we try to hide, God knows us for who we truly are.

Let's Pray.

Dear God, we may be frightened of showing others our true selves, but we ought not be frightened of you. You already know us; you know all our dark and hidden places; and yet you love us anyway. Thank you for your love, and may your light shine in those places we wish it would not. Amen.

Today's Thought Is: **God sees through all disguises.**[47]

*J*esus had a younger brother named James—poor imperfect James. Just imagine what it was like growing up in a household with the Son of God. Talk about the perfect child. I'm guessing James could never measure up. He was probably always blamed for everything; Jesus probably never was. Anytime anything was broken in the house, it was "*James*, come in here right now!"

Yet when James was older, and he understood who his big brother was, he became a follower. Later on, long after his death, James was declared a saint. Was James some sort of perfect person? Hardly.

I used to believe that saints had to be perfect people. They had to be pure of heart, and holy of body, and must seldom, if ever, sin. But looking closely at all the apostles makes it clear that they were just plain old human beings who made plenty of mistakes and were, in fact, no different from you and me. What makes a saint then? A saint is a person who loves God with all her heart, mind, and soul; and who loves her neighbor as she loves herself.

Let's Pray:

Dear God, we aren't perfect. We are broken and yet you love us. Send us your love, that we might love you back, love ourselves, and love our neighbors. You don't have to make us saints; just give us love, so that we have love to give. Amen.

Today's Thought Is: **God loves those who love themselves.**[48]

*C*hin tucks, eye lifts, dental veneers, nose jobs, jaw enhancements, liposuction, enlargements, and reductions are primetime TV. Cosmetic enhancements use medical means for nonmedical ends. However, extreme body makeovers transform lives. The self-effacing ugly duckling becomes the lovely swan, complete with the new self-confidence and hope that beauty brings. Let's face it: exquisite looks open doors. Of all the prejudices—like sexism and racism—in our God-given world, the preferential treatment given to the gorgeous cuts across all socioeconomic and racial lines.

A while back, an hour-long TV magazine had two young people apply for the same jobs. They carried hidden cameras and hidden microphones. The handsome applicant's résumé was not as strong as the unattractive candidate's résumé. Guess who got the job over and over again? Is it any wonder then to what extremes we will go to look gorgeous?

Add nonsurgical procedures like teeth whitening, retin-A, Botox, Minoxidil, and hair dye. Throw in health club memberships. What we have here is the great desire to look our best for our own advantage. In the olden days, we might have called this vanity; now we call it maintaining the edge, getting ahead, and seeking the advantage in our relationships, in business, in life.

Let's Pray:

Dear God, the pursuit of beauty is as old as henna in the hair, perfumed oil on the skin, and charcoal eye shadow. Now we reshape the body. Help us to remember that the body is God's temple. Amen.

Today's Thought Is: **Is beauty only skin deep?**[49]

He landed at our airport at midnight and finally opened his back door, totally exhausted, at two A.M. To test if the contractor had installed plush new carpet while he was away (as promised), he kicked off his sneakers before flicking on the light. In his bare feet, he felt the deep soft wool. Then he felt something unexpected. First, there was a tickling on his legs. Then there was a bite, then another bite, and another, then ten bites! As he leapt up onto the countertop, he scrambled for the light switch. In the light, he could see thousands of black dots leaping knee high off the carpet and landing, leaping and landing. Fleas! Fleas in the carpet! The fleas of a thousand camels were infesting his brand-new plum-colored carpet and were trying to bite his fresh flesh!

Fleas or not, it was time for bed, so he dashed across the carpet. After treating his bites, he slept, rose the next morning, and called the carpet company.

This man had arranged to make a change, had opened a door, and had then found a thousand complications resulting from that change. How often do we arrange for a change in our lives only to discover unforeseen ripple effects?

Let's Pray:

Dear God, we do the best we can, making choices and changes as we go. If our choices result in painful or undeserved consequences, help us to find a remedy, or at least help us to endure. Amen.

Today's Thought Is: **May God guide our choices.**

*T*n *Beatrix Potter's Nursery Rhymes* there is the famous story that begins:

"You know the old woman who lived in a shoe?

And had so many children she didn't know what to do?" . . .[50]

No matter how big her shoe was, that little old woman who lived in a shoe must have lived in cramped quarters.

An old islander from Penobscot Bay told me there once was a woman who lived on the island who'd given birth to a baby every year for twenty-one years. Twenty-one babies! Can you imagine trying to house that many kids? One family in the neighborhood where I grew up had twelve kids. Their house was bigger than a shoe, but it wasn't a mansion. Housing kids in big families isn't easy, but God has room for everyone.

Let's Pray:

Dear God, the word is that you have room in your home for all your kids—all the billions and billions of us. Keep a bed open for me. Amen.

Today's Thought Is: In God's house, there's room for all God's children.[51]

*W*hen my racing skipper announced that Thad, who won an Olympic gold medal in sailing, was going to join our crew of misfits for an afternoon, I figured I'd learn a thing or two. Instead, I learned 222 things. Among them was how a sailboat moves forward. Like most people, I had thought the wind pushed the sail like a big windbag. Duh!

That's not quite how it works.

Sailboats move because of the curved shape of the sails. The wind on the back (concave) part of the sail moves across the sail slower than wind on the front (convex) side of the sail. The wind on the backside creates high pressure, which pushes the boat forward, but only because the faster wind on the front side creates a low-pressure vacuum that likewise *pulls* the boat. It's like a blow-dryer on one side and vacuum cleaner on the other side. A sailboat has to be pushed *and* pulled forward; otherwise, it won't move. It's got to be both.

I don't know about you, but I'm stubborn enough that I need God to push and pull me at the same time to get me to move forward. If I don't get pushed and pulled, I ain't moving forward. Spiritually speaking, I need a desirable goal in front of me and a bit of threat behind me.

Let's Pray:

Dear God, draw us forward; push us toward your goal for us. Let us resist little, and gain much, by your insistence. Amen.

Today's Thought Is: **God pushes, and God pulls.**

On the Isle of Springs, on a warm afternoon, the gorgeous bride, Anna, stood beside her lovely sister, Kim. Both were beaming, blond, and blue-eyed. The handsome crowd of well-dressed guests sat still as the cello and flute finished a musical interlude just before the vows were spoken. Anna spoke her vows with all her heart. Rick, her groom, charming in every manner, repeated his vows with love. His best man, Matt, handed the minister the rings. The minister prayed a blessing on them, handed them one at a time to groom and bride, who each in turn placed a ring on the other's finger. The mood was sweet and tender, and tense at the immensity of the pledge. "You are committed each to each other," the minister intoned. His hand on all four of theirs, he looked intensely at Rick and Anna, and briefly glanced at the eyes of her sister, Kim. He pronounced, "Rick and Kim, you are husband and wife with God's bless—"

Anna interrupted loudly, "You called me Kim!" The tension shattered into laughter. The minister stopped, blushed, and said, "Anna, Anna, and Rick, you two, Anna and Rick, are wife and husband."

One thing's for sure, when God calls your name, he's never going to make that mistake.

Let's Pray:

Dear God, you know our names, you know our souls, you know our hearts and the core of who we are—call us by name, call us to you. With all our heart, we await that joy. Amen.

Today's Thought Is: God's never going to mix you up with somebody else.

ouseflies like people. I'm convinced of it. They must get pleasure from us or, worse, food out of us. Or maybe they have a form of undetectable superintelligence that just likes to toy with us. In my house, I am the eliminator. I swat pesky flies whenever and wherever. Unhappily, my enthusiasm has led to some broken objects.

In my zeal to cleanse the world of houseflies, I've made mistakes. Christianity's sometimes like that—smashing the wrong things while trying to do right. During the Spanish Inquisition, they didn't use comfy chairs to convince nonbelievers. The Crusades weren't any better, and neither was turning a blind eye to concentration camps. Judging me by the objects I've smashed is as shortsighted as my blindly slapping flies. Judging an entire religion by seeing only the horrible human mistakes of its believers is shortsighted as well. We've all got flies on us.[52]

Let's Pray.

Dear God, we all make big mistakes. So do institutions like religion. Forgive us our errors, help us make amends, show us how to love. Amen.

Today's Thought Is: God, please forget our mistakes.

*H*olding a phone to her ear, she sits alone on a folding chair, under a white sun high above and behind her. The sun casts her shadow on the grass, a contrast of light and dark. She's speaking to a friend about the woes of life, the choices that must be made. In the middle of her shadow, on the ground, at an angle from head to hip, a singular beam of light appears to cut her in half. It doesn't belong there. Shadows don't have light beams inside them. Shadows are the absence of light. Yet there it is—a white beam bisecting her shadow on the grass. Intellectually, she knows that the narrow beam is a reflection off the tall window by her side. Nevertheless, that's not how it seems. It seems like the Light of God is cutting through her. She feels God, always does, but that reflected light beam bisecting her shadow is symbolic of how her life now feels—fragmented, cut into two. Either choice she faces is right, but choosing either one means pain for somebody.

God is present in our pain, in the choices we must make. That doesn't mean God will choose for us. The best we can do is pray, trust, and try.

Dear God, why is it that we're faced with dilemmas, in which either choice is right, yet both cause pain to one or another? We wish it were not so, and beg for your guidance. Amen.

Today's Thought Is: It's not always a choice between right and wrong; sometimes it's worse—a choice between right and right. May God guide us.

*W*hat's done is done. There's no changing that. When the phone call came at 7:38, reminding her of where she was supposed to have been at 7:30, it was too late to get there on time. It was an hour's drive, and at the other end were angry and disappointed people who had gathered expecting her attendance. She was their soprano soloist. The trouble was that the date had just never made it onto her calendar. Her reputation as a responsible person was seriously damaged. The concert was in a week. There were public expectations. It didn't matter that this was the only rehearsal she'd ever missed. It didn't matter that she was good at what she did. All that mattered was that she had missed a rehearsal.

The next night she was again scheduled to rehearse, and there was no hiding, no backing out. She had to go and face them. The respect they had for her as a professional was gone. Part of her job was showing up on time, as expected. Not showing up was worse than bad form; it was irresponsible. It's the kind of behavior that gets people fired, and she felt terrible about it, was truly sorry. But she had to go and face the music.

Let's Pray:

Dear God, when we make a mistake, when we inconvenience others or hurt persons unintentionally, help us mean it when we ask for their forgiveness and then help us forgive ourselves. Amen.

Today's Thought Is: Forgive others as they forgive you; and as they forgive you, forgive yourself.

*T*his is edited and reprinted with permission from *Homiletics* journal. The author is unknown.

A young marine and his commanding officer board a train headed through the mountains. They find two seats across the aisle from a young woman and her grandmother.

After a while, it is obvious that the young woman and the young marine are interested in each other; they're giving each other looks. Soon the train passes into a tunnel and it's pitch-black. There is the smacking sound of a kiss, followed by the smacking sound of a slap. When the train emerges from the tunnel, the four sit silently.

The grandmother thinks to herself, "It was brash of that young marine to kiss my granddaughter. I'm glad she slapped him."

The commanding officer thinks, "I didn't think the young marine was brave enough to kiss that girl, but I sure wish she hadn't missed him when she slapped and hit me!"

The young woman is thinking, "I'm glad the soldier kissed me, but I wish my grandmother hadn't slapped him!"

The young marine sits with a satisfied smile and thinks, "Life is good. When does a fellow have the chance to kiss a beautiful girl and slap his commanding officer all at the same time!"[53]

It's difficult to know exactly what happens in the dark. When we're in the dark, misunderstandings and miscommunications can predominate.

Let's Pray:

Dear God, there is darkness in life. When we cannot see, when we are alone and without guidance, shine your light so that we may see. Help us so that we may understand. Amen.

Today's Thought Is: **Who illuminates your darkness?**

The man was thirsty in his brother's house, and opened a cabinet near the sink to grab a glass. There he found, among the tableware glasses, a work of art. A clear glass goblet, hand turned, mouth blown, whose stem was a colorful round marble. It was strangely light in his hand, and it fit perfectly. He filled it with well water from the tap and drank, his lips lying on the rim as if the rim had been made for his mouth.

The man's brother came in and, seeing the glass on the counter, lifted it and said, "This is unbreakable. It's made of laboratory glass." The brother dropped it to the floor. It was shocking and slightly frightening for the man to see his brother drop the piece of art. The glass bounced. Picking it up, the brother said, "I've seen the blower purposefully drop his artwork to a concrete floor hundreds of times to prove it's unbreakable." So saying, the brother again dropped the glass from waist height. Again, it bounced. "You try," said the brother. The man took the glass and dropped it to a carpeted floor. It shattered. Sudden silence filled the room; and then apologies, forgiveness, and the vacuum cleaner. All glass, even laboratory glass, has an unpredictable shattering point. The man must have dropped it just right . . . or just wrong.

Let's Pray:

Dear God, even that which is seemingly perfect about our lives can be strangely fragile, and may shatter when we least expect it. Be with us when it shatters; help us pick up the pieces. Heal us. Amen.[54]

Today's Thought Is: **Nothing is unbreakable.**

They were out of state visiting family for a reunion and decided to take a side trip. It was pouring a steady cold rain. The car was parked at a meter on a busy street on a hill, very near the granite curb. It was getting dark on the Saturday night of a holiday weekend. The sidewall of the tire had struck the sharp edge of the curb when he was backing in. They thought nothing of it and went on their way to visit the university and to see the town. Hours passed. More unexpected rain came, and fell hard. The tire that struck the curb was now flat. This once-cheery family dissolved into a sopping, chilled mess. Earlier, on the ride down to the valley, a child had been carsick. The boyfriend of an aunt, who was coming from Boston to meet the family, had been hospitalized with a stomach illness. Another aunt found that she wasn't quite over the flu, so she went home. The family reunion faded.

After changing the flat tire, the family drove back up into the mountains on the skinny spare, itself nearly flat. That night, they stayed at the best motel in the area. Best does not always mean nice. The rooms were moldy, with broken fixtures, thin walls, and loud neighbors. As it turned out, despite all the trouble on that cold wet weekend from hell, the family found time for meaningful conversations between the teens and their parents.

Let's Pray:

Dear God, open the doors of conversation within families, and let the hard times become the best times for talking. Amen.

Today's Thought Is: **Talking with family is worth almost any price.**[55]

*I*n the capital city of Sierra Leone was an orphanage where twenty-six children and their American caretaker, Pinky McCann, lived. Among the orphans was a little girl about to be adopted by a Maine couple. A war raged outside the orphanage—bullets broke windows and riddled walls; mortars exploded in the streets. Fearing for the life of their new daughter, the couple in Maine contacted everyone they knew. Within days they organized an international rescue mission. Their team included a Maine senator, the U.S. president, an ambassador to Italy, a U.S. Navy admiral, the U.S. State Department, a navy ship, and our U.S. Marines. Eventually, enough strings were pulled, enough favors called in, so that a ship was moved and helicopters arranged so the Marines could airlift the children and Pinky to safety.

Pinky's boyfriend used an old Toyota to ferry the children, a few at a time, through a battle zone to a churchyard across the city. Bullets hit the car; mortars burst beside them. His mission was successful. No child was hurt. Night fell. Rain fell. Barefoot, cold, and wet, they all waited by the church steps. Sierra Leonean soldiers arrived at dawn, pushing their AK-45 muzzles into the children's necks; their officer decided whether orphans should be allowed to flee or should die. Just as he decided they should die, the U.S. Marines arrived and rescued the children, all of whom were flown to a U.S. warship.

The determined actions of a handful of people an ocean away saved the lives of the orphans that day. The Prophet Isaiah says, ". . . learn to do good; seek justice, rescue the oppressed, defend the orphan . . ."[56]

Let's Pray:

Dear God, we thank you for those determined enough to save lives. We thank you for those willing to use their resources to do your will. Amen.

Today's Thought Is: **Determined action changes lives.**

On July 20, 1969, *Apollo 11* landed on the Moon's equator. As Neil Armstrong stepped onto the surface, he meant to say, "That's one small step for a man, one giant leap for mankind." If he had said this, as planned, his meaning would have linked the small action of one man with a colossal accomplishment for all humankind. Instead, he flubbed his line, leaving out the article "a" and saying, "That's one small step for man, one giant leap for mankind."[57]

Can you imagine having the entire world listening to you as you flub a line that will go down in history? How embarrassing! Did Neil Armstrong's oral error diminish his, his teammates', and NASA's achievement? No, not at all. Even as a boy of ten, I understood what he was trying to say. People all over the world understood what he was trying to say. We all saw on TV what he was doing, and we all understood that one man was representing all of humanity, all of us.

There are times when we all flub our lines. I meant to say this; I didn't mean to say that. Neil Armstrong's flubbed line made history. At least ours don't.

Let's Pray:

Dear God, we say stuff we don't mean, and mean stuff we don't say, hurting those who love us. Say, God, can you help those we are talking to hear what we mean, even when we don't say it well? Amen.

Today's Thought Is: Think first, then speak.

In Wyoming's Teton National Forest, three friends led twenty-three college students on a backpacking trip. As the sun set they shared delicious food and mountain stories and strictly followed the park's grizzly bear safety rules.

The three leaders slept cramped and overcrowded in a two-person tent. Late at night, the three were startled awake by a guttural grunting, snorting, and scratching just outside their tent. A large, soft-furred creature leaned against the man who was sleeping on the left side of the tent. The beast slowly slid down his back, eventually covering him head and toe, and then rolled over on top him and his two pals—covering all three—with an incredible softness and an astounding weight. The load of a full-grown grizzly bear crushed the breath from them, making it impossible for them to scream, if that had been their inclination, while helplessly pinning them to the ground. When their breath was used up and the weight impossible to withstand or remove, when they believed the ignoble end had come for them, it was at that time that the bear simply rolled off and wandered away.

We don't need a bear's crushing weight to understand that some of life's worst burdens feel unbearable. Yet even in the hardest, most difficult circumstances God is with us. Just bear with it, trust God, and take a breath if you can; say a prayer and trust that no matter what, no matter the burden, God is present.

Let's Pray

God, let our burdens be light; if not, give us endurance to hang on. Help us bear the pressures on us. Amen.

Today's Thought Is: **Faith bears all things.**

ho was the Prophet Muhammad? He was born in 570, in Mecca, located in modern Saudi Arabia. Before he was born, his dad died. Not long after he was born, his mom died. His uncle of the Quraysh tribe raised him. Like most people in those ancient days, he was illiterate. While he was growing up, his tribal people noticed that he was honest, generous, and sincere. He was also reliable, so much so that they nicknamed him Trustworthy.

He was a religious man who took to spending quiet time in a cave outside the city. When he was forty, Muslims believe that he received his first visitation and revelation from Gabriel, one of God's angels. He soon began to recite those revelations and to preach to a small group of followers.

Together they suffered fierce persecution from the rest of the tribe, forcing them to leave Mecca for Medina, about 260 miles to the north, in 622, which became the start date for the Muslim calendar. In 630, he and his followers peaceably returned to Mecca and forgave their enemies. His revelations continued until his death at sixty-three, by which time much of the Arabian peninsula had converted to Islam, thus ending the tribal factionalism that had ravaged that land for such a long a time. Within a century, Islam had spread west to Spain and east as far as China. Collectively, his revelations are called the Koran.

Let's Pray:

Dear God, we pray that we might learn to understand something about those who believe differently from us and, in understanding, learn to live peaceably on your Earth. Amen.

Today's Thought Is: **Ignorance is not bliss.**

A rich man is dying. On his deathbed, he negotiates with God to let him bring his treasure into heaven.

"God, please, I've accumulated riches. Let me bring them."

"It's not customary," says God, "but you've been faithful, and have supported my work, so bring one suitcase." Immediately, the rich man fills a suitcase with gold bricks, and thereafter, he dies.

At the pearly gates, Saint Peter stops him, saying, "I'm sorry, but you know the rule: 'You can't take it with you.' You may enter, but your suitcase stays outside."

"But God told me I could bring one suitcase," the rich man protests.

"Well," says the saint, "if God says it's okay, okay—but I'll need to look inside before you bring it in here."

Saint Peter takes the suitcase, opens it, looks inside, and says in a puzzled tone, "You brought paving stones?" (Get it? Paved with gold . . .)

Okay, so it's not a funny joke, but it does have a point: You *can't* take it with you. In heaven, wealth is valueless, but as a stockbroker once said, "You can't take it with you, but you can leave it to your kids."

Actually, the Scriptures advise *not* leaving it to your kids. Instead, Proverbs says, leave it to your children's children—to your grandkids. It's a wealth-building technique that gives a leg up to the ones most likely to need it. Our kids may want it, but wisdom counsels those *leaving* life to leave wealth to those *starting* life.

Let's Pray:

Dear God, money management is a spiritual issue.
Help us take the long view. Amen.

Today's Thought Is: Leave an inheritance to your
children's children.[58]

*M*aking applesauce is easy. Peel a pile of apples. Core them. Quarter them. Boil them. Mash them. Add cinnamon, sugar, or honey to taste. Cool. Eat. Easy! Peeling a pile of apples is easy if the paring knife is sharp. I tried peeling my apple pile recently with a paring knife that was duller than my garden hoe. It was time to sharpen the knife. The sharpener is a handheld rod of rough steel, like real chefs use. I applied steel to steel until the honed blade was sharp enough to slice paper—and apple skins.

Steel sharpens steel—that's how the knife is whetted. There's an adage from the Iron Age: "Iron sharpens iron, as one person sharpens the wits of another." It takes challenges to sharpen our wits. It takes friends of the same mettle willing to shove against us a little, to push back on us, to hone us. Who needs friends who love us so little that they prefer us dull?

Let's Pray:

Dear God, sharpen our wits. Present us with people and challenges that increase our acumen, hone our minds, and whet our thinking. Amen.

Today's Thought Is: As iron sharpens iron, a friend sharpens a friend.[59]

A scuba diver off Mount Desert Island, Maine, was fixing an underwater mooring chain when he felt an eerie presence close behind him. Turning to look, he was face-to-face with Poco, the smiling wayward beluga whale that entertained coastal humans with his harbor antics. At fifteen feet when full grown, belugas are small by whale standards, but they seem giant to divers. Naturally social like all belugas, lonely Poco allowed the diver to stroke its skin, which I imagine was a memorable experience, even while wearing gloves. After a time, the diver remembered he was running out of air and had a job to finish, so he returned to his work. Poco began bumping into him to regain his attention. Frustrated with the friendly creature, the diver finally told Poco to "get lost!"

No one likes to stop having fun, and apparently that goes for belugas, too. The diver was wearing a tool belt hanging diagonally across his back. Poco intentionally hooked the diver's tool belt in its snout, and then good-naturedly zipped away with the diver in tow![60] Poco had a playful spirit like human children do. Even belugas need somebody to play with. We all do.

Generally, humans are social creatures who need companionship, yet many of us are lonely and alone. We can help change that by reaching out, touching a hand, or simply smiling.

Let's Pray

Dear God, if we are lonesome, send a smiling face to visit us; if we have empathy, send us to visit someone lonely. Amen.

Today's Thought Is: **A smile shared dispels loneliness.**

*H*umans do it. Every songbird that sings does it. Even mice do it. Do what? They sing love songs. Humans, birds, and mice sing songs to woo those they love. A study published by Washington University scientists explains that mice sing love songs in voices pitched above human hearing. How did the scientists discover this? They recorded the vocalizations of forty-five male mice after exposing those mice to female mice pheromones. Smelling pheromones makes the mice sing. Their ultrasonic utterances contain recurring phrases similar to those of songbirds.[61] Birds sing to woo mates—the better the song, the better the mate. Is this true for mice? Perhaps. What is certain is that mice songs are love songs. Humans react to pheromones, too, perhaps making us sing love songs.

Human love songs are ancient, and love songs can make us go weak in the knees. Our Scriptures contain one book that seems to be dedicated to human love. It's called the Song of Songs, or the Song of Solomon. It is a poem for two voices, male and female. Perhaps in ancient days it was sung as a love duet. If you read the Song of Songs aloud, you will hear words that speak provocatively of the powerful human desire for true love.

Let's Pray:

Dear God, you love us. Give us a chance to experience true love in this lifetime. May the songs of our hearts speak aloud the love that lies within. May songs of love give us joy. Amen.

Today's Thought Is: The Song of Songs, or the Song of Solomon, shows that God loves creatures loving.

On a rare and warm autumn day, he casually drove up the narrow road on Tibbett's Neck in his compact convertible, with his teenage daughter beside him. The ragtop was down, the radio was blaring Bette Midler, and the trees' rusty leaves played against the true blue sky on either side of the road. "There's a bald eagle," said the teen, pointing with a finger. Almost overhead, twenty feet up, was a huge eagle soaring in tight circles, trying to rise on the thermal lift coming off from the sun-heated pavement. Right there in the middle of rural Maine Highway 69, they stopped. There was no traffic—the tourists were gone and few locals were out that day. They watched the eagle. "She's young," said the father.

The teen asked how he knew she was young.

"Because of the mottled, speckled coloring under her wings," he replied.

"Why isn't she flapping her wings?" she asked.

"The eagle doesn't need to expend that energy. She knows to stay in the heated column of rising air, to let the air do the work; by keeping her wings in place, she lifts ever higher. Eventually, she'll touch the sky." They sat there for a few minutes watching the eagle and listening to the music.

On what column of air do you rise? God will lift you if you allow it.

Let's Pray

Dear God, we circle around on your rising breath, keeping steady the parts of us that need to be kept steady so that you can lift us to yourself. Lift us. Amen.

Today's Thought Is: **God lifts us.**

*T*alk about a possible flu pandemic turns my thoughts to the Greeks. Why? Because the word *pandemic* has the same prefix as my last name, Panagore, and is derived from *panagaris*, which means, I was once told, "he who takes all." I don't know if it's an accurate translation, but I rather like it. Maybe my people were gamblers, or clever men of business, or pirates. The word *pan* means "all." In *pandemic*, the *demic* comes from the ancient word *demos*, which you might think means "demons," but if you do, you are wrong. *Demos* means "people." Therefore, *pandemic* means "all people." Everybody—meaning we're all in this together.

The ancient historian Thucydides was the first to record a pandemic. It probably wasn't the first pandemic, but it was the first one recorded. In 430 B.C., at the height of the Peloponnesian War between Sparta and Athens, a disease struck Athens. In four years, the pandemic took one-third of its citizens, including the army and the great military tactician Pericles. Over the next 2,500 years pandemics have been recorded in Europe, the Middle East, Africa, and eventually in the United States, with surprising regularity. The last one was the Spanish flu, in 1918.[62]

Often pandemics arrive with the accompaniment of reactionary voices claiming it's the end times. It wasn't and isn't the end times. Bad times, yes; end times, no. What's the good news about this? The good news is that for the first time in history, humans have the chance to stop it before it gets started.

Dear God, help us use science and the resources of public health
to stop it before it starts. Amen.

Today's Thought Is: It's not the end of the world.

*H*is dream skates were at a sporting goods store. They weren't top of the line, but they had a factory-stamped signature of his favorite player on each skate. He *needed* them; he had to have them. He believed that with those skates on his feet, he'd fly and stop, start and dart, and play like a pro. He didn't really know much about skates, or hockey, for that matter. He just played on the pond after school with the kids almost every day. Unconvinced, his mom gave in, saying, "We'll buy them big so that they'll last a few years."

When unlaced and worn over two pairs of thick socks, the skates fit okay. The shop owner told his mom that he'd grow into them. But after the owner laced the skates up tight, the boy felt a sharp pinch on both of his big toes. He wanted the skates so much, however, and hoped so much that all the other boys would admire his skates and him, he chose to ignore the pain, saying they fit just fine. Those skates hurt his feet every day that season, and every day for the next three years. They hurt so much that eventually he stopped playing. But when asked, he never mentioned why.

Sometimes we talk ourselves into making choices that cause us pain, and then we seal our lips tight. It might be skates, relationships, or jobs. Admitting aloud that there's a problem is the first step to fixing it.

Let's Pray:

Dear God, give us courage to speak our pain, admit our troubles,
and make our changes. Amen.

Today's Thought Is: **If the skate hurts, don't buy it.**

*P*eekaboo is a game often played with babies. I'd hide my face behind my hands. If my wife was standing by she'd say, "Where's Daddy?" I'd pull my hands away, saying, "Peekaboo, I see you," and my baby would laugh.

From the baby's point of view, when I hid my face, I vanished—out of sight, out of mind. Or so I believed. It turns out babies are smarter than we thought. According to the *Atlantic Monthly*, babies understand that objects, or people, persist over time even if hidden. Show an object to a baby. Hide the object behind a screen. Wait a while. Remove the screen. If the object is missing, the baby will act surprised.[63] I can imagine my baby's surprise if, when I removed my hands while playing peekaboo, I wasn't there.

We all appreciate that, even when we can't see those we love, when their faces are hidden from us or they are far away, our love for them persists. God has designed the human heart to love even when we can't see or be with the ones we love. Inside our hearts, they persist; in our hearts, we feel they are there.

Let's Pray.

Dear God, when those we love are hidden from us, or deceased, let our love peek out and reach across the distances to touch them. Amen.

Today's Thought Is: **Love lasts.**

I was talking to this minister friend who said, "I've been thinking. I'm kinda tired of officiating at weddings. Jesus went to a wedding in Cana. We know this, and we know he didn't officiate at that wedding. He was smart enough to stay at the bar and make sure there was enough wine for everybody. I wonder if he made a toast to the couple? I wonder if there was an Aramaic saying they used to toast the bride and groom like the Hebrew term *l'chaim*, to life?"

What my friend said made me think, What happens when we toast somebody? Why do we raise a glass and clink? I don't know if it's true, but I was told that when we make a toast we use all our senses. We see, we hear, we touch, we taste, and we sniff. Our whole body is involved. We toast in celebration, in joy, in remembrance, or in giving honor. Often when a toast is offered, we stand. It's an act that involves everyone present and all the senses of each person. In the moment of the toast, we share one mind and act as one body. When we worship God together, shouldn't we be as fully and joyously present in that moment as we are when we lift a glass?

Let's Pray:

Dear God, we lift our hearts to you, we honor you, we worship you. Amen.

Today's Thought Is: *L'chaim!*

reak storms washed almost every crab ashore—thousands of them, millions, even. By using bucket loaders and dump trucks the Crabby Pickin' and Freezin' 'em Factory collected more crabs than the workers could process. Knowing that crabs had to be cooked, picked, packed, frozen, and shipped before the pile started to stink, the owner went down to the local labor pool at six A.M. and hired everybody there, promising $100 for a day's work. By eight A.M. he could see the crab pile wasn't getting smaller, so he went back and hired more people. At ten, noon, two, and four he hired more. By six P.M. the pile was next to nothing. He told his paymaster to pay the last hired first, and the first hired last, and everybody else in between. The serpentine line put the first hired right near the last hired, so that the first hired saw that the last got paid $100 each for two hours' work. A quick calculation had the first imagining $50 an hour, or $600 cash, for the day's work. When it came time for them to collect their pay, the first hired each got just the $100 they had been promised.

"This isn't fair! Something's fishy!" they shouted.

"Nothing's fishy," said the owner. "I paid you what I promised."

"You did," they agreed, "but you paid everybody a hundred dollars, but we worked all day and they didn't."

"When I promised a hundred dollars, weren't you happy?"

"We were," they admitted.

"Then what's it to you?" asked the owner. "Are you jealous because I'm generous?"

This parable describes heaven and God's unreasonable generosity. God is more charitable to us than even the good owner was to all his workers.

Let's Pray:

Dear God, call us into heaven, and thanks for the favor. Amen.

Today's Thought Is: **God is generous.**[64]

After a week of backcountry skiing on ten feet of snow and living in snow caves, the college boys emerged from the Valley of the Ten Peaks near the Wenkchemna Glacier on the very western boarder of Alberta, Canada. The boys needed supplies. Having left their skis and backpacks at a ranger station, they hitchhiked up the Ice Fields Parkway to Jasper. Back in the winter of 1980, Jasper's Main Street was as populated by mule deer as it was by people. North of there was only wilderness for hundreds of miles. The local bakery catered to its clientele by offering "backpacker's bread," guaranteed to keep its shape by withstanding shmushing inside a backpack. The loaf measured six × three × three and weighed four pounds. It was moist, dense, and nearly impossible to chew. Back in the wilderness, that loaf lasted three days of hard biting and slow chewing. The baker had said, "There's no yeast in it. It's so solid it'll last for weeks."

Yeastless bread. It's almost a shame to call it bread. Better to call it nutritious, nearly edible rock. Of course, chewing that bread meant the boys didn't have to bother brushing their teeth.

A little leaven lightens the loaf. A little yeast, kneaded in and spread around, makes the loaf rise. The Teacher says heaven is like yeast. A little goes a long way.[65]

Let's Pray.

Dear God, leaven us today. Let your words rise in us like bread yeast,
and may we share your bread. Amen.

Today's Thought Is: **A little heaven spread around goes a long way.**

When the Department of Health and Human Services bears down on deadbeat dads, those dads sometimes pay their debt in full. They might not have paid child support for years and years, but when it's time finally to pay, sometimes they come in with the whole sum in cash—ten thousand, even fifteen thousand dollars.[66] Was it stuffed in a mattress or buried in the cellar? Personally, I can't imagine keeping that much money anywhere but in a bank. I'd be afraid I'd keep moving it around so a robber couldn't find it and then forgetting where I put it. I'd end up having to tear the house apart looking for it. Imagine the fear you'd experience if you lost ten grand and had to tear the house apart, and then the relief you'd feel when you found it. If you didn't owe it to the state or somebody else, you might be inclined to shout about it, maybe throw a party in celebration of finding it.

That kind of rejoicing is the kind of feeling the woman in the gospel parable felt after finding her lost coin. She kept looking until she found it, and when she found it, she was ecstatic! The Teacher says that that overwhelming feeling of joy is what God feels when, after you've been lost from him for a while, you are found.

I'm guessing that's similar to what single moms feel when they get a check for back child support.

Let's Pray:

Dear God, if we are lost, find us. Amen.

Today's Thought Is: **Let yourself be found by God.**[67]

The year is about 900 B.C.E. Eliab, the eldest son of Jesse, is hanging with his homeboys down at the battlefront when that sneaky little pipsqueak of a brother of his shows up at the Israeli military camp. Encamped just across the field, with their bow fingers itching for war, is the entire Philistine army. It's no place for a baby boy. Eliab overhears little David chatting up the soldiers, and so he gets testy. "You can't fool me," Eliab bites out. "What're ya doin' here? Who'd ya leave the sheep with out in the wilderness? There're lions and wolves and bears out there. If we lose one single sheep, it'll be your *tokhes* Dad'll kick. I can't believe you're here! I know why you're here, you little nebbish. You've come to see the battle, haven't you? This is no place for a presumptuous, naughty-hearted, little sheep boy like you." Red-faced, Eliab is towering over David, leaning in a little, glaring, bearing down on him in voice and gesture.

Like all little brothers everywhere, David (the future king of Israel) mounts the usual irritating defense, "What'd I do now? I was just asking a question." With that said, David disrespectfully turns his back to his eldest brother and acts like Eliab isn't standing there glaring at him. Worst of all, the men actually answer David's questions.[68]

Getting snubbed by family or friends is ancient, and it isn't any easier now than it was then, even when we deserve it.

Let's Pray.

*Dear God, when we're given the cold shoulder, give us the poise
we need to endure. Amen.*

Today's Thought Is: God never turns his back on us.

*T*alented film actors, who could be stars based on skill or sparkle, and who can do much more than just play supportive roles to the superstars, are often left in the background because they lack a pretty face. But that's the way it is in Hollywood, where face is fate. One such actor is Yale-trained Paul Giamatti—a talented man whom you've certainly seen in films, including *Sideways* and *The Illusionist,* opposite—ah, what's his name, ah, Russell Crowe. Giamatti has a face you may have seen and then forgotten, and a name you may have never known. He says that he's content with his role as a character actor in supportive roles. He's not a complainer. Directors like Ron Howard have seen his talent, and they have fought to get him the roles he deserves, but Giamatti knows that, in Hollywood, face rules. Films are loaded with such less beautiful but terrifically talented people— the character actors, those who assume the supporting roles, the extras. Without these people, there isn't a movie.[69]

In Hollywood, face may be fate. In heaven, face isn't fate. In heaven, it doesn't matter if your face is perfectly symmetrical, with lovely skin and eye-catching beauty, or if it isn't. We humans love beauty, but God loves love. A heart filled with love, hope, faith, charity, or kindness has more beauty to the eye of God than any Hollywood star's face has.

Let's Pray:

Dear God, in our culture, where beauty is honored, give us eyes to admire those whose hearts radiate beauty beyond compare. May our hearts shine as brightly. Amen.

Today's Thought Is: **Face isn't eternal fate.**[70]

*O*ld Yankee skiers say that the best skiers come from New England because the skiing here is wicked icy. Cindy had grown up leaping logs, roots, rocks, and streams on ungroomed trails, while negotiating the ice pack at high speeds. She'd been skiing since she was seven, back in the days of lace-up leather ski boots, bear-trap binding, and fiberglass-topped wooden skis. At twenty-one years old, with six years of National Ski Patrol experience under her fanny pack, Cindy knew a thing or two about skiing East Coast ice. That year she went west to Bridger Bowl in Montana—hip-deep fluffy power, two huge snow bowls, a twenty-six-hundred-foot rise, and access to extreme skiing. It was a hotdogger's dream. She'd been skiing on shorter skies, which weren't suitable to deep power, so she bought herself a pair of long powder boards.

As an expert skier, Cindy tried to convince the ski shop man that she needed the bindings tighter than normal for somebody her weight. The shop man didn't listen. On her first run, flying through the fresh powder, Cindy shot out over a vertical headwall, feeling young and alive; then, in midflight, Cindy watched her left ski simply fall off. The binding had been too loose. Dead ahead was a midmountain lift line. Cindy tried a controlled landing on one ski, but failed. She crashed, then tumbled thirty yards smack into the line, knocking down the skiers like dominos.

Let's Pray.

Dear God, maybe we've gotten ourselves into compromising situations because we trusted somebody we shouldn't have trusted. Help us discern when and where not to be trusting. Amen.

Today's Thought Is: "Trust, but verify."[71]

A friend owns a six-foot narwhal (whale) tusk that once belonged to his father. Before that, it belonged to a narwhal. Holding it is mesmerizing. The tusk is bone hard and spiral shaped. Its whitish hue and sharp end make it easy to see how it played into myths of unicorns.

Unicorn tales were started in the fifth century B.C.E. by the Greek physician Ctesias, who told of a creature in India whose horn had magical and curative qualities. We call that magical creature a rhinoceros. Six hundred years later the Roman naturalist Aelian said the unicorn horn was spiral. After that, the rare narwhal horn became a commodity. In the sixteenth century, Queen Elizabeth paid the equivalent of an entire castle for one horn.

After years of research, a team of scientists have a bona fide theory about this odd tooth. What makes narwhal tooth unique among teeth? Two aspects: one, it's the only tooth with soft tissue on the outside and hard structure on the inside; and two, its spiral shape. It was believed that the tusk was used for defense, or to poke holes through thin Arctic ice. It is now understood that the narwhal tooth, owing to the soft exterior tissue, is responsive to gradations in barometric pressure, water salinity, and temperature. In short, it's a one-piece weather station.[72] When science debunks a myth, the truth is more fascinating.

Let's Pray:

Dear God, we thank you for our minds that you give us to use to discover the intriguing truths of the reality that you create. Help us appreciate your world more when myths are debunked and truth revealed. Amen.

Today's Thought Is: **Truth is stranger than mythology.**

*I*n a café, over hot chocolate, my friend Trisha sat with me and her ten-year-old daughter, listening to Lyle Lovett singing on the stereo.

"I've got Lyle Lovett's signature on my jean jacket," Trisha volunteered. "It was a July night at the Merrill Auditorium, and my friend Susan and I hung around backstage for hours waiting for him. I was surprised," she continued in a near whisper, "to see how short he is. He was wearing pointed boots and had dyed his hair, but maybe it was to please his young girlfriend. I have a niece who was born the year Lyle Lovett released his first album. We were listening to it while I was watching her being born. Now my niece is going to have her own baby."

To me, my friend looks almost like she did when I first knew her twenty-five years ago, in college. I had a lot more hair then. These days, she spends her time driving her ten-year-old to dance lessons, or worrying about her seventeen-year-old driving the family SUV. She spends summers gardening and works winters in a clothing shop. Not much has changed about her. Her hair remains long, although with tints and hints of years gone by. She's trim and funny, but as time passes, Trisha and Lyle continue to age unstoppably. We all do. Time is relentless.

Let's Pray.

Dear God, we can't stop the clock. Why is it that we age, God? Why is it that our bodies slowly wear down? There's a time for everything—getting gray hair, having babies, and passing on—but, God, couldn't we have more time?

Amen.

Today's Thought Is: Under heaven, there is time
for every matter.[73]

When she needs to escape her thinking, when she's stressed, when she needs focused relaxation, she drops thirty or so bullets into her hip pocket, lifts her old Mossberg rifle off its hook, unlocks the trigger lock, slings the plinker's strap over her right shoulder, and then walks out in the woods behind her rural house. Ten minutes down an old Abenaki footpath, the woods open up into a clearing where she has a homemade target range ending halfway up on the side of a steep hillock. The target is a steel plate that makes a satisfying plink whenever a round hits it.

Placing one bullet at a time in the bolt-action .22 rifle, she loads and fires the plinker at the target. The more she shoots, the calmer and more focused her mind becomes. At first by force of will, and then by relaxation, her breathing slowly becomes steady as she exhales whenever she gently squeezes the trigger. When she shoots well, she feels an emptying of self and a letting go of all distractions. To say she becomes one with her rifle, each bullet, and the target is not an exaggeration. When she is not one with them, she misses her aim.

Do you have an aim in life? Do have a target you wish to hit? If you do, what do you do to reach it? Do you have an aim in the afterlife? If so, what do you do to reach it?

Let's Pray:

Dear God, if we are aimless, give us aim. If we are unfocused, give us focus. Make you our target. Amen.

Today's Thought Is: Aim at heaven.

*T*hom's family was headed back to Connecticut early the following morning, and since they had a busy day of cleaning and packing ahead of them, their visit with us was short. From end to end, from top to bottom, their van was packed, items pushed, shoved, crushed, and jammed tight with broken-down brown boxes, big green trash barrels, clear plastic bags of colored bottles—brown, green, clear, milk, and returnable—bundles of newspapers, piles of paper, and black plastic trash bags galore. It was rubbish from a long holiday-weekend party, including the trash of half-a-dozen stay-over guests. It had taken two hours to collect, sort, and load.

As Thom explained a pressing need to have an empty van for the journey home, it came to his attention that the dump was closed that day.

"Closed?" he said. "That can't be."

Thom called the dump. It rang, and rang, and rang, and no one and no machine ever answered. Thom laughed, saying, "We'll put it all back in the cellar. This isn't the first time I've done this. God is a patient teacher."

Let's Pray:

Dear God, you made us flawed and loving creatures. Teach each of us the lessons you want us to learn, and teach us repeatedly, if need be. Amen.

Today's Thought Is: God is love, and love is patient.

*L*ong ago when the Creator was making everything, he sprinkled cosmic dust into the mud to make a whale. Some of the dust stayed in the mud, and the mud awoke and sat up. That mud man took fistfuls of mud, packed it onto his body, and built himself until he was a giant. Over eons, the mud solidified into rock, and that's how the stone giant was made. He believed that he was self-made.

At the end of my road that same stone giant sleeps. I didn't even know he was sleeping there until the other day. My guess is, not many people ever knew he was lying there on the edge of Royal Beach. From a certain angle across the cove, it's obvious a gigantic creature is lying there on his back. His boulder block head is twelve by twelve, with a proportionately long body. He—please pardon me—is decapitated, but like I said, he's sleeping, not dead. Reattaching his head to his body would reawaken him. There's a vertical line where his torso ends and where his strong thighs begin. There's a line at his knees, and the calves end without feet. Tumbled off his side is a huge stone plate shape that could have been a shoulder. It's leaning against his long right arm.

This story is part legend, part fiction. There was no stone giant, not really, but there is a Creator who made everything, including us, out of Earth's elements. We may think we built our lives, but none of us is self-made.

Let's Pray:

Dear God, if in our stone hearts we forget you, forgive us and teach us otherwise. Amen.

Today's Thought Is: **We are made of mud by the fingers of God.**

*L*ong ago, an old monk lived in the Arabian Desert. He spent his days in prayer and labor. He prayed for wisdom and wove baskets to sell in the city. Once a month he carried his baskets to the marketplace, spread his carpet on the ground, arranged and sold his baskets, and talked with the people. His baskets were renowned, and his wisdom was praised. On market day, people would gather around his carpet asking questions, listening to answers, and nodding with approval. They started to call him the Holy Man and revered him.

Back at his camp, he wove himself a basket. This basket could hold a hundred pounds of sand, and could be worn strapped on his back. In one lower corner of his basket, he cut a tiny hole. Filling his basket full to the top with sand, he walked to the city, spilling a trail of sand behind him. At the marketplace, a large crowd awaited him and was surprised when he didn't sit as they expected. Instead, he walked silently through the city all day long, spilling a trail of sand behind him. At the end of the day, before sunset, he returned to the marketplace.

"Holy man," a boy asked, "why do you wear the basket with the hole, letting the sand spill?"

"This basket is my body and my life," the man replied. "The sands are my sins, which pour out behind me. I am no more holy than you."[74]

Dear God, only you are holy. Let us never mistake the messenger for the message. Amen.

Today's Thought Is: **Our sins spill out behind us.**

he sign on the café door read, "We'll be back at 3:45." The young teens didn't see the other smaller sign saying that the owners had gone to New York City for the weekend. This friendly group often hung out at this café, so they waited patiently, or almost patiently, on the porch.

Naturally, they began to horse around. A cap was snatched off one head and tossed around in a game of keep-away. One kid tried to catch it and, in doing so, backed up and bumped a potted plant, tripped over a chair leg, and accidentally bumped his butt into a window. The window broke. All the kids took off. All the kids, that is, except the breaker-boy and his pal. These two waited on the porch. Eventually, the other kids came back. The breaker-boy phoned his dad. The dad came with a staple gun and plastic sheeting to cover the window. He suggested that they might want to write a note, and if they did, the owners might not ban them from hanging out in the café.

Together, the kids drafted a letter to the owners, explaining exactly what had happened to the window, who they were, and adding their phone numbers. Breaker-boy took responsibility by offering to pay for the repair costs himself. Two days later the owners called breaker-boy, saying that, because the kids behaved so responsibly, not only were they welcome to come back but they didn't even have to pay for the window.

Let's Pray:

Dear God, when accidents happen, give us courage to face our responsibilities, and may we find forgiveness. Amen.

Today's Thought Is: **Accepting responsibility shows character.**

*E*ventually, you must empty the ashes from the woodstove or shovel out the fireplace. There's no way around it. Unless the ashes are cleared out, they pile up and up until there's no room for logs. Then what? That bucket of ashes makes a perfect antislip agent when the world outside your back door has become a hockey rink. Turns out that one Vermonter used half her ashes on her backyard ice rink one day last winter, sprinkling it down the stairs and along the path in order to get to her studio workshop. Later on, she left her ash bucket safely perched on her porch.

Embers inside ash buckets can stay "live" by being insulated under old ashes, even in subzero temperatures. That night the wind blew a gale, blowing the bucket over and spilling ashes and embers. The wind blew the hot embers into the backyard, where they melted into the ice instead of burning the porch. Dumb luck, some might call it; Providence, others might say.

Let's Pray

Dear God, thanks for taking care of us when we get careless, even when we think we're being careful. Amen.

Today's Thought Is: God watches over fools and saints, and hopefully the rest of us, too.

*G*ive a man a fish and you feed him for a day; teach a man to fish and you feed him for a lifetime." The Heifer Project International has held that philosophy since 1944. This organization tries to end world hunger by turning its recipients into donors, because one gift turns into many, and lives are transformed through the passing on of that gift.

While traveling in Nicaragua, I visited a village that had been destitute until Heifer Project gave the village a flock of chicks. Those chicks grew up to provide eggs and income. It was a flock of five hundred when I was there. Every year that village gave away chicks to other villages, and those villages did the same, continuing to pay it forward.

The Heifer Project donates water buffalo, heifers, llamas, goats, sheep, pigs, honeybees, rabbits, chicks, ducks, geese, and trees. Today, millions of people who were once hungry are nourished by milk, eggs, and fresh vegetables, thanks to the Heifer Project and the people who donate to them. When I served as a minister in Downeast, Maine, the children of our congregation raised funds for Heifer Project animals, which were given away in our own county.[75]

Let's Pray:

Dear God, maybe it's crazy to pray for the end of world hunger, but it sure isn't crazy to try to end it. Help us help others help themselves. Amen.

Today's Thought Is: **Giving brings unimaginable blessings.**

ver lunch at the China Dinah (Maine vernacular for a Chinese restaurant), a friend told me how one day he was struggling with having to put his beloved dog, Al, to sleep. The poor thing was sick, and the vet had advised him to do the right thing. Before the event, my friend was digging a proper grave for his pooch, but tears forced him to stop. He went inside, literally knelt down, and prayed to God for a sign. "What should I do, God?" he asked. "Don't give me a little sign I'm going to have to sit around thinking about. Give me a clear, big, obvious sign so I know what to do." Just then, there was a knock on the door, and in walked his next-door neighbor, who said, "I saw you digging for Al, and wondered if you'd mind if I tossed a shovelful or two?"

I ask God for signs and direction, too, but I don't always get what I'm looking for; if there is a sign, maybe I don't always notice it. It'd be wonderful if every time we needed a sign, or prayed for one, God gave it to us, loud and clear. It doesn't always work that way. Unlike my fortunate friend, most of us ask, and few of us receive. Or maybe it's that we just don't see, or don't want to see, the messages God gives us because they're not what we expect, or they're not big enough or dramatic enough.

Let's Pray:

Dear God, give each of us the sign we need to make whatever choice we must make, but, God, please, let it be obvious. Amen.

Today's Thought Is: God listens, but do we?

The boys were hitchhiking from western Montana using a cardboard sign that read "Boston—Home to Mom." Days into their trip, they got stuck in Cleveland's rush-hour traffic. They figured they'd wait until after rush hour, when, just then, the local ice-cream truck pulled over, ringing his bell and offering them a ride. The boys climbed in, dropped their backpacks to the floor, and hung on for a wild ride. "Have an ice cream bar on me," shouted the driver, adding, "Going to Boston, I see. I'll get you to where you need to be." An hour later, he let them out in the darkness. The street scene didn't look right. They seemed to be in the middle of nowhere. City or country? They couldn't tell. Under a highway lamp, they started hitching. A car slowed and stopped. It was an old Cadillac all tricked out, blaring Spanish music. Inside were four scary-looking gangbangers—red bandanas, lots of thick gold jewelry, and big bulges where there shouldn't have been bulges.

"Going to Boston," they laughed. "Yeah," said the boys. "White boys, what are you doing out here? It's not safe. You're thirty miles from Route 90. There's a train station a couple miles from here; get in, we'll take you." It wasn't a request. They got in. The ice-cream man had done them wrong; the gangbangers did them right.

God uses who God chooses to set us on the right road, and it isn't always who we expect.

Let's Pray:

Dear God, if we are on the wrong road, send us any guide you choose to point us home to you. Amen.

Today's Thought Is: **God shows us the path of life.**[76]

The teenager with the thick chestnut hair turned to his middle-aged dad, looked hard at his dad's thinning hair, and quipped, "You know, Dad, you'd probably have more white hair, if you had more hair."

"My only son," replied his dad, "I'll tell you what my dad told me, when I had long hair, on the day I started kidding him about his ever-gleaming bald patch. My dad said, 'Son, remember this day and this conversation when your son says something similar to you.'" The teen smirked and said, "Yeah, right." Baldness is old. It goes way back, and I don't just mean from the forehead to the crown. Baldness turns out to be biblical. On a list of other terrible things, like turning off the sun at midday, making parties into funerals, and turning every joyful song into a dirge, the Prophet Amos includes becoming bald! Sounds like Amos believed baldness was a curse, or a sign of mourning. Most men might agree. I'll wager that Amos himself probably had a nice head of luscious locks, and that he was a bit nervous about future prospects.

Baldness is one of those let-me-accept-what-I-cannot-change situations.

Let's Pray:

Dear God, there are parts of our bodies we don't like. Help us change the things we can, and accept the things we cannot change. Amen.

Today's Thought Is: Our bodies are beautiful.

*I*nside Tompkins Square Park, tucked between Avenues A and B in New York's East Village, is a children's playground. On Saturdays, neighborhood kids of many colors and languages run freely, swing wildly, and play happily. Parents are chatting, sipping Mud Truck coffee from orange cups, pushing swings, taking pictures.

Whenever a soul comes through the playground gates, everyone smiles in that direction. It's a safe place, a friendly neighborhood. Children are happy. Parents keep an eye on one another's kids, break up fights, wipe noses, and change diapers. Kids share balls and bikes, dolls and toys.

If a camera is raised to take a picture of a growing child, whoever might be crossing the lens stops and waits for the picture to be taken. This gesture of civility, of neighborliness, isn't unusual in the East Village. It isn't unusual to the city. The whole city seems friendlier, where neighbors watch out for one another and help one another. Gone is the urban animosity. Gone is the trash. Gone is the I-don't-see-or-care-about-you attitude. Did 9/11 change the city? Can good come from bad? I think it can.

Let's Pray:

Dear God, when the trouble is past, let good come from bad. Amen.

Today's Thought Is: God makes everything work together for the good of those who love him.[77]

*T*he crosswalk rule in Manhattan is fair: Cross when the traffic has a red light. Do not cross on green, or you will be threatened by a speeding taxi. Being an ex-urbanite turned hayseed, and lost in conversation, I ignored the crosswalk rules and stepped off the curb on a green light. My conversation partner grabbed my shirtsleeve and yanked me back, perhaps saving my life, just as a horn-blaring taxi flew by. That familiar heart-pounding metallic taste of fear rose instantly to my tongue, reminding me of the paralyzing kinds of fear that freeze up our faith. I have felt the fear one feels when stepping out in faith—such as risking your job for the truth, or telling somebody that you believe in the God of Christ when every social pressure is screaming for you to shut your face.

Then there's another kind of spiritual fear that doesn't taste metallic. The fear of God is talked about in the Bible. God can be scary because he is so big. But that word *fear* doesn't get to the full meaning. Another translation of the fear of the Lord is having reverence for, or being in awe of, God. It's more like being at the top of the Empire State Building, where you can see the whole city. Up there fear might be present, but it's inspiring, too, combined, perhaps, with an overwhelming feeling of amazement and respect.

Let's Pray:

Dear God, touch us with your overwhelming love that we might feel awe.

Amen.

Today's Thought Is: Reverence for God is the beginning of true wisdom.[78]

ad things happen. Even terrible things happen. Sometimes it's through our own fault; other times we have nothing to do with the cause, we just suffer the results. At times like that we might blame God, or believe ourselves accursed. We shout to God, "Why me?" Or, "What did I do to deserve this?" The likely answer would be nothing.

The strange thing about feeling cursed is that curses can turn out to be blessings. The author Henri Nouwen wrote a simple and profound book entitled *The Wounded Healer*. In that book, Nouwen tells us that, as people of faith, we need to identify the wounds in our hearts and in our lives, to identify those places where we suffer, and to make those places the starting points for lives of faithful service to others.[79]

Who better to help a battered woman than another woman who was battered herself? Who better to counsel those suffering an incurable disease than those who understand it personally? Who better to help a parent through the loss of a child than another parent who also lost a child? Who better to understand than those who suffer in similar ways?

Life cuts us a raw deal sometimes. The wounds we find, or that find us, may feel like curses, but with faith and with the help of others, those curses can be reoriented into blessings that will empower us to help others.

Let's Pray:

Dear God, I am not pleased about this situation. My circumstance—I didn't deserve it. I know it can't be changed. So change me. Amen.

Today's Thought Is: A curse is a coin with a blessing on the back side.

In the rain, Flo's fourteen-year-old son Lenord was vomiting from his cancer treatments as they walked to a New York subway station. Commuters ignored them as she struggled with her suitcase. "You need help, lady?" somebody asked. Flo saw a homeless man in jeans, sneakers, and a cutoff army jacket. Feeling afraid, she declined. He insisted, picked up her suitcase, and led them to the subway, which he boarded with them. After they got off, he hailed a cab for them. As she closed the door, Flo gave him five dollars, and heard him say, "Don't abandon me."

Flo Wheatley didn't abandon him. Back home, using old clothes, she sewed together her first sleeping bag. It was 1982. She delivered it to a man sleeping in a Manhattan doorway. She made eight more. As word spread, neighbors brought fabrics to her house. A church asked her to show them how to make the sleeping bags. She named her project My Brothers' Keeper Quilt Group, and she calls the sleeping bags Ugly Quilts, hoping that the name will show how easy they are to make.

There's a one-page instruction sheet. Materials include bedspreads, drapes, blankets, mattress pads, fiberfill, and neckties. Ugly Quilts spread nationally. To date, the quilt group estimates that a half million Ugly Quilts have been sewn and distributed nationally. In 2006, the project was still going strong.[80]

Flo believes her encounter on that walk to the subway wasn't chance at all. She believes she encountered Christ in the homeless man.

Let's Pray.

Dear God, chance encounters change lives. Give us ears to hear your voice today, give us gumption enough to listen. Amen.

Today's Thought Is: Don't just sit there; do something.

*A*t the Boston Seafood Show, a Connecticut company showed a videotape of frozen lobsters coming back to life. So far, twelve out of two hundred frozen lobsters awoke after their subzero hibernation.

How's it work?

First, each lobster's metabolism is slowed by bathing it in below-freezing seawater, and then each crustacean is immersed in a minus-forty-degree brine. The freezing happens so quickly there's minimal cell damage. Next morning, the frozen-stiff bottom crawlers are thawed in twenty-eight-degree seawater. In less than three hours, they're swimming about and whistling happy tunes, so to speak. University of Maine's Lobster Institute's Dr. Robert Bayer was skeptical but intrigued. Like all scientists, Dr. Bayer needs proof. A videotape and somebody's word for it doesn't meet the scientific standard.[81]

Faith isn't like science. There's not going to be any measurable, repeatable proof about Easter. There's no videotape; we only have witnesses' words for it. The Apostle Thomas, for one, was skeptical but intrigued by the reports about the risen, living Christ that he was hearing from his pals. Thomas wanted proof. He got it when, according to the Gospels, he saw the risen, living Rabbi with his own eyes. Science isn't going to explain it, and it's not repeatable.

Let's Pray:

Dear God, thaw our frozen hearts, bring our faith to life, enliven us with the grace of your presence so that we may feel your living love. Amen.

Today's Thought Is: **Blessed are those who believe but never see.**

On a twisting rural road, on a Sunday after dark, a man in a pressed dress shirt stood bewildered beside his oddly angled airport van stuck inside a ditch. He'd driven three hours north of the jetport to deliver a piece of lost luggage. Thinking he'd passed the house he wanted, he tried turning around in a driveway. He didn't see the drainage ditch.

Andy was driving in the first car that happened by. He stopped, asking if the van man needed help. He did. "Be right back," said Andy, and went to get his one-inch rope and to call his neighbor, Crusty, who owns a pickup truck. Crusty came and brought his boy, Ben. After looking over the van, they decided it needed a four-wheel drive. Crusty fetched William and his son, Pete. When the five men, two trucks, two flashlights, one boy, and one stout rope were gathered, the work began. The rope was tied to the van and the four-wheel drive. On the first tug the rope snapped. It looked bad for a minute until Crusty tied a square knot, rejoining the heavy lines. They tried again. The van leapt out of the ditch. The rope was untied and coiled. Thanks and good-byes were said. Everybody started to get in his vehicle. As the van backed down the driveway, Crusty shouted, "Stop! Look out!" And the van stopped—once again caught in the ditch. Wearing smiles, everybody came back and pulled out the van a second time. This time everyone waited until the van drove away; then they all had a good laugh, because, with the exception of the van driver, they all had had an enjoyable time.

Let's Pray.

God, thanks for the chance and fun of helping folks, especially when no one's hurt. Amen.

Today's Thought Is: Do something for somebody everyday for which you do not get paid.[82]

On a sunny summer Sunday afternoon, a ponytailed hippie nature boy was driving home from a church service. Although he believed in God, he didn't attend church regularly, but a pretty woman had invited him to the Sunday service. The wild preacher had shouted, "God's calling someone here to the ministry! I can feeeel it!" Lots of "Amens!" Course nothing happened.

On his way home, this happy hippie had his convertible Bug's top down. Overhead was blue, blue sky; a mile in the distance was a localized thunderhead cloud, dark as night and tossing lightning and hail. The thought—"Is God calling me?"—had crossed his mind, but he brushed it off. At the same time, he wondered to God if he should put his convertible top up.

He saw it coming. A bolt of lightning reached out of the black mass, striking his backseat and sounding like a bomb. He turned to see as an arch left the seat, entered his thigh, and exited his shoulder, and rejoined into the main bolt. It was over in a flash. No pain. Just shock and amazement. He put up the top. Two troubled years later, he found himself answering the call.

God's usually more subtle than lightning. Maybe you've had a pesky idea that God's calling you. Try to shake it off. If you can't shake it, talk to a religious pro, or go to www.dailydevotions.org to see a list of divinity schools and seminaries.

Let's Pray:

God, strike the hearts of those you choose to lead, set them afire with love and desire for you. Leave out the lightning strike, but draw them strongly to yourself. Help them discern your will. Amen.

Today's Thought Is: Do you hear God's call?

*I*t was late in the tourist season, long after the leaves had fallen, and snow was threatening. A tour bus parked in the harbor village. After the bus disgorged fifty or so respectable-looking visitors, all bundled brightly for warmth, wearing name tags and smiles, the group leader organized them for a walk about town, pointing out the various quaint sites. As they were passing by a roughly dressed old fellow seated on a bench, sipping his coffee, the group leader stopped, then quieted her group. The leader turned to the old fellow, speaking loudly in a rather patronizing tone, "Excuse me, sir. Please tell us, were their any great men or women born in this little town?" The old fellow stared at her for a half moment before answering, "Nope, only babies born here."

We are all born with potential, not with greatness or with failure. Sure, some folks are born with a leg up, some with two legs up, but as babies we're all much the same. We eat, cry, sleep, love, fuss, laugh, and require regular clean up. We're equal in our dependence, equal in our needs. From the human point of view, there are greater and lesser people. Some babies grow to be presidents, noble scientists, or renowned artists. The rest of us are just regular folk—sales reps, lift operators, ministers, loggers, teachers, floor sweepers, tour guides, business owners.

From God's view we are all much the same—just children, just babies, of God.

Let's Pray:

God, if we're great in someone's sight, so be it. If we're great in our own sight, show us your point of view so that we may see ourselves as you see us. Amen.

Today's Thought Is: We're all the same in the eyes of God.

The bachelor professor had it all—an endowed chair at Yale University, respect in his field, brains, publications, charm, parties, friends, a fine Victorian home in a nice neighborhood, and a place in his home for his ill mother. He was living the good life.

Over time, his mother's illness worsened. Her hospitalizations lengthened, her pharmaceutical costs increased, her home care required round-the-clock nursing. The professor had insurance through the university, but it wasn't enough. He found himself under financial strain. He spent his savings and cashed out his retirement to pay the bills. Living in the city meant he didn't need his car, so he sold it.

Other bills mounted. After a time he cut back on the nursing expenses by caring for his mother alone. He began missing classes when his mother needed him. He missed faculty meetings; he missed publication deadlines. His mother mattered most. Eventually, the university fired him. After his mother died, he sold his home to pay the remaining bills, and he found himself destitute at sixty-three years old.

I met him one morning on the Green as I walked past his park bench, where he had spent another night under newspapers for warmth. This professor, still brilliant, was homeless. His career was ruined; his reputation was shattered. I tell you this story to let you know that homeless men, women, and families come from diverse backgrounds, and many work full time for inadequate wages. Even the brilliant and hardworking can find themselves without shelter. It could be you. It could be me.

Let's Pray:

God, bless your children who struggle to make ends meet. May they never find themselves living on the street, but if they do, give them hope, help, and friendship. Amen.

Today's Thought Is: There, but for circumstance, go I.

On a snowless late December day, when frozen fields remained a November brown, and russet apples clung frostily to knuckled branches, I wandered outside to see what nature could sermonize to me. Nothing I was writing that day was beautiful. I walked out into the field beside our former farmhouse home, and down the hill toward the saltwater pond. I ducked under the overgrown apple trees and bushwhacked through the brambles, finally bursting free into the open meadow, which I had mowed on a hot Monday months before.

My twig-snapping walk and loud leaf-crunching carelessness spooked a snowshoe hare from her hiding place beneath the blackberry thorns. She shot out like a streak of fur, then froze midmeadow, as if she were camouflaged by her winter-ready white pelt in a snow-filled field—only there was no snow. That hare wasn't hidden, just perfectly still—bright white fur on the brown ground. I approached slowly, carefully, in stride, watched all the time by one unmoving eye of the solitary hare. I knew the hare had been in the meadow for months. I'd found her tracks in the mud one day. On numerous occasions, I'd hunted her—not for fur or food, merely for a long look. I hadn't seen her till that day. Closer I came—eight feet, seven, six; at five I froze, looking intently long while she believed in her invisibility. Her misconception of reality was flabbergasting. After a time, I turned toward the salt pond, and, as I turned, she scooted, stopped, then scampered to bramble safety. In the long winter of the year, with dark nights and lonesome days for some, you may believe you are alone, invisible, unseen, solitary. Not true. Right now, God sees you and loves you.

Let's Pray:

God, for the isolated and lonely, let them feel your care and love. Amen.

Today's Thought Is: God sees even the invisible.

*T*he bitter cold created perfect pond ice—hard, white, and smooth from end to end, snow free. Don is out there alone. Since boyhood, Don has skated on rivers, reservoirs, lakes, bogs, and ponds. He understands ice, and he always measures its thickness before skating. Don finds a open ice-fishing hole and, using his hockey stick, measures the ice—eighteen inches. It's thick enough for a ten-ton truck. Doing laps around the pond, he skates faster and faster each time, and closer to shore each time as well. It's a challenge to duck branches, leap logs, shoot sharply in and out of little coves with quick turns. Into an inlet, he sees a black ice patch. Black ice late in the winter means thin ice, dangerous ice, certainly there's a spring hidden beneath. It's too late because he's going too fast. The black ice breaks beneath his blades, and suddenly he's in the icy and dangerous water. He twists left, pushing his hockey stick out over the thick ice. As quick as he's in, he pops himself out again, but he's soaked to the waistline of his winter-wool pants.

Skating quickly toward his car, his pants freeze solid, wrapping his stiffening legs and freezing feet in half an inch of ice. Teeth chattering, he pulls his knife from its sheath. He cuts the frozen skate laces, climbs out of his frozen-solid pants, and climbs into the car. In an hour's time, it's nothing but a memory.

Let's Pray:

God, we may feel our lives are thickly buttressed, strongly secured, and invincibly solid; but the veil between this world and the next is astoundingly and unexpectedly thin sometimes. Protect us as we go out this day. If there's any thin ice beneath our feet, or the feet of those we love, please turn us, or them, toward a safer direction. Amen.

Today's Thought Is: **Life is fragile.**

When the winter ice is perfectly smooth, or close enough, and safely thick, every skater in town, young to old, frolics on the longest pond on weekend afternoons. Figure skaters of shapely dexterity perform leaps and spins to entertain those of lesser ability. A fast yet courteous game of hockey is played—padless—with players ranging from six to sixty-eight; no one is ever hurt, not badly anyway. When a little one has possession of the puck, or anyone much less skilled, allowances are given. Plays are made; goals are scored—but no one cares who wins so long as the game is fun. A log fire burns by the ice to warm the fingers and toes of frozen children. Mothers and fathers tow brightly bundled toddlers on sleds, while skating siblings tag along, begging for a turn. Preteen girls zip off, giggling, in bunches; then stop to talk, then zoom again. If any child should fall on the ice with a cry, any nearby parent, or able adult, or neighborly teen will rush to the rescue. Such a town-wide skating event is rare now. Back a few years ago, there were weeks when townies and urbanites cavorted on the ice and found fun and friendship in the red-cheeked joy of being together.

Let's Pray:

God of ice ponds, glad children, adults, and dogs, thanks for the times when we are worry free while whirling around with neighbors we know in a town we love. Amen.

Today's Thought Is: **Community events build stronger people.**

We are what we eat. Our bodies are built, cell by cell, by the foods we consume. In a similar way, we are what we think. Our worldview is shaped by what we feed into our heads and by the thoughts we hold. The following was sent to me. It supposedly came from a Cherokee American, but I could not find its origin.

An old man is teaching his grandson about life. "A fight is going on inside me," he says to the boy. "It's a terrible fight, and it's between two wolves. One is evil—he is anger, envy, sorrow, regret, greed, arrogance, self-pity, guilt, resentment, inferiority, lies, false pride, superiority, and ego. The other is good—he is joy, peace, love, hope, serenity, humility, kindness, benevolence, empathy, generosity, truth, compassion, and faith. This same fight is going on inside you—and inside every other person, too."

The grandson thinks about it for a minute and then asks his grandfather, "Which wolf will win?"

The old man replies, "The one we feed."

We bear responsibility for our inner life—who we become, how we live, how we treat those around us. Whichever wolf we feed—whether we swallow wicked thoughts or good thoughts—then that undoubtedly is who we will become. Our minds are like our bodies—they both consist of just what we consume.

Let's Pray:

God, give us the right food to feed the good wolf inside us. Help us eat a steady diet of joy, peace, love, hope, serenity, humility, kindness, benevolence, empathy, generosity, truth, compassion, and faith in you. Amen.

Today's Thought Is: **We are what we think.**

*C*ompleted in 537, Istanbul's famed Hagia Sophia, or Holy Wisdom Church,* was the grandest church in Christendom for one thousand years. In 1453, the Ottoman Sultan, Mehmet the Conqueror, seized Constantinople, renamed it Istanbul, and changed the Holy Wisdom Church into a mosque. In 1935, it became a popular museum. My ten-year-old daughter and I were walking down the narrow, twisting, cavelike rampart from its upper level to its magnificent main floor, when suddenly there were several men dressed in dark suits rushing toward us. One pinned me up against the ancient wall, efficiently frisking me and ordering, "Do not move." Meanwhile, I tucked my daughter behind me. Around the corner strode President Putin of Russia. I could have reached out past his bodyguards and touched him, but I didn't. Outside there were hundreds of armed guards, armored vehicles, and even tanks. Putin wouldn't remember me, didn't see me, and will never learn about the brief fright he gave my daughter and me. There we were, in one of the holiest and most magnificent buildings for God on Earth, near one of the most powerful men on Earth with armies guarding him, but I could see that, like me, he was just a little human being inside the grand house of God.

Let's Pray:

Dear God, in your eyes we are all the same—human creatures you have made. It doesn't matter if we're presidents or pastors. We belong to you. Amen.

Today's Thought Is: Only God is great.

---

*Ayasofia is another way of writing Hagia Sofia.

I love this scriptural line for its sinister beauty: "He enjoyed the taste of his wickedness, letting it melt under his tongue."[83] It's a tasty sentence that most of us would quickly deny as ever applying to us. However, at certain times, we all can brandish a cruel tongue that we skillfully use to produce pain.

As a grammar-school boy, when a mean kid called me names, I'd chant what my mother had taught me: "Sticks and stones may break my bones, but words will never hurt me." I always said this, even knowing (just between you and me) that the words actually did hurt. Mean words are powerful. They sting. They bite. Wicked words wielded by a sharp tongue are like razors, like a flogging to the heart. Even as adults we are harmed by hurtful words—which is why we sometimes use them. Now we have a report in *Scientific American* backing up what we all experience as true. The report says that social rejection elicits a brain response similar to the one triggered by physical pain. Subjects snubbed in a virtual game of catch exhibited activity in a brain region called the anterior cingulate cortex, which also plays a role in processing pain. So there we have it—sticks and stones do break bones, and words can break a heart.

Let's Pray:

Dear God, if my tongue is ever too twisted, or too wickedly quick in retort,
if hurtful words escape my mouth and wound loved ones or strangers,
help me regain control, help me keep silent rather than unnecessarily
break a heart. Amen.

Today's Thought Is: "Gentle words bring life and health."[84]

In *Aladdin,* that cartoon parents and children have watched millions of times, the genie of the lamp appears with a big song-and-dance routine, promising Aladdin three wishes. Whatever Aladdin wants, Aladdin may have. There are a few provisos, but pretty much he can have anything. Given a similar chance, for what would you wish, for what do you pray?

If God appeared, saying, "I've had my eye on you. I'll give you whatever you want. Just ask." What would you say? This actually happens to Solomon. God shows up one night, saying, "Sol, you're such a mensch. You're going be king, and soon. So I'll give you whatever you want—just name it."

Sol says, "God, give me wisdom and knowledge because how else can I govern your people?"

God says, "Good choice, Sol. You could've asked for riches, possessions, vengeance, long life, or honors, but you didn't. Since you ask from your heart, it's wisdom and knowledge for you. Moreover, since you made such an excellent choice, I'm going to throw in riches, possessions, and honors, too."

We all ask God for things. God, give me this or that. God, the Teacher says, will give us what we need. But God isn't Santa Claus, or a genie who grants wishes. God gives blessings, and answers prayers, but not always in ways we want or expect.

Maybe we'd get further if we follow Sol's example of praying for selfless spiritual gifts like wisdom, compassion, kindness, strength, fortitude, or hope.

Let's Pray.

Dear God, there are so many things we want; instead, we ask that you give us what you think we need. Amen.

Today's Thought Is: **Prayer is a practice of selflessness.**

or their honeymoon, they rented a tent in a national forest campground in the Virgin Islands. It was classy: two rooms, wood floors, gas stove, electricity, a small fridge, with a sea view and a sandy beach. When the wind was up, he talked her into renting a Sunfish, which is a surfboard-sized vessel with barely enough room for two people. Once they were both aboard and under way, she was white-knuckled, and he was ecstatic. They cruised out at good clip. "Ready about," he shouted. If he'd been an astute husband, he'd have noticed the questioning look of his new bride, who did not understand nautical talk. Instead, he shouted, "Coming about," deftly swung the tiller, ducked the boom, and watched as his stunned bride was banged on the brow and knocked overboard into the sea. She was not exactly cooled off by her unexpected dip.

It turns out that she had no idea what "ready about" or "coming about" meant. The first means "Get ready to duck the boom, I'm going to turn the boat." And the second means "I'm turning the boat right now, so duck the boom." But she didn't know the lingo, and he didn't know she didn't know. A miscommunication that resulted in a bruised brow for her and groveling from him.

For some people, the lingo of faith is just as off-putting. Either they don't understand it, or they did understand when they were younger, had a bad experience, and can't tolerate it now.

Let's Pray:

God, if churchy lingo gets in the way of some folks' faith, please find other words or ways to reach them. We need you. Amen.

Today's Thought Is: **God speaks your lingo.**

*T*here's a man who has everything. After a career at a brokerage house, he retired at forty-seven, sold his West Coast home, moved back to his East Coast home, and rebuilt the family cottage in Maine. He's a success—three smart, good kids in excellent private schools; a smart, kind, loving, and beautiful wife; good health; expensive clothes and cars; lots of time; gobs of money . . . but there's trouble in paradise. He's dissatisfied. It's the classic story of the kid who scores the goal, wins the prize, gets the girl, and drives off in the Land Rover—but knows something's still missing.

The man is bewildered by this. At everything he's ever done, he's succeeded. He's solved every problem, except this one, which, as it turns out, is a classic story, too. He's gained the world but has never found his soul. His solution, our solution, to the question—where is God in my life?—is right inside his heart.

The Teacher said, "Ask, and it will be given; search, and you will find; knock, and the door'll be opened. Everyone who asks receives; everyone who searches, finds; everyone who knocks, the door will be opened." God's at the door knocking. If you hear the knock, open the door. God will come in.

Ask, seek, open—it's as easy as it sounds.

Let's Pray:

You're not lost, God, but maybe we are. Maybe we don't know how to search, or where to knock, or how to ask. Help us with these things. Amen.

Today's Thought Is: Heaven's door is within you;
just knock, ask, open.[85]

The Prophet Elijah is on the run for his life. The first thing he does when he gets to the desert is to complain to God that he's messed everything up; that he's no good, just like his no-good ancestors; that the best solution to his troubles is just dying. Getting it off his chest by complaining aloud to God was the right thing for him to do. Elijah was upset, shook up, and bursting with major stress from all that had happened—Israel abandoning God, the people killing God's prophets by the sword, Elijah single-handedly killing all the prophets of Baal, Queen Jezebel all angry and seeking his life, and Elijah leaving, on the run.[86] If he'd kept it all tightly bottled inside, he'd have exploded like a dropped bottle of seltzer water. Instead, he cracked his dry lips and spoke to God, thereby easing the internal pressure and ensuring he'd get a good nap under a broom tree.

When we're facing terrible trials and tribulations in the wilderness of our lives, when we're facing illness, loss of employment, family tragedy, or any life-blistering experience or bone-chilling misfortune, talking to God is good place to start. In Elijah's story, the first thing God does for him right after his complaints is . . . absolutely nothing at all. God just lets Elijah have his say, vent his frustrations. Many times in life, just venting is good enough, for starters.

Let's Pray:

God, life can be stressful. While we run from this to that, sometimes bad things happen and we may feel we've messed everything up. Listen to our pain, God. Be with us. Amen.

Today's Thought Is: **Give burdens to God.**

What do you think heaven's like? Boring? Quiet? Or a blue sky smiling at you? White fluffy clouds? Chubby little cherubs flitting about, carrying gold harps humming in holy harmony? Halos? Angels' wings? Golden roads? Pearly gates? Saint Pete standing guard? These are images in the popular imagination. Whenever we see a cartoon about heaven—complete with clouds, harps, halos, and wings—we say, "Yep, that's heaven." Beyond the cutesy images, when you think about heaven, what do you imagine? Or is it just too scary to consider?

In her book *Amazing Grace*, Kathleen Norris shares her favorite definition of heaven, which came to her from a Benedictine sister. "As her mother lay dying in a hospital bed, the sister ventured to assure her by saying, 'In heaven, everyone we love is there.' The older woman replied, 'No. In heaven I will love everyone who's there.'"[87]

I will love everyone who's there, even my enemies, even the people I now dislike, even those who've hurt me and those I've hurt. Heaven isn't about me or you the way we are now. Heaven is about our changing in the twinkling of an eye, sloughing off our biological bodies while keeping our *beingness*, keeping our *self/soul/mind/consciousness*, and not changing because of anything we do but because of the *supernatural* order of things—because God made us, God loves us, and God forgives us. Death is like being born again into real love.

Let's Pray:

Dear God, help our belief in you diminish our doubts, and guide us in life so that in death we find our way home. Amen.

Today's Thought Is: **Heaven is home.**

The ice was good, but it was covered in snow. Lou trucked over his snow thrower to use to create a hockey rink. After a few games the rink surface was bladed into a choppy mess. Joe happened to have an industrial water pump from the shipyard where he worked. So the gang chopped a hole in the ice with an ax. They dropped the three-inch intake hose into the hole. They ran power to the pump and fired it up with a roar. It was better than a Zamboni and way more fun! A fresh surface! Ha!

Suddenly, the intake hose slipped to the bottom of the shallow pond. Instantly, a brown mix of water, sand, and stone sprayed the rink surface with grit, and then the pump broke. In silence, they watched the sand-topped rink freeze. That was the end of the season that had started with such hope. Perfect ice; a minor problem; a fine solution. Pumping water had seemed like a such good idea. Then the whole thing fell apart. The rink was wrecked, the season was over. Boo-hoo.

Married couples start out life with high expectations for a shiny and perfect marriage. A little snow might fall, but nothing that can't be dealt with, nothing that can't be cleaned up. Then one person gets an idea to do something imprudent and slips up; a mess is made, a marriage is ruined. Ask yourself—before you do anything careless—is it really worth the risk of ruining everything?

Let's Pray:

Dear God, for the folks struggling in their marriages, give them strength to face their situation and opportunity to work through their troubles. For those suffering through divorce, give them self-confidence and courage, remove their anger, show them love. Amen.

Today's Thought Is: **God heals marriages, and broken hearts, too.**

*H*itchhiking was safer in the seventies. Don's thumb was his means of travel back then. He held a sign that listed his destination: "Yellowstone." Or "College Student Going Home to See Mom." That one always worked. Once he took the wrong ride.

In Montana, he was hitching north to Glacier Park. The driver who stopped was the only car Don had seen in an hour. After stuffing his backpack into the cramped backseat and barely climbing in himself, she sped off.

Instantly, Don knew it was a mistake. The driver said she was headed to kidnap her son in south Kansas, but they were actually driving north. She said that the son had been awarded by the court to her ex, and that God had given her Don to help her with the kidnapping, just as her cult leader had said would happen. "Here's the plan," she said. Don wasn't paying much attention. He had already decided the next exit would be his. She slowed down, then literally began driving in circles on the highway, saying she wasn't sure which way to go, or if she should let him out. Around and around they went until he demanded she stop. She did. He escaped. Luckily there wasn't much traffic in Montana in those days.

When starting out on a faith journey, we sometimes naively hop into the first car that comes along. But be careful out there. You don't want to be taken for a crazy ride by a false messenger of God, or by one of the messenger's gullible lackeys.

Let's Pray:

Dear God, help us be wary of spiritual predators and charlatans who pretend to know what's best for us but who are in it for themselves. Amen.

Today's Thought Is: Cults and false teachers prey on the vulnerable. Take care.

*S*imon came from London to spend his summer vacation working in Ohio at a faith-based summer camp. At the first meeting of the counselors, the camp director asked if anyone knew how to shoot a .22 rifle. Simon had learned riflery at Boy Scout camp and had eventually earned his riflery merit badge. He got the job as a head rifle instructor. A week later a canoeing instructor, who been a counselor at this camp the previous summer, said that the canoe pond was beyond the rifle range, about a half a mile away, just past the cornfield, and that if they wanted the attention of the folks on the pond, the rifle instructor should just aim for the bell on the canoe shack. Plink it. Last year's rifle instructor had done it all the time. The Brit took the Yank's word for it, although he shouldn't have.

One morning Simon tried it with one round. At lunch another Brit counselor came up to him, white-faced, and said that the rifle instructor's bullet had struck a post six inches from this Brit counselor's head, just below the bell. He continued, "Don't do it again. I'll not tell anyone, but I'm not your friend." Even smart folks can be led in strange directions, against all common sense, and played for a fool. There were two fools in that near unlucky game—the rifleman for listening and acting, and the canoeist for seeing danger as sport.

Let's Pray:

Dear God, prevent us from speaking wrong words or performing wrong actions. Help us not to foolishly endanger the innocent or guilty. Teach us wisdom and right action. Amen.

Today's Thought Is: Doing wrong is like sport to a fool, while wise conduct is a pleasure to the wise.[88]

*T*he little boy nicknamed Sandy loved trucks—backhoes, dump trucks, graders, bucket loaders. Sandy loved reading his picture book about big trucks. When his neighbor, Pat, started new construction, the little boy begged his mom to watch the construction every day. Together they would watch the yellow backhoe digging the foundation hole. One day, the backhoe operator waved to Sandy. The little boy waved back. The next day, the backhoe operator stopped working, got out of his cab, and walked over to the mom and little boy. "If it's okay with your mom, how'd you like to dig the foundation with me?"

"In the backhoe?" Sandy whispered in awe.

"In the backhoe," the backhoe operator laughed.

His mom thought it was fine so long as she could watch. The man and the boy climbed inside the cab of the noisy machine. The man sat on the torn black seat, the boy sat on his lap, eyes wide and smile huge. Placing the boy's hand on the levers, and his hands atop the boy's hands, the two of them set to work. The backhoe operator's face was serious with concentration. The boy's face was joyful glee.

It turns out the backhoe operator let little children from all over town dig big holes with him in his backhoe. Many children joyfully remember the power and fun of running his big machine. Kindheartedness toward children is brilliant. Children know the real thing when they see it. The Teacher was kindhearted toward children. The Teacher said, "Let the children come to me. Don't stop them. Heaven belongs to such as these."

Let's Pray:

Dear God, let your blessings fall on your sons and daughters who are kindhearted toward children. Amen.

Today's Thought Is: **God's heaven belongs to children.**[89]

A college-aged troupe of traveling performers had six nights off during their ten-week tour of sixty-four shows. One free day was spent on the Oregon shore at a driftwood beach. Barehanded in the sand, the troupe dug a trench and erected a wall of upright driftwood logs as a barrier to the prevailing wind. To the leeward, they lit a roaring bonfire, then sat and sang, lounged and ate.

Come early evening, Kerri went for a lonesome walk away from her friends to mourn her missing beau, who had left the tour for home. Atop a sandy bluff above the sea, embraced in fog and sadness, she was praying for a sign that someone loved her still. Imploring with her heart and eyes, she raised her head to the gray, gray sky. Suddenly, just above her, in slow motion, soared an American bald eagle. The eagle was eight feet from tip to tip, and seven feet off the ground, and he craned his head to watch her as he drifted out of sight. His size alone overwhelmed her, but his exquisite presence answered a prayer for her, because, she says, in that moment her heart was lifted up on that eagle's wings by understanding that God still loved her.

We're never alone in life, even if it seems so. A faithful heart turns to the one whose love is promised and delivered.

Let's Pray:

Dear God of signs and miracles, use any means you wish to touch our hearts today and show that we're loved. Amen.

Today's Thought Is: **God's love heals hearts.**

The chairlift wasn't moving up the mountain as they dangled twenty feet off the snowy trail with nothing better to do than teeter in the wind, wait, and talk. The cheery man on the chairlift said he'd been skiing seventy-one years that very day. He'd started skiing in 1933 and had spent his war years as part of the U.S. Army's 10th Mountain Division. Those soldiers trained specifically for high-altitude mountain warfare, in the toughest and coldest conditions, using downhill and cross-country skiing techniques while carrying military guns and ninety pounds of gear. They combined military training with superb mountaineering skills.

"It kept me out of trouble," he said. "At eighty-six years old, I'm blessed with good health and the same crazy brains I had when I signed up for army." In recent years, his friends either had died or were restricted to riding their front-porch rockers. "God's given me a chance to continue doing what I love," he said, adding, "I know I'm lucky." Not many of us get to live that kind of blessing—to live doing what we love. Lots of us fall into our lives, hoping to make the best of things while dreaming of weekends, good times, or a better future. Whatever God's plan is for your life, be it riding a rocker or hopping a lift to the top, realize that your choices do make a difference, and so does your attitude.

Let's Pray:

Dear God, as our bodies and minds age, help us adjust with gracious cheerfulness to our aches and pains, and help us continue to love living. Amen.

Today's Thought Is: Celebrate life!

Spending all her nights spinning fantasies of her future, this young woman seldom rises early enough to seek work. At the crack of noon, she rises to find nothing to eat in her apartment, her rent overdue, her phone disconnected, her life in shambles, and nothing much to do. "God," she pleads, "help me." She dines on dreams. She dreams of being an artist, but her talent is raw and untrained. She dreams of singing in a band, but she never practices her voice. She dreams of being a model, and she could be, if only the circles beneath her eyes from her sleepless nights hadn't given her such a desperate look. She dreams of having money, but she refuses to work more than twenty hours per week, because work cuts into her life. If only she could win the lottery! If only she could meet a prince. If only she'd be discovered, then she'd never work again. Here's the thing, though—artists work at their art, singers work on their voices, models pose for long hours. It's all work—whether it's prying blue mussels from the seaside muck, or flipping burgers, or writing books. It's work that makes life work. Surely, God would help if only first she'd learn to help herself.

The lazy person says, I can't go out to work; the phone might ring. I might miss my dreams.

Let's Pray:

Dear God, help the lazybones awaken from their dreams and set about working toward them. Take fear from them. Amen.

Today's Thought Is: The cravings of lazy people will lead to ruin, because their hands refuse to work.[90]

*M*y friend recalls every word he's read since second grade. In one conversation, he can quote from Dr. Seuss's *Marvin K. Mooney Will You Please Go Now!* and *The Biography of Samuel Adams*. He remembers everything that's ever happened to him, including all the things he struggles to forgive. Maybe there's a moral superiority in having a poor memory. I heard a reporter talking about an international debt one country whose name is . . . uh . . . I forget . . . anyway this one country owes another country a billion dollars. The reporter said, "It'll take serious diplomacy for the debt to be forgiven and forgotten."

Forgive and forget—I'm pretty sure I'd remember if some individual, or some nation, owed *me* a billion dollars, even if I forgave the debt. The reporter was using a figure of speech that most folks believe comes from the Bible. Forgive and forget, the common wisdom holds, amounts to moral superiority. Only it's not in the Bible.

Of course, those of us with poor memories could be considered morally superior by virtue of actually forgetting many of the slights we've suffered. If anything, most of us are more likely to forgive and remember. That's tougher to do anyway when you think about it. When the Teacher talks about forgiveness he says, "Forgive others and God will forgive you." There's never anything about forgetting.

My friend will say, "How can you be nice to that person? He's so-and-so who said such-and-such that hurt you so much." And I'll say, "Jeez, I don't remember that." It may look like moral superiority on the outside, but really it's just my bad memory.

Let's Pray:

Dear God, we ask for the courage to forgive those who've hurt us. Heal us of our wounds and grudges. Amen.

Today's Thought Is: Forgive and be forgiven.

*Y*ears ago, an American tourist traveling in Bombay, India, happened upon an American nun who was kneeling by a river bathing a diseased child. After watching for a minute, then taking a picture or two, the tourist ventured, "Sister, I wouldn't do that for a million dollars." As the sister continued cleaning the child, she replied, "Neither would I."

The Xaverian brother who told that story said that the sister spent her life caring for the poor because she saw the treasure inside each soul she helped. It wasn't that she wanted to live among the poor, bathing their wounds and feeding their bellies. She claimed she had no choice. It was plain to her eyes that each human being was a living temple of God. To ignore this, to pretend she couldn't see that, would have been a denial of her faith. How the nun saw this light inside the poor was never explained; that she *did* see it was as plain as the smile on the child's face, and it has roots in Scripture. The Apostle Paul wrote, "Don't you know that you're God's temple and that God's Spirit lives in you?"[91] This isn't to say we are God. We're not. But God does and can live in us, if we allow room. Each of us, no matter who we are or how we live, is a holy temple of God.

How do you treat your temple?

Let's Pray.

Dear God, help us see your light reflected in the eyes of everyone we meet this day. May we, like the nun, have the heart to see many temples of God, and may we treat our own temple with respect. Amen.

Today's Thought Is: **Not for a million dollars.**

*T*he station wagon was two decades old when a group of poets, dancers, and actors drove it from the University of Massachusetts at Amherst to Worcester to attend a performance of the great mime Marcel Marceau.

Monsieur Marceau's performance was remarkable, but it ended late on a dark and starless night. A thick fog settled in the valley where they drove. The farther from the city, the denser the fog; the denser the fog, the slower they drove. Eventually, their nervousness about the conditions forced them to turn off the stereo, preferring to pray silently while driving. They weren't a particularly religious group. A moment of silence was normally about as close to prayer as they got. But that night, prayer to God was constant. At the bottom of the valley, the fog became impenetrable. Barely inching along in the zero visibility, their headlights useless and the road invisible, the driver opened his door to watch the double yellow line pass beside them, ensuring they stayed in their lane. It worked. They found their way in the fog, made it out of the valley, and finally reached home safely. Ignoring whether or not it was smart to open the car door, this group of young bohemians found themselves in a challenging circumstance and suddenly forgot all their hipness and gladly returned to the faiths of their childhoods through prayer.

Let's Pray:

Dear God, for those who've wandered from their faith, for those caught in a disorienting fog, help them find you again. Amen.

Today's Thought Is: Raising a child in faith provides later bearings in the darkness.

A Congregational minister, his fiancée, and two other couples rowed a dory from Sylvester's Cove in Sunset out to Eagle Island in Penobscot Bay, Maine, for a picnic. It was a beautiful day until the weather soured. The young couples hurried to their dory and began the difficult row to shore in chop and wind. The dory took on water, and, after a time, it foundered. All hands tried to swim ashore. The women—in their long dresses and petticoats, as was the fashion at the turn of the twentieth century—were unable, unassisted, to make it to land. The men attempted rescue, but all six were lost at sea that day. A newspaper, which reported the unfortunate event, carried this curious headline, "Three Women, Two Men, and a Minister Lost at Sea." Notice the headline didn't say three women and three men. It singled out the minister as being neither male nor female. Whether this was a customary subtle separation, an elevation, or a diminishing of the minister, the point is clear—clergy were alien. We're more subtle these days, but clergy are often considered outsiders, not because of who they are or what they believe, but often because of what is believed *about* clergy.

Religious and nonreligious people may stereotype ministers as old white-haired men, with stodgy ways, round bellies, and narrow ideas. While occasionally this is true, for the most part it isn't.

Let's Pray:

Dear God, bless those who chose a life of religious service when they could have taken an easier road. Amen.

Today's Thought Is: God calls all kinds of people to the ministry.

*O*he's standing in the grocery line eyeing the candy rack, one hand on the loaded wire cart, while her mother skims a tabloid. The girl reaches, takes, and pockets a Hershey bar. No one's looking. No one sees. With groceries bagged and loaded, mother and daughter exit through the automatic doors. Inside the car, in the back seat, the girl pulls out her Hershey bar and quietly, guiltily, removes the brown wrapper. Mother hears, and says, "What are you unwrapping?"

"Nothing!" The answer is too quick, the girl's voice too high and too scared for her mother not to notice. Again, her mother asks, as she pulls the car to the curb, "What do you have?"

"A Hershey bar."

"Where did you get it?" Silence. "Where did you get it?"

"I took it from the store."

"Then you must return it."

"Noooooo. They'll be mad. No one saw. Don't make me."

"Yes, they'll be mad. But it's right to return it and wrong to steal."

"Nobody saw me!"

"God saw you and that's reason enough."

The Hershey bar was rewrapped, uneaten. Together they walked into the store; together they waited in line at the customer-service desk while the girl, frightened, cried quietly. The manager took the candy bar, saying he was glad she had returned it. "Promise me you'll never steal again."

She promised, and although she was forgiven, she never has forgotten.

Let's Pray:

God, bless the children who learn honesty through their mistakes. Amen.

Today's Thought Is: **You shall not steal.**[92]

One wickedly freezing and windy day a skier stood atop the Sugarloaf/USA snowfields, otherwise known as "the sheer glacial sheet of your icy death." It's a double-black-diamond kind of trail where, when you stand above it, half the length of your skis hang in midair because the trail drops away at an improbable angle. It's the type of trail that should come with a sign that reads, "Danger! Only Experts and Fools Dare Descend." Of course, there is no warning sign, other than a quickening pulse, sweaty palms, and the knowledge that you've done it before and lived.

And you realize in a flash of winter inspiration that, should you fall, it's a good day to die. You also believe that you are both expert enough *and* fool enough—so you descend, trusting your skill, courage, and quickness. It seems like a big deal, like a bragging point told over a beer—"*I* skied the snowfields!"—until you meet someone with *real* courage, who has overcome the terrible odds of illness, or has returned unscathed from war, or has learned to face a difficult truth about himself. Those things take real courage. Then life slides back into perspective. Reality becomes clear. You understand again that some people live double-black-diamond lives and never talk about it.

Nowhere in the Bible does Jesus say, "You guys! Did you see me walking on that water! I could've drowned! Did you see me change that water into wine. It was so cooool!"

Let's Pray:

Dear God, keep our egos out of it. Whatever it is that makes us feel like boasting, just keep our mouths shut. Amen.

Today's Thought Is: Christ never bragged.

The unfriendly city where he went to school was dangerous after dark. Only thugs, gangs, and those who had no choice remained outside after the sun went down. A cold torrential rain fell on that winter's evening as he slowed down and found a parking spot near his apartment. Hurrying on the slick sidewalk was a slouching grandmother dressed in a wet, dark coat. She was tugging a loaded two-wheeled grocery cart behind her. She reminded him of his own grandmother, who lived in his hometown and walked each day to the market pulling her cart.

On an impulse, he stopped, hopped out, and said to the old woman, "You're getting soaked. I'll give you a ride home." The look of fear on her face prompted him to add, "You look like my grandmother, and you're wet. I hope somebody'll give my grandmother a ride if she's caught out in weather like this." The old woman climbed in as he loaded her grocery bags and her cart in the back. It was a short three-block drive to her apartment. When they got there, she said, "I've been thinking—you're an angel sent by God."

"Thanks, but, no." He smiled. "Just a student."

"I don't think so," she said. "You look human, but you're an angel. I was praying God would get me home safely, and he did."

Today, you could be God's answer to somebody's prayer.

Let's Pray:

Dear God, when we respond with compassion, may it truly be your work we are doing. Amen.

Today's Thought Is: A compassionate impulse may be God's prompting.

*D*on and Kath were concerned when Chas and Linda came for a visit with their nineteen-month-old baby, Jordan. In the time since they'd seen their favorite couple, Chas and Linda had changed. For the entire visit, the young parents focused much of their attention on the baby and little to none on their friends. Adult conversation, to which the two couples had once been accustomed, was nonexistent. In its place was a series of chopped-up dialogues that revolved exclusively around the baby. It was an unpleasantly memorable visit. Don and Kath figured they'd lost their friends forever. A year later, after Kath had given birth to their own baby, Ozzie, they suddenly understood the change in their friends' behavior. Unexpectedly, Don and Kath had become members of a club neither had known existed—the Parenthood Club.

Sure, they knew couples had babies, but they didn't know and couldn't understand what that change meant until it happened to them. They had to experience it. They weren't the same people they'd been before. Ozzie became their focus; sleep became precious; selfless giving became the norm. They saw the world and themselves with fresh eyes. They had changed.

It's that type of life change that overcomes a person who suddenly and fully believes in God. It's like entering a world they'd heard about, didn't understood, and couldn't comprehend until they entered it themselves—until they *experienced* it. Seeing it from the outside isn't enough for belief, only a heart touched by God's grace changes and sees.

Dear God, open the eyes of the spiritually blind so that they may see your light. Amen.

Today's Thought Is: **Dare to see with new eyes.**

*I*n the film *Bruce Almighty*, God explains to Bruce that being God is complicated work. Everybody wants something—a cure, a fix, a benefit, height, a miracle, money, weight loss, beauty . . . whatever. When God grants Bruce his powers, Bruce is so overwhelmed by all the prayers that he grants the wishes of everybody. They all get a yes, causing a complication of cross-purposes.

Often people mistakenly see God as a genie who grants material wishes, or as a Santa Claus who brings life's desire. When Santa doesn't deliver the goods, when the genie runs out of magic—poof! Their faith disappears. Faith isn't about getting something physical from God. Faith, real faith, is about God, just God, only God. It's about experiencing the wings of grace and the touch of love. It's believing, not owning. It's not about getting, or receiving, or having, or winning, or healing.

The gifts of God are nice to get, maybe even needed, but don't base your faith on presents. You don't love your family because of what they do, or what they give you; you love them just because you do. The same is true for any honest and loving relationship. Sometimes it's just about love and being near to the one you love. That's the same with faith. It's not the gifts, or the cures, or the hopes—it's the love, it's the grace. Being a person of faith is simply learning to love God for who he is and not for what God gives, or doesn't give.

Let's Pray:

Dear God, set our faith straight. Help us understand that loving you and being loved by you is enough. Let us feel it. Amen.

Today's Thought Is: **Pray for wings of grace.**

*I*t was prom night when Tommy took his daddy's Caddy to drive his date, Lynn; his friend, Gary; and Gary's date, Debbie, to the dance. Debbie lived two towns away. The ride back to the city, with the stereo blasting and the AC on, was quicker than Tommy had realized. Pulling into town, Tommy glanced in his rearview mirror and saw three cruisers about a half mile behind him, their blue lights flashing. They were too far back to have anything to do with him, so he ignored them—but then he saw the roadblock just ahead. Six city cruisers impeded his path. There were flashing blue lights and police everywhere. Naturally, he slowed to a stop.

Officers stared at him, with their hands on holstered pistols. The three speeding cruisers slid to a stop, boxing his car in where it was. It was then Tommy suspected he'd been driving a little too fast.

Nine cruisers, each with two cops—eighteen police officers surrounded his car. As the sergeant in charge approached his window with a menacing look, Tommy recognized his uncle Al. Uncle Al looked at Tommy, shook his head, and smiled. Turning to the other officers, Uncle Al said, "It's all right, boys; he's my nephew. I'll take care of him." The other cruisers and cops vanished. Two of the cruisers behind Tommy had followed him through two towns but couldn't catch him. The third one, from the most recent town he had passed through, had joined the merry chase a couple miles back. They'd radioed ahead for the roadblock. Tommy would've paid a big price if his uncle hadn't interceded.

At heaven's roadblock, God will intercede for you and make your indiscretions go away—just believe.

Let's Pray:

Dear God, help us understand our spiritual advocate is available to all who seek you. Amen.

Today's Thought Is: **God's there for you.**

*W*hen Cindy came home from college for January break, her younger brother, Jeff, joined her in her room, where they discussed her classes in science, French, and tae kwon do. Cindy said her martial arts class focused on form and was noncontact. Jeff asked her to show him a punch, a block, or a kick. Having earned her yellow belt, she was confident that she could show him a side kick. "Stand still," she said, "I won't hurt you." Trusting, as only a brother can be, Jeff stood still. Cindy assumed her stance, and then, moving with force and speed (and mismeasurement) she "ki-yahed" Jeff in the chest, sending him flying backward across her bed and slamming him into the wall. Cindy was mortified. Jeff was sore, but forgiving.

Life can be something like this. There you are, innocently standing by, all trusting when—*ka-pow*, an unexpected blow catches you unaware, causing your head and life to reel. The strike can come from anywhere. It doesn't have to be a loving sister with poor aim. It can be a large and unexpected bill, a sudden and serious health issue, anything difficult and unexpected.

At times like these we often say, "Why me, God? Why now?" Those are spiritually rhetorical questions—questions that probably won't be answered. Ask them anyway. Pray to God, anyway. It's okay to say, "Hey God, what's up with this?" Just add, "A little help here, please."

Dear God, when life coldcocks us, help us get on our feet again,
help us understand that you are with us and that we'll make it
through it somehow. Amen.

Today's Thought Is: **God rewards persistence.**

One hundred and forty-three children, ages eight to seventeen, traveled on three buses from Maine to Manhattan. The kids were part of a choir going down to sing on NBC's *Today*. While there, the kids took in the sights of the city. To ensure no child would get lost, they divided the kids into manageable-sized groups led by parents. Inside Madame Tussaud's Wax Museum, one blond boy disappeared. Suddenly, in a crowd of many hundreds of tourists, he vanished. His absence was quickly noticed. His chaperone handed the other boys to another parent, then dashed back through the museum, looking and calling his name. The blond boy was nowhere.

Parents and older chorus members were recruited, museum staff alerted, and the sidewalk checked up and down for two blocks. Twenty minutes had passed. He remained lost. Eventually, a museum staff member spotted a small blond boy crouching in a corner of the incredibly crowded lobby. When questioned, the boy said, "I got lost." To lose your own child is scary; to lose somebody else's child is dreadful. The boy had gone astray, but then, thank God, he was found.

The Rabbi believed that any lost lamb is valuable enough to find. He said, "A shepherd leaves ninety-nine sheep to find one lost lamb."[93] We do the same thing for our children.

Sometimes being lost isn't a geographical issue. It's a theological one, a spiritual one. If you're feeling lost in life, turn to the one who knows you, loves you, and will find you wherever you are. Turn to God.

Let's Pray:

Dear God, find the lost; lead them home. Amen.

Today's Thought Is: Seek and you will be found.

I saw this shaggy-haired teen wearing a shirt silk-screened with the faces of the seventies' rock band KISS. Unmistakable.

It was like if, in 1973, I had been sporting a flat top and wearing a "Benny Goodman and His Orchestra" T-shirt. The teen said that he had tickets to KISS's next concert and that he would never cut his hair. "Eventually, we all do," I said, adding, "I had an original KISS tape back when I had hair."

We who love music of any type—whether it be swing, rock, bebop, reggae, hip-hop, funk, R and B, country, opera, classical, religious, or international—share one thing in common. Music touches us intellectually and emotionally. We love the notes, the rhythm, the percussion . . . the sound. It stirs us where we live. It speaks to us.

That's what we want from our God, is not it? A God who can touch us where we live, in ways we understand, in ways that move us. So maybe we go to different churches, or synagogues, or mosques, or not at all. Maybe our styles of faith differ from one another, but there is this one binding love, this one celestial music, that supersedes our differences and joins us at our hearts, into God. Loving music of any type makes us similar. Loving God makes us one.

Our problem is that we tend to notice the differences, not the similarities.

Let's Pray:

God of all people, God who sent prophets and the Teacher to us, bless all who love you. Bind us as one people, your people, in our hearts through love, this day. Amen.

Today's Thought Is: Loving God makes us one.

*O*ne evening my daughter and I enjoyed dessert in a local restaurant crowded with tourists. Seated near us was a mother with her cute two-year-old. Just after their dinner was served, the little girl erupted in tears, complaining of a hurt wrist—but of course she wouldn't show it. The more her mortified mother consoled her, the louder her crying became. It soon evolved into a wailing chant, "I want to go home." A doggie bag was quickly organized.

As they left I scanned the restaurant and saw every eye looking—expressing sympathy, understanding, and relief. Although we sympathize, few people enjoy being in the presence of pain—emotional or physical, real or imagined. When those we love are suffering, they need us, as much as that child needed comfort from her mother.

When the problem is bigger than tears, like an injury or an illness, words of comfort may help. When words fail us, what remains is the kindness of showing we care—a phone call, a brief visit, a hug, a prayer, a card, flowers. It's not so much what we say, in the card, on the phone, or in person. What matters is showing we care, thus lightening the burden of fear and loneliness.

This is sometimes the most healing gift we can give.

Let's Pray:

Dear God, help us remember with kindnesses those who are hospitalized or bedridden. May our presence, cards, calls, and prayers, be healing to them. Amen.

Today's Thought Is: Visiting the sick is an act of faith.

*I*n my fifth-grade class was a girl no one liked. I don't know why we didn't like her, we just didn't. Everyone, it seemed, picked on her. Her name was Peggy, which became . . . Piggy. We all, it seemed to me, taunted this girl every time the teachers were out of earshot. I guess we thought we were better than Peggy. One day Peggy was called out of class. In marched our principal—strong-armed, stern-faced old Mrs. Wallace. She gave us the worst scolding of our lives. We were *never* to call Peggy "Piggy" again. Intimidated, we all agreed.

For some reason, in line on the way out the door over by the chalkboard, at the end of the day, I decided to whisper to her, "Piiiggy," one last time. My best friend, Steven, overheard me and told the teacher. I was mad, and scared. After school, I had to clean the tops of all thirty-six desks in the classroom "with elbow grease." I had to write "I am sorry, Peggy" one hundred times on the chalkboard. I had to apologize to her in person. I learned my lesson—how words, name-calling, and other forms of bullying can hurt just as much as a punch in the nose.

Here's a word: *empathize*. It means to feel someone else's pain.

Let's Pray.

Dear God, sometimes we are the bully. Maybe we use words, or maybe we shove around a little kid for no other reason than that we can. We're sorry, and we promise, with your help, never to do it again. Amen.

Today's Thought Is: **Empathize with the victim.**

*I*t was dark—really, really dark. We had candles, kerosene lanterns, and a propane stove, so we had light and heat. Outside, a full-faced moon served as a big white night-light casting shadows in our yard. We went to bed. At midnight there was a pounding at my back door. I fumbled for the flashlight and stumbled down the stairs. At the back door there was an entire crowd, and I knew them all. Each one of them wanted to come in. I tried to bar the door, but they shoved in anyway.

In came cowardice, in came fear, in came joy and pleasure, depression and laughter. Malice and sorrow and boredom squeezed in, too. Some were welcome, some were not. What did they think this was? A guesthouse? Turns out it is. I run a house that has frequent guests, coming alone or in groups. God sends them over. They come whether I am ready or not. A few knock over the furniture and shove it aside, clearing space inside me, preparing me for some unknown delight. Others carry quieter gifts and sit down for a cup of tea. Some I like; others I don't. But each arrives as a guide from God to help me get ready for whatever comes next. My job is to welcome them, whether I want them or not.

Let's Pray:

Dear God, guide us. Whether we expect them or not, send your emotional emissaries to be our teachers; let them lead us into your desire. Amen.

Today's Thought Is: **Welcome them all.**[94]

*L*iz, an able sailor, went sailing in her sixteen-foot Hobie Cat on a small-craft-warning day. Why? She was young and believed herself immortal. Hers was the only boat at sea.

The swells were six to eight feet that day. Liz was flying from wave crest to wave crest when suddenly she was flung from the boat. She saw the sail split as she hit the water, but the unmanned Hobie Cat sped away. Liz spent seven hours in rough waters, clinging to lobster buoys. Half the time she spent gasping for air, forced under water by fat waves. By the time she was rescued, miraculously, by a passing trawler, Liz was nearly dead from hypothermia. After her ordeal, she spent several days hospitalized.

Normally Liz never wore a life jacket. For some reason, as she was preparing to sail that day, she thought, "I'll put on my life jacket." The only life jacket she had was too small for her frame. She wore it anyway, and it saved her life. Liz's father told her that at about one-fifteen that afternoon he said a prayer, "God, make Liz wear a life jacket today." It was a one-fifteen when Liz put on that life jacket.

Prayer works. Maybe we don't always get what we want. Maybe our prayers are answered in unexpected ways. There have been several studies on prayer, conducted at major universities, that show that, even when a sick individual is a hundred miles away and being prayed for by strangers, the healing is measurably faster.

Let's Pray.

God, please answer our heartfelt prayers in whatever way you prefer. Touch our lives with minor miracles. Amen.

Today's Thought Is: **God listens.**

*E*very year there's a sweetest-water-in-Maine competition. We don't enter. Without filtration our well water is so discolored that, if a brown duck was hiding in a bucket of it, you'd say, "What duck?" After four years, the well pump was hauled out and replaced just before guests arrived. The water pressure tank died that day, too. Meanwhile, I'd been noticing that matching my clothes was getting easier and easier, since everything was colored a subtle shade of rust. The day after we replaced the pump and tank, after twenty sort-of faithful years, we also replaced the high-tech water-filtration system in our dirt cellar. *Chaa-ching* and voilà! White shirts and sparkling sheets.

Basically, around here, you make do with the well water God gives you—sometimes it's award-winning water; other times it's liquid mud.

The Rabbi says, "Out of the abundance of the heart the mouth speaks." Whatever's in there, whatever's down there in the well—be it sweet or mucky, pain or comfort, beauty or anger, love or fear—it's going to come out of the tap, out of your mouth. It'll be plain to see then whether it's palatable or not. We can't change the water in our well; we can only filter it.

What's in the well of your heart? That can be fixed. Sure, it takes time, but mostly it takes God, guidance, faith, deep self-reflection, and a willingness to change.

Let's Pray:

Dear God, if the words out of our mouths are mucky, nasty, or ugly because of the pain we carry in our hearts, we ask you to heal us. Amen.

Today's Thought Is: "Rivers of living water will flow out from within."[95]

*I*t was the very last car they impregnated with rust before it was shipped to the U.S. market. They had to sell the last rust model to somebody and we bought it. We're not martyrs, but we just needed a small, used, four-wheel-drive wagon. The price was right. Now, with 140 thousand miles on it, it'll cost twice what the car's worth to fix the oil leak and the rust. Eventually, it'll be unsafe. Meanwhile, the engine, transmission, seats, heat, radio, lights, wheels, everything else is shipshape. The engine might make it to 200 thousand miles if the body doesn't give out, but the body is going to give out.

That's how it is for some older people. The engine, minus a leak or two, is in excellent shape and could keep going on forever, while the body is decaying faster than a rusted fender on a wet, salted road. We hear folks say, I'm eighty on the outside, but I'm twenty inside. It's too bad the body isn't more durable. There's a time limit built into us. Botox, chemical peels, health clubs, good diets, stretching—they keep aging at bay, but they don't stop the rust.

The Apostle Paul refers to the body as a temple. It's a holy dwelling place of God. It doesn't matter if it's covered in rust, or the oil leaks, or the brakes squeak, or the seats aren't comfortable. In any condition, the human body is a holy dwelling for God among us.

Let's Pray:

Dear God, thank you for loving us the way we are, for seeing beyond the rust spots to our bright souls within. Amen.

Today's Thought Is: **Rust can't touch the soul.**[96]

A mallard swept down from the sky with its webbed feet extended, expecting a soft-water landing on our pond. Instead of touching water, he touched down on thin black ice, quickly lost his footing, landed on his bottom and spun across the ice. He crashed softly into the tall brown grass on the edge of the pond. Collecting his wits, he stood and shook himself off like a cartoon character. He waddled two steps, and then, with his neck craned to watch his own left foot—he skated—left foot, right foot, left foot. He didn't fall.

Over toward the other edge of the pond the sun had slightly melted the surface ice. The water was a half-inch deep. Duck wanted to swim. He waddled over. Tail up, he dropped himself in—or tried to. His breast hit ice. Duck shook his head, as if asking, "What the . . . ?"

Ducks make good cartoon clowns. God has clowns, too. These everyday people might not look like clowns, but seeing their joy of being in God brings us merriment. God's actually pretty funny. After all, God gave us ducks to watch.

Let's Pray.

Dear God, you can be funny. Make us snicker today. In amusement let's feel joy, and in joy let's feel you. Amen.

Today's Thought Is: **God gives joy.**[97]

*G*rowing as a weed in Mexico—from Cancun to Campeche and back to Tulum—is a spiderwort plant of mythic proportions. It's commonly called the wandering Jew. I often wonder who named this plant. Was it one who had left his own country—a minion on a military migration, a member of the Spanish War machine, a soldier engaged in a global hunt for gold or glory?

Perhaps it was a European soldier who named this unusual plant. After all, who would name a plant after a centuries-old legend featuring a Jerusalem shoemaker who was told that he would wander the Earth until the second coming of Christ?

My neighbors with green thumbs grow wandering Jew plants. Its stems are hues of purple; its delicate three-petal flowers bloom pink, white, or purple. It's prolific in sunny windows.

Are you surprised that it reaches to the light? Plants, people, nations need light—outer and inner. Elohim, the God common to Christians and Jews, gives light to both. Living in the light brings buds to blossom. This scrambling spiderwort grows, spreads, and prospers wherever its need for living Light leads.

Let's Pray

Dear God, you are the living Light. Live in us as a nation, as a people of Light lovers. Amen.

Today's Thought Is: Love the Light.

enry Ford built the Gristmill in Sudbury, Massachusetts. It's a three-story fieldstone building, complete with a two-story waterwheel, nestled next to a stone dam that pours a wide waterfall from a millpond. It's surrounded by ancient trees and millstones are scattered in the yard like gigantic granite wheels. A long and low stonewall sets off the gravel parking area from the building and the irresistible beauty surrounding it. This flour mill works at grinding grain into flour, as a tourist trap, and as a favorite parking spot for young lovers.

On their first high school date, Steve and Lynn parked at the Gristmill. It was dark, they kissed, they talked, it grew late and, as if they were in a grade-B film, his car would not start. Steve's dad was out of town, so they had to call Lynn's father, a protective man who was perturbed at finding his innocent daughter in the hands of a teenage Casanova. In a controlled voice, her father paraphrased the Scriptures: "If you cause a girl to stumble, then it would be better for you if a millstone were hung around your neck and you were thrown into the sea, or into a nearby millpond, as the case may be." As misdirected as his paraphrase was to those innocent teens—well, not totally misdirected or innocent, either—his message was clear: "You better not get my daughter into trouble."

Let's Pray:

Dear God, keep us from becoming temptations to others;
let us lead no one astray. Amen.

Today's Thought Is: Am I the cause of another's stumble?[98]

*R*esearchers wanted to compare the dietary habits of pre-industrialized Americans to those enjoyed by our modern-day population. They studied the Amish and came up with the Amish diet. It's a diet plan where you don't give up fats, sugars, and carbs; you don't join a gym; you don't have your stomach stapled. Eat whatever you want—you can have meat, potatoes, bread, pasta, butter, pies, and cakes, every day—and don't worry about calories.

Here's the catch: like the Amish, you must walk a minimum of ten thousand steps a day. Two thousand steps equal a mile. Amish men average eighteen thousand steps (nine miles), and women walk an average of fourteen thousand steps (seven miles). One overachiever, coming in from the fields with a team of Belgian horses, showed he'd walked fifty thousand steps, or twenty-five miles, that day. His comment? "Yup, and it weren't no easy walking either."

For people with weight struggles, it's not easy walking to better health. It's a burden. But "many hands make light work." It's true for diet and exercise. Within a community context, diet and exercise are easier to pursue and maintain. It's easier to go for a walk when there's somebody to walk with, especially when sweet temptations surround us.

The same is true of our faith. It's much easier to face temptations, to succeed in our spiritual lives and to walk with God inside a community of motivated people who share similar goals. We'll find an improved faith in a community who together breaks bread and walks with God.

Let's Pray:

Dear God, support the seekers who desire a leaner soul, who want to walk with you but somehow find it a burden to start. Get them started, God. Amen.

Today's Thought Is: **We live on bread and the word of God.**

*G*od says to Abe, "I hear that the people in the city are wicked. So I've decided to destroy it."

Abe says, "Hold up there, God. You're planning on obliterating the innocent and the guilty together? Suppose you find fifty innocent folk in that city. You wouldn't destroy the good folk along with the bad, would you? That's not justice."

God replies, "Fine! If I find fifty innocents, I'll spare the city. Satisfied?"

"Actually, no," says Abe. "Suppose there're forty-five? Will you squash the whole place for a lack of five?"

God replies, "No! Not if there're forty-five. Okay?"

Abe presses, "What if there're forty?"

God replies, "Okay. Not if there're forty."

Abe pleads, "Don't be angry, God. Just a thought—maybe there're thirty?"

God replies, "Listen, if there're thirty, I'll leave it alone, okay. Are we done here?"

Abe says, "Okay. That's good, but since I've dared to speak to you— maybe there're twenty?"

God says, "Twenty? Fine. Not for twenty."

Abe finishes, "Listen, God, don't get angry; but maybe there're just ten?"

God, a little exasperated, says, "If ten, I'll leave the city alone. Are you pleased?"

Abe says yes. God goes on his way. Abe thinks, God can be reasonable. You can talk with God. You can negotiate with him. But in the end, the city was destroyed because there were fewer than ten innocents.[99]

Let's Pray:

God, we can't always get what we want in prayer, but if we try, if we pray, we believe you'll treat us justly. Amen.

Today's Thought Is: **Pray—you just might succeed.**

*P*etro's grandmother came from Greece. She dressed in black every day. None of his schoolmates' grandmothers dressed in black. He loved her, but her house smelled funny—like garlic, yogurt, and roast lamb. And he never knew what he'd find in the fridge—could be goats' brains. She cooked funny, too—delicious, but funny. Even her scrambled eggs turned green and tasted different. His grandmother talked funny, and the house was filled with old, odd things: a pedal-operated sewing machine, a gramophone with old-time scratchy black records as thick as two CDs stacked together, a lemon tree with lemons growing on it.

When he was a grown man, he accidentally discovered the cause of the green scrambled eggs. His grandmother had used dark green olive oil, which accounted for the "different" flavor, too. And it was once he reached adulthood that he learned that being different, coming from a different culture or attending a different church, isn't wrong, or bad, or evil . . . and that there's more than one way to scramble an egg.

When the early Church was forming, there were those living in Jerusalem who thought that there was only one way of doing things. They believed members had to be Jewish—no Greeks or Romans—nobody else was allowed. If you wanted faith but were from a different culture—no way.

It was the Apostle Paul who forced the issue, eventually convincing everyone that there was room for more than one type of faith.

Let's Pray:

Dear God, isn't there room enough in heaven for all of us? Help us get along on Earth when our perspectives differ. Amen.

Today's Thought Is: God has room for all.

A New Yorker flew in to Lake Chesuncook in northern Maine for a fishing holiday late one summer. One night by the campfire, his guide entertained him with tales of severe winters. "There're snowdrifts taller than spruce trees; Canadian winds come so frosty that the breath from your mouth freezes solid as soon as it leaves your lips and falls in a lump to the ground. And there're only two seasons up here—winter and the Fourth of July."

"Well," said the urbanite, when the guide was catching his breath, "we've got cold snaps in the Big Apple, but nothing like what you describe. How do you manage under such conditions?"

"Me?" replied the guide. "I don't try to stand it, not anymore. Before it freezes up solid, I pack up my gear, find the wife, get outta here; we go down south to stay warm for the winter."

"Florida?" asked the New Yorker.

"Nope," said the guide. "Portland."

Portland was plenty cold in winter's last snap. Makes you wonder about all the folks who need heat assistance, or those who are barely making ends meet, or the homeless. Thank God for the Salvation Army, homeless shelters, food pantries, Goodwill, and houses of worship—all of which provide a safe harbor for a brief time by giving away emergency money, or heating oil, or food, or coats and mittens in the dead cold of winter. If you're cold, or hungry, turn to one of those organizations. If you are able, give to one.

Let's Pray:

Dear God, we pray for those whose homes are cold, who lack food because they chose heat, who need coats or a place to stay. Let our helping hands be your hands, God. Amen.

Today's Thought Is: When you give to one of my family, you give to me.[100]

*U*p the ancient, tropical trail, through a lush grove of impossibly towering trees, toward Wailua Falls, along the Wailua River, on the island of Kauai, the two men—the local Reverend David Kamaaina and his friend, Mr. Peter Hoale, a mainland developer with a scientific bent of mind and an eye for opportunity—talked of the ecology, considered the climbing, clinging leathery-leaved philodendrons and the marching roots of wild ginger, and then they discussed how the entire setting would be perfect for a high-end development.

Dispassionately, they analyzed and subdivided the beauty. Then suddenly, inexplicably, and simultaneously, the palpable presence of God overcame them, weakening their knees. The majestic grove in which they walked seemed a sacred place where the holiness of God readily leaked through creation, touching their human hearts. All talk of taming nature ceased. Wonder returned, awe overwhelmed them, and they stood in childlike silent appreciation of what God creates.

If we approach God, and all life, only analytically and dispassionately, without wonder or curiosity, devoid of any childlike spirit; if we choose to subdivide God into tiny proportions and usable propositions; if we mistakenly choose to possess God, by grasping only indisputable religious facts— then we may miss the sacred nature of all life and creation. Instead, let's live in our work and in our homes, in the living richness of the Divine who loves us, who touches us where we stand, who sustains us right now.

Let's Pray:

Dear God, leak through creation now, touch us with your sacred presence, open us to contemplation. Amen.

Today's Thought Is: Now is the perfect time to commune with God.

*T*his is an intriguing story that circulated simultaneously on both Christian and Islamic Web sites. The author is unknown.

A ship was wrecked. Two men swam to a desert island. Their only hope was to pray to God. To discover whose prayer was more powerful, they divided the island and stayed on opposite sides. One prayed for food. Soon he saw a fruit tree on his side. He ate. The other man ate nothing. After a week, the first man was lonely and prayed for a wife. Soon another ship was wrecked. The survivor was a woman who swam to him. For the other man, there was nothing. The first man prayed for a house, clothes, and food. All were granted. The second man still had nothing. The first man prayed for rescue. A ship arrived. This first man and the woman boarded. They decided to abandon the second man. The first man considered the other unworthy, since none of his prayers had been answered. As the ship was leaving, the first man heard a voice from heaven, "Why are you leaving your friend behind?"

"My blessings are mine, since I prayed for them," he answered. "His prayers remain unanswered. He deserves nothing."

"You're wrong!" the voice rebuked. "He had one prayer only, which I answered. If not for that, you would've received nothing."

"Tell me," the first man asked, "what did he pray for that I should owe him anything?"

"He prayed that your prayers be answered."

Let's Pray:

Dear God, give your blessing on those we care about, that their prayers might be answered. Amen.

Today's Thought Is: Our blessings may not come from our own prayers, but from others praying for us.

*B*ack in 1949, an orphan seal appeared at Jane's home in Castine, Maine. The seal, whom Jane named Junior, was obviously ill and out of sorts. Being a wild baby seal, he didn't know how to take a bottle. Jane's mom called up Mr. Goodridge, a friend of the family, who was also a friend of the famous Andre the Seal. Mr. Goodridge and Jane's mom were on the phone nonstop. She tried all of Mr. Goodridge's methods to get Junior to eat. Nothing worked. After Junior slipped slowly into a coma, Jane's mom stayed up all night with him. She forced an enema tube down his throat and into his tummy, and fed him homemade eggnog—fresh eggs, canned milk, and Karo syrup—by the teaspoonful every twenty minutes or so. By morning, Junior had regained consciousness. He eventually thrived and became Jane's preferred water playmate. That summer, Junior mostly lived aboard the schooner *The Stephen Tabor,* which was owned by her dad.

That fall, after the windjammer season had ended, Junior lived on their back porch. On land, whenever Junior got hungry, he'd pull open the screen door, and the family's dogs and cats would jump all over him, which forced him to duck. Then he'd flippity-flop into the kitchen, saying, "Whaaaaa," and wait for his formula. Late that fall Junior disappeared into the sea. Jane, who is an adult now, remains hopeful that his instincts helped him catch fish, find a mate, and lead a wonderful life.

Let's Pray:

*Dear God, if we have to figure a way to make the improbable work
—whatever it is—give us the moxie and resourcefulness we need,
just like Jane's mom had. Amen.*

Today's Thought Is: By combining diligence, effort, ingenuity, and necessity, we'll find a way to thrive.

*P*arked on a street in a not-so-nice neighborhood, the car was locked shut. As the sun set, Pete returned to the car and realized his keys were still dangling from the ignition. He tried the passenger door, but it also was locked. Pete stood there, alternately looking at the keys and at the new dent that appeared mysteriously in the front fender. Not a good car day.

A car stopped next to him, and the driver lowered his window. "Got a problem?" he asked. "Two problems," Pete said. "Keys are locked in the car and there's a new dent." "No problem," replied the driver. "I can fix both, for a small price." Reaching over to his passenger seat, the driver lifted a tool specially designed for illegally popping ignitions out of steering columns. The driver held it up. "I'll pop that dent for twenty bucks."

As he got out of his car, he grabbed his portable drill. "I don't usually do this kind of work," he joked. Skillfully, he drilled a tiny hole in the fender, inserted the tip of his special tool, gave it a yank, and *bang* the dent was gone. Next, he produced from his car a two-and-a-half-foot-long, one-inch-wide flat piece of metal with a handle. This he snaked between the rubber gasket on the passenger door and the window. In a jiffy the lock was open. "Twenty'll cover it," he said, but then he added, "Ah, forget it. It's my good deed for today."

Let's Pray:

Dear God, no matter our flaws and failings, shine your light through us, that others might see it through us. Amen.

Today's Thought Is: God puts lamps in unexpected places.

*I*n the Western Way, a rip-roaring and roiling channel between Mount Desert and the Great Cranberry Islands of Maine, the helmsman called, "Minke whales off the starboard stern!" As all eyes turned to see the whales, the twenty-four-foot sloop, *The Darian*, was running downwind on the incoming tide, rocketing up, over, and down the mounting swells. Suddenly *The Darian* jerked and stopped dead in the water when she should've been sailing free. Captain Teke spilled his drink. Cousins Andrew and Annabel landed on their Scottish fannies. Only the helmsman kept his feet, but he lost his dignity. By ignoring his course, he had snagged a lobster buoy, which had in turn become a sturdy, immovable anchor. Hanging him by his ankles, Captain Teke dangled the helmsman over the stern to see if, by sheer muscular strength, the helmsman could haul their craft astern against the rushing current and steady wind. Impossible.

The only choice for the helmsman, given sore bottoms and spilled drinks, was to don his birthday suit; tie a line around his wrist; grasp a serrated blade, piratelike, between his teeth; and dive into the nippy North Atlantic. Cutting lobster buoys in Maine is like stealing cattle in Montana. The helmsman hated to do it, but he had little choice. Under the water, he sawed until, with a snap, the line parted. The freed sloop shot forward. The helmsman was hauled back aboard.

One kind of stealing is taking what isn't yours and keeping it. Another kind of stealing is making the other fellow lose his property permanently.

Dear God, forgive us our unprincipled ways and unavoidable errors as we forgive those who mistreat us. Amen.

Today's Thought Is: If you forgive others their trespasses, God will forgive you yours.[101]

his kid, Don, is a natural. At second base, Don doesn't always pay attention. He'll be scuffing the baseline with his cleats when the batter hits a line drive that zooms past the pitcher. Then, like somebody flicking a switch, this second baseman flashes to life and makes a leaping, lightning-fast catch. Don's like this all the time. At bat, his form is slouchy, with the bat just hanging and his feet weakly planted. As the ball crosses the plate, an instant transformation turns him into a mini–Babe Ruth. Don runs fast, too, and doesn't expect to be caught as a base runner. It doesn't matter what sport he's playing—baseball, basketball, football, kickball. In every event, he's a natural. Being a natural, Don's come to expect winning without effort.

One evening, he was on first base, ready to steal, when the catcher bobbled the pitch. The natural took off. The catcher saw him and burned a straight throw past the ducking pitcher. The ball arrived a nanosecond before the runner. The umpire called, *"Out!"* Don couldn't believe it. He stomped, shouted, stamped, protested, and marched off the field. He'd never been caught before. He'd never lost. But he gained by losing. He gained perspective, empathy, and self-understanding.

He's not the only one who can gain by losing. The Rabbi tells us that in order to gain life we have to lose it.

Let's Pray:

Dear God, losing is no fun; but if losing ourselves in you means gaining our souls, then so be it. Amen.

Today's Thought Is: To get what's worth having, maybe we must risk losing everything else.[102]

e said, "I come here only for the soda and the cookies." I didn't believe him, even though I was watching him guzzle a can while munching some cookies. It was early evening, and we all should have been finished an hour ago, but there had been a delay that nobody really minded. I had just been walked to the long table set up in the gymnasium for the day. The Red Cross nurse told me to have something to eat and drink, to do no heavy lifting for the rest of the day, and to wait ten minutes before leaving. Ten minutes. Dinner been scheduled for half an hour ago, and my evening meeting was to start in a half hour. Not much time to sit, drink juice, eat a cookie, dash home, eat dinner, and then drive back to the office.

"The life you save could be your own." Or it could be your mom's, or a stranger's. The first time I gave blood was at the end of my senior year of high school, and I did so because all the volunteers got out of class for a half day. Two weeks later, the kid with the locker next to mine needed blood. He was hit by a car because, stoned on hash, he stepped out into traffic while crossing the street on his way to a school dance. Suddenly, we all understood what was at stake.

Let's Pray:

Dear God, your life pulses through us; it beats in our hearts, it courses through our bodies. We thank you for this life, and we thank you for the chance to share life. Amen.

Today's Thought Is: Give the gift of life.

*S*itting on the hillside on the cool grass under a warm sun, the spectator watched the Little League game spread out on the diamond below him. It was a hard-fought game. A team's benchwarmer came over and sat beside him on the grass. "Look what I can do," said the boy. In his hand, he held a twelve-ounce aluminum bat. He placed the bottom of the bat on his palm so that it was sticking up toward the sky, and then, staring at it, he tried to balance it. It kept falling. He kept trying. The boy kept saying "Darn, darn, darn" as the bat kept falling, and "Look what I can do," although he wasn't actually doing it.

The man wanted to watch the game, but he was distracted by the boy. After about ten minutes, the spectator figured the only way to watch the game was to spend time showing the boy how to balance almost any object. Taking the bat from the boy, he said, "Watch this." The man balanced the bat on two fingers. It didn't wobble. "Wow," said the boy, "howja' do that?"

"Easily," said the man. "Keep your eyes glued on the very top of the bat." The boy practiced silently. The spectator watched the game.

Let's Pray:

Dear God, sometimes it's like you've taken your eye off us,
and we feel off balance. We don't want to badger you, but that seems to be
the only way to get your attention. So we're pestering you again, until
you pay attention and respond. Amen.

Today's Thought Is: It's okay to pester God.[103]

nside a state office building there lives an illegal fish. It's a frilly red fish that swims about in a clear glass vase among the roots of a living plant. On my visit there, a respectable official said, "I was hoping a pastor would stop by and that he'd be able to bless that fish, because, even though everybody here believes this fish has been living in that vase for a year, it hasn't actually been the same fish. The fish keeps dying, and we have to keep replacing it." This respectable official figured that if I blessed the fish and the water, then the fish might live.

I smiled, nodded politely, and said nothing, hoping to avoid the entire situation. But that was not to be. Later on, when I was done with my business, I mistakenly hung around instead of exiting. The smiling official found me, saying that he knew I hadn't blessed the fish or the water. As he dragged me along, I asked him, "After I bless this fish, what happens when it dies? It will die, you know. Then the story won't be about the minister who blessed the office fish, it'll be about the minister who blessed the office fish *that then died.*"

The official just smiled at me and insisted.

Trapped, I prayed, "Lord, bless this water. Bless this fish. May it live until it dies. Amen."

Let's Pray:

Dear God, it's sure easier when we pray for what we know will happen. When we don't know, which is most of the time, it's better for us to pray that your will be done. So let your will be done today. Amen.

Today's Thought Is: **God's will, not mine.**

The rotted bottom planking of the old lobster skiff let in more sea than it kept out. Hauled ashore and rolled over, the man attached sheets of marine plywood, a hundred stainless steel screws, caulking, epoxy, and fiberglass matting to make his boat float again. The old Evinrude, eighteen horses built in 1959, drinks gallons of gasoline but pushes the skiff at a reasonable rate, albeit at a sound decibel too loud to allow for talking. The man gave it to his teenage daughter and taught her how to use it.

She needed a ride to reach her summer job, and she wasn't old enough to drive a car. But the bay beckoned for a boat, and so she made a daily trip across the water, around the point, and up into the harbor. There she tied the old skiff onto the town float and walked the short remaining distance to her job. This hardy sea girl runs her skiff with the ease of an island-born and bay-raised child. It's as natural to her to be aboard a boat as it is for a seagull to fly, or a razorbill to swim, or a city kid to ride the subway. Besides, you can't flip a skiff, and a wood boat always floats.

Some see the sea as dangerous for a teen on her way to work, but she knows her craft; she knows the sky and the sea. She feels at peace and free on the waters where she lives. On flat-water days, she'll "open 'er up"; on chop, she motors slowly; on stormy days, her boat stays moored. The girl has had able teachers.

Let's Pray:

Dear God, in our boat of faith, with skills learned from able teachers, we cross from birth across the wide bay of life to you. Amen.

Today's Thought Is: How safe is your craft of faith?

*I*n the spring of his senior year, after rowing on the crew team for four years, the coach cut him from the varsity squad. He was too short. He had always been the smallest, so he rowed in the bow position, where his weight was an advantage. Over that particular winter his teammates had grown. He hadn't. The entire team was a head taller. His stature caused the length of his stroke to be shorter than his teammates', ruining the necessary symmetry and balance of the shell. He wanted growth hormone shots but was refused.

Growth hormone is regulated. What about the kid of average size who wants to make the basketball team? What about the child who wants the advantage of height in the business world? Who should have access to growth hormone—perhaps anyone who can afford to pay for it?

Why should a person's genetic code limit height or anything else when remedies are at hand? Why should genetic traits be treated as if written in stone?[104] These questions relate to our place in the God-given world, to our relationship with the ultimate Creator, and to our inborn tendency for innovation.

Let's Pray:

Dear God, your humans are on the verge of species re-creation,
or at least genetic manipulation. We aren't you, and do not want to be you.
Show us how to use these new and remarkable tools. Amen.

Today's Thought Is: In whose image?

The children hurriedly opened the wardrobe door to hide from the visitors who'd come to view the professor's old, odd house. It wasn't an ordinary wardrobe with an ordinary inside. Beyond the long fur coats that smelled of mothballs, beyond the place where the back of the wardrobe should have been and wasn't, was a land of destiny for Peter, Susan, Edmund, and Lucy. Unexpectedly, through the wardrobe, they entered a bewitched world where winter never stops and Christmas never comes; where animals talk and plot; where nymphs and fauns suffer under an evil witch turned Queen, who turns her enemies into stone statues; and where hope comes in the form of a kind and fierce lion, who isn't tame.

There are horrors and hags, wars and betrayals, dangers and honors. It's a world whose future is balanced on the lives of these four unsuspecting children, who must find courage inside themselves, for if they fail, their lives will remain in the icy fingers of the coldhearted Queen, their world will forever be a land in winter. This is the world of Narnia, a world envisioned and created by author C. S. Lewis in his acclaimed series, the Chronicles of Narnia, beginning with the children's book *The Lion, the Witch, and the Wardrobe*.[105] It's easy and engaging reading for any child who says, "I'm bored."

Let's Pray:

Dear God, in fantasy stories we sometimes see ourselves reflected, and maybe we might even recognize you, God, in certain stories; let our summer reading fill our minds and souls with goodness. Amen.

Today's Thought Is: **Certain books open windows to God.**

In my high school, I was famous for basketball, because my cumulative score in four years of playing during physical education class once a week was four points. That's not four points a game. It's not even four points a season. That's four points total in four years of playing. Other than the kid who never played because he figured out a way to cut every gym class for four years, thus scoring *zero* points—other than him—I held the record for the least number of baskets ever. I believe my record still stands. It's not like I didn't try, but I just never figured out how to shoot that ball so that it might land inside the hoop. Consequently, as you might guess, I was always the last one picked. Actually, I wasn't ever picked or chosen, I was just the last guy standing there. One team had to have me. I could pass, I could steal, I could dribble, I just couldn't shoot.

Not being chosen, being passed over, or being the last one standing there isn't easy. It doesn't matter if it's playing dodge ball, or being maid of honor, or losing out on a promotion at work. At one point in life, everybody's not chosen. Quarterback Tom Brady, who led the New England Patriots to three Super Bowls, was finally picked in the sixth round of the 2000 NFL draft. That's almost like being the last kid picked.

Who chooses you when you feel unchosen, or unworthy? Take a guess. It's God. Asking God to pick you helps.

Pick me, God. Choose me. I'll follow. I'll play. Amen.

Today's Thought Is: "For we know, brothers and sisters beloved by God, that God has chosen you . . ."[106]

*T*hey told him, "You can't possibly, not ever, lock your keys inside this car." The car had one of those push-button keychain lock mechanisms. Push the button and the headlights flashed, the horn beeped once, and the car locked itself. Push the other button and the lights flashed, the horn tooted, and the car unlocked itself. The fellow behind the counter repeated, "You don't need a spare key, because I promise you can't lock the keys in the car, and besides, the key has a computer chip. It costs forty-three dollars to buy another key, and two weeks for it to get here. Do you really want to spend that money and wait?" Convinced, no extra key was bought.

About eight months later, while attending a wedding, he unlocked the car with the button, got what he needed, then decided to toss the keys onto the floor of the car and leave it unlocked. Preparing to leave later that night, he could see the keys on the floor, *and* he could see that the car was locked. Using a metal coat hanger, he got the door unlocked. A couple weeks later, it happened again. So for a second time he had to break into his own car. The promise had been that the car couldn't lock itself. The car locks itself to this day.

It's tough to believe in promises when they're are broken. We, accidentally or intentionally, break promises, or maybe we make promises we shouldn't make. God doesn't, hasn't, won't, can't, and never will break a promise.

Let's Pray:

Dear God, you promise that the key to new life, and life eternal, is belief. The Rabbi said so. We believe, God, but help us when we don't. Amen.

Today's Thought Is: **The promises of God are rock solid.**

On July 7, 2005, four barbaric and deadly terrorist bombs exploded in downtown London during the morning rush hour. Many innocents—children, women, men, shoppers, tourists, commuters—were killed. A group calling itself the "Secret Organization Group of al-Qaeda Jihad Organization in Europe" claimed responsibility.

Once more, innocent and law-abiding Muslims went into panic mode, fearing blind reprisals and vengeance as the world stumbled and staggered over the debris scattered through the London streets. There are cowards in this world intent on destroying any positive relationship that exists between people from differing religions. Sectarian brutality has frequently and historically been at the root of war, terror, oppression, and violence. It is never correct to blame an entire faith system for the cruelty of zealots.

The British Chief Rabbi, Sir Jonathan Sacks, was quoted by the BBC: "These terrible events have brought home to us the full evil that terror represents. It is not the weapon of the weak against the strong but the rage of the angry against the defenseless and innocent. It is an evil means to an evil end. I will be asking all our congregations to say special prayers for the victims and their families this Sabbath. We grieve for the dead, pray for the injured, and share our tears with the bereaved."[107]

We would do well to heed the words of the Rabbi Sacks.

Let's Pray:

Dear God, we pray for the dead, we pray for the injured, we pray for the bereaved, we pray for the innocent victims of terrorist violence. Bless them all, Adoni. Amen.

Today's Thought Is: **Vengeance is mine, says God.**[108]

*P*am hadn't intended to get pregnant. She was cautious. It wasn't love; it was attraction, convenience, and opportunity. Until that time, she'd considered herself a good Catholic, if not always an obedient one. It took her a week to decide. It's not what she wanted to do.

Either way, that one night of passion had altered her forever. She was too young to have a child. As one of seven children, she knew about the responsibilities and challenges of parenthood. She had no job. Her parents lived abroad. Her brothers and sisters were in struggles of their own. Pam was on her own. Where was the man? He was there, but it's not his story.

Pam chose. He supported her. When the day came, he drove her and waited for her, and then he was attentive to her for months. It was a devastating choice. She grieved and felt shame. She believed she did the right thing, but it was not a simple thing. It's an enduring thing, an unspoken thing. It exists between her and God, unforgotten, unavoidable, and, she hopes, forgivable. Pam is like many others who believe in God, who love God, who find themselves in a compromised position. Perhaps it is pregnancy, or divorce, or war in which we take actions we never believed we would take and then continue to live.

Let's Pray:

Dear God, there are things that we do that we know are hurtful to you, to us and to others. Sometimes we make choices that lead us on paths we never believed we could walk. Forgive us, for at times we know what we do. Amen.

Today's Thought Is: **God forgives.**

I hate peas. I hate winter. I hate mice. I hate reading. I hate talk radio. I hate licorice. I hate hats. I hate crybabies. I hate winners. I hate rich folks. I hate welfare cheats. I hate TV preachers. I hate. . . . What a word—*hate*. We use it as easily and as freely as we use the word *love*.

I love your skirt. I love pizza. I love that idea. I love talking with you. I love your coffee. I love. . . . I used to think I knew what hate was. I hated Brussels sprouts. Now I just don't like them. *Hate* is a powerful word. On talk radio one day, I heard a caller from an infamous church talking about how God hates America, gays, and Canada. It wasn't just what she said. It was her tone, her belief, her conviction. Hate fueled her. Hate consumed her. Hate was her identity.

The teacher tells us to do good to those who hate us. It's not an easy command. Did he think that by doing good we would make them love us? Does love conquer hate? What does doing good mean? Should I open a door for her? Should I feed her if she's hungry? Should I give her broadcast time? Recently I heard that 98 percent of the Gospel can be summed up in one word—hospitality. I don't know what the other 2 percent is.

That's my answer to hate. Treat the hater with hospitality.

Let's Pray:

Dear God, we're called to love, not to hate. Open our hearts to showing hospitality to those who hate us. Amen.

Today's Thought Is: **Do good to those who hate you.**[109]

At the beach I noticed my swimming goggles were missing. Call me paranoid, but when I swim in the ocean, I like to see what's in the water with me. But not having my goggles didn't stop me. I dove in and swam out forty yards. Something out there nibbled at my toes. Without my goggles I couldn't see what was chasing me. With my head out of the water, I looked back. It wasn't a shark, so I kept swimming. The nibbler kept nibbling. Enough was enough. I sprinted toward shore. Fish friends must have joined him, because halfway back there was nonstop nipping on my kicking toes. I didn't panic, but knowing a group of mysterious sea creatures think that your toes are delectable delights makes it hard to concentrate on getting to the beach.

When I arrived at where I could stand in water up to my waist, I did so. Whatever those nibbling nippers were, they vanished into the deep. Being pursued by unknown and potentially hostile forces was both rousing and disconcerting. Sometimes fear drives us forward.

Some folks' faith is all about fearing the unseen God who pursues us. Fearing God's wrath is what motivates them. Other people don't want to hear anything about fearing God. They believe it's wrong to fear God. I ask, is fearing God wrong if the fear of God's reprisal is all that prevents somebody from intentionally injuring another person?

Let's Pray.

Dear God, fear of you can motivate us, but we'd rather be drawn in by your love than driven away by our fear. Amen.

Today's Thought Is: Is faith the opposite of fear?[110]

*B*ack in college, I died from hypothermia. It was about three in the morning while I was trying like hell to get off a mountainside. I was ice climbing in the Rockies, still 150 feet up on a cliff, when I suddenly felt warm and sleepy. The next I knew, I was in a place I can only describe as an infinite void. I was still me, only a soul me, without a physical body. In front of me was heaven's gigantic door and the proverbial tunnel.

After judgment, after God's forgiveness, I was filled with an intense and unspeakable love and beauty. I was fully loved and fully known. I said to God in a wordless communication inside my mind, "I can't die." At that time and for many years previous, my sister had been missing. She had vanished—run away. Her absence had caused my family great emotional suffering. I said, "I can't make my parents lose another child."

Wordlessly inside my mind, God replied, "I love you. I have always loved you. In the same way that you feel my love now, I have always loved you, only you could not feel my love on Earth because your human form prevented you from knowing my love. In the same way that I love you, and have always loved you, I love your family, and have always loved them, only they do not know it. Because I love them, all will be well."

Even though we don't feel it now, God loves us with an immense love.

Let's Pray:

Dear God, show us your love; don't make us wait. Amen.

Today's Thought Is: God loves us unspeakably.

Wrapping around the medical clinic grounds in Pinelajo, Honduras, is an eight-foot-high chain-link fence. The entrance gate holds a padlock. The groundskeeper has the only key. Since the gate isn't topped with barbed wire, one can climb it and hop over it, which is what we did one night when we wanted to go to the corner store to buy juice.

I scaled it and landed outside. Matt did the same. Lizzy, dressed in a short denim skirt, was hesitant to climb. Gallant Jeremy quickly took to his hands and knees, insisting that Lizzy stand on his back to begin her assent. We goaded her into it. Shoes off, she stepped on his back, and bare-toed, climbed the chain links. Her skirt cooperated on the climb up, but as she teetered on top, her skirt gave her inches of creeping trouble.

On her descent, her skirt hitched itself higher. We had promised not to look, but we didn't want her to fall. Her skirt never entered the danger zone, but it required her to stop descending in order to readjust. At the moment Lizzy placed one foot on the ground, while exclaiming her incredulity at having been egged on into climbing, a little Honduran child, still inside the clinic grounds, arrived, looked at us quizzically, lifted the gate handle, opened the gate, and walked through, saying, "It's unlocked."

Let's Pray.

Dear God, heaven's entrance gate is easily opened; open the gates of our hearts, and let us enter your heaven. Amen.

Today's Thought Is: The Teacher says, "I am the gate, enter through me."[111]

*T*his is the clinic—one room built of cinder block, never stuccoed; two wooden doors; two windows, with no glass, no screens; no electricity, an inch of dirt and dust covering the poured floor. This medical clinic, which is normally closed, is high in a hot pine forest of the Honduran mountains, in the poorest village among poor villages. The clinic is normally staffed only when the visiting nurse who has no car, no truck, no horse, no bicycle, arrives on foot. She reaches each village only infrequently.

The clinic also opens on the rare occasions when a missionary doctor visits, as when we were there. Any missionary doctor might be overwhelmed by two hundred or three hundred villagers hoping to see her. Some patients walk for as long as four hours over mountain footpaths to visit the clinic when they hear that the mission doctor might be there. And the doctoring doesn't end until the last patient is seen. No one has money for medical care. Few have money for shoes, so they walk barefoot, both the young and the old. Some lack money for food. Medical care that we take for granted—aspirin, cough syrup, vision checkups, stitches, and the setting of broken bones—are, for these people, luxuries they cannot afford. Yet, for all this poverty, their clothes are always clean and their yards are neatly maintained. Poverty isn't squalor. Their courtesy, generosity, joy, and pride are unmistakable.

It turns out that the greatest joy the doctor on our team ever experienced is by serving those who have nothing.

Let's Pray:

Dear God, we went, hoping to give of ourselves, but once there, we found we received more than can ever be repaid. Thank you for teaching us that in giving, we receive. Amen.

Today's Thought Is: It is in giving that we receive.

y neighbors include a nurse, a sports trainer, a retiree from South America, a hospital maintenance worker, and a radiologist. All of different ages and backgrounds. There's one thing that we share—each of us has had a near death experience, an NDE. Some say such experiences are dreams, or the brain's natural response to dying. Maybe so. But for those who have experienced one, no amount of reasoning will change our minds. The impact is profound, deep, and lasting.

I had mine in 1980 while ice climbing in the Canadian Rockies. I've not been the same since. I felt overwhelming, inexpressible love. Beauty. Sweetness. Comfort. Peace. Judgment. Forgiveness. Contentment. I was truly, absolutely home, and I was allowed to return.

People who've had an NDE may say nothing about it for years. It's lonely. It's bizarre. It can be depressing to return here, until we readjust. A great Christian thinker wrote, "We are not human beings having a spiritual experience; we are spiritual beings having a human experience." Jesus, who raised Lazarus from the dead, tried to teach us that heaven is among us now and heaven awaits us at death. It truly does. Fear not. God is merciful.

Let's Pray:

God of heaven, lighten our hearts from burdens we carry about those we love who have left this world. Touch us with the assurance of your love that we might know that all is well with those who love you. When we face our own deaths, bless us with peace. Amen.

Today's Thought Is: "We are not human beings having a spiritual experience; we are spiritual beings having a human experience."[112]

All the soccer players in a Honduran valley had uniforms, but few wore cleats, or shoes of any kind, even. On their stone-strewn field, no grass grew from the packed, rocky dirt. I saw barefoot players expertly playing the game as if they didn't feel stones and hard earth underfoot. The soles of their dirty feet must have been as hard as leather.

Watching them reminded me of an old story about dirty feet, about the day when the Teacher ate dinner in the home of a community leader. During the meal, an uninvited guest burst into the dinning room, bent over, washed the Teacher's dirty feet with her tears, dried them with her hair, and poured oil on his leathery feet. The host thought, "If this teacher really was a prophet, like people say he is, then he'd know what kind of woman this is. He'd see her dried-up soul inside her." The Teacher, perceiving his host's heart, said, "I see your soul clearly enough. When I came to dinner, you didn't bother washing my feet. You showed me no respect."[113]

In those ancient days that's what a proper host always did. Maybe the host didn't bother with the Teacher's feet because, in the eyes of the host, the Teacher just wasn't the right kind of player. This does call into question the leather-hardened nature of the host's soul, doesn't it?

Let's Pray:

Dear God, when we measure one another's worth, let's not judge others by their shoes, or their lack of shoes, but, with your eyes, let us see into their souls to see the treasure carried there. Amen.

Today's Thought Is: Rich or poor, money is all the same to God—valueless.

*D*ick grew up in Brazil, the child of American Presbyterian missionaries. More than seventy years ago, when Dick was a baby, he contracted dysentery. In those days, especially in the tropics, and particularly among young children, dysentery was frequently fatal.

In a darkened room in their home, Dick's grieving dad had been sitting a vigil with his dying child. Dick died and so his father left the room. When the father returned sometime later, to go about the grim task of preparing his boy for a funeral, he saw a miracle. Dick's eyelids fluttered ever so little, ever so gently. From that moment on, Dick began to recover.

Like many churches who send missionaries overseas, the Presbyterians provide their stateside congregations with a prayer calendar listing the names, locations, and work of their missionaries. On each day of the year, people all across the states pray for one family. The day Dick died, and then recovered, was the day designated for his family to be prayed for.[114]

Let's pause for a moment and pray for someone, anyone, whom we may not know well, or even know at all, and ask God to bless him.

Dear God, let your ears hear our prayers; let your heart be moved.
Even if we don't know the needs of those we pray for, you know them,
so bless them. Amen.

Today's Thought Is: Pray for one another.[115]

*I*n the ancient and ruined Mayan city of Copán, in the western mountains of Honduras, in the treetops lives a clever monkey who, it is said, feeds the deer. In the driest season, when all low leaves have been eaten, and when the deer become hungry, this monkey, high above, plucks and drops leaves down to the deer so they may eat.

What makes this story stranger still is that this monkey has been sighted riding bareback on the deer. Picture a white-faced monkey riding silently on a small deer that is leaping through the forest. A monkey riding a deer—just when you think you've seen everything, you haven't.

In a Honduran village lives an intelligent but handicapped mother, with shining cinnamon eyes, who walks mountain paths on the tops of her upside-down and backward-facing feet; there's also a boy with iguanalike eyes that move independently of each other, seeing the world from two views at once. Closer to home, in Maine, there was a hard-nosed cop who took back a ticket from an old woman whose husband had just died and whose house had just burned. I heard, too, of the father who superhumanly lifted a car off his daughter to save her life. There was even a man who, so long ago and far away, walked on water. You may not have seen everything, yet suddenly, nothing seems impossible.

Let's Pray:

Dear God, this is a crazy world where the unexpected and unanticipated reveals your quirky nature. Blessed are you, God, who allows room for the new and the unexpected. Amen.

Today's Thought Is: **You haven't seen everything.**

*A*fter two years with a cell phone, I canceled my subscription because I didn't get reception at my house or in half the area of the rural town in which I live. After I canceled my service my parents wondered how they'd ever reach me again as if landlines didn't exist. It's gotten to the point where cell phones are nearly essential. Two years later, I resubscribed. I'm not the only one who needs a cell—so do my teenage daughter, my teenage son, and my wife. Four people in our household who need a cell phone for communication and safety. Cells are convenient, but it's another monthly bill to pay.

Nowadays, like everybody else, we pay the ever-increasing light bill, the phone bill, the mortgage, the car loan, the Internet bill, the water bill, the heating bill, insurance bills, rising taxes, and probably a few more I'm forgetting. We'd be paying for cable TV, too, but we had to draw the line somewhere, and besides, we get the best local station, WCSH 6, on the aerial for free. The cost and number of items that we all consider to be essentials of modern living just keep increasing. On top of these expenses, we choose to give to charities, too, and we feel good about it. It sure seems like whatever we give away comes back to us in other ways.

Let's Pray:

Dear God, although we feel pressured by finances, thanks for the chance to give back to you through charity. Amen.

Today's Thought Is: Give, and it will be given to you . . . for the measure you give will be the measure you get back.[116]

*Y*ou've probably heard this story . . . The river was rising. The radio advised residents to leave. "I'm not leaving until God rescues me," said Tom. The river rose and was flowing down his street. There was a pounding at his door. A voice announced, "Get out before the river rises." Tom said, "I'm not leaving until God rescues me." The river rose over the first floor.

A boat came by. A voice shouted, "Get in the boat before the river rises higher!" "I'm not leaving until God rescues me." Tom retorted. The river rose. Tom was up on the roof. It was a crisis. A helicopter came and tossed Tom a line.

Tom shouted, "I'm not leaving until God rescues me." The water rose and Tom died. At the pearly gates Tom yelled at God, "I prayed that you would rescue me and you didn't."

God said, "I spoke to you on your radio. I knocked at your door. I shouted from a boat. I sent a helicopter. What more do you want from me?"

When God speaks to us, do we listen? If God is trying to get a message to us, he whispers, then speaks, and then shouts, and lastly he gives us a crisis. The trick is have the wisdom to listen early on.

Let's Pray

Dear God, when you whisper, let us hear. When you speak, let us hear. When you shout, give us ears. When crisis comes, let us gain understanding. Give us the wisdom to act on the whisper, or the courage to act in the face of crisis. Amen.

Today's Thought Is: Through whispering, speaking, shouting, and crisis, God speaks to us.

*J*an said, "I'm uncomfortable with religion. When I hear it, all I can think about is the violence of the church and all the wars, and the greed, and the discrimination, and the lust for power that permeates history. Organized religion has used God for their own ends."

My first thought was humorous. "Jan," I thought to myself, "most of the well-meaning churches I have belonged to were closer to disorganized religion than organized. Just attend a few board or committee meetings, and you'll see what I mean." What I said aloud was, "Jan, many people agree with you. A survey of history shows that you're right. In our lifetime, it was the Catholics against the Protestants in northern Ireland. Long ago there were the ever-popular Crusades, as well as dozens of pogroms against the Jews in Europe. I don't think God had much to do with those things. Those were about people—about power, money, control, hatred, ideologies, dogmas, bigotry, scapegoating, and land."

Humans have frequently used religion as an expression of hate. It's not just Christians either, Sunnis and Shi'is are duking it out in Iraq, and neither Sunni nor Shi'i is fond of the Sufis. Hindus and Sikhs have fought for centuries. Unfortunately, anybody anywhere can do wrong in the name of God.

Let's Pray:

Dear God, please don't let the history of religion get in the way of those who seek you. Let those who are troubled by history see beyond the human flaws in religion. The only perfection is you, and you are love. Amen.

Today's Thought Is: God doesn't misuse religion, people do.

*S*cientists studying a group of wild bottle-nosed dolphins in Florida made a startling discovery—the dolphins talk to one another by whistling other dolphins' names. They know one another's names and can even mention by name a dolphin who isn't present. Scientists recorded dolphin vocalizations. They removed intonations from the vocalizations, leaving only the syllables. It'd be like recording a human voice, removing my accent and vocal characteristics, and leaving only the frequency modulation. Basically, my voice would be completely understandable, but wholly unrecognizable. They played these recorded names on an underwater microphone to see if close dolphin relatives reacted. They did. Essentially, the Wild Dolphin Project has determined that dolphins have rudimentary language skills.[117]

It's long been believed that only humans could name objects or creatures. In God's great wisdom, he has given humans a brain to penetrate the mysteries of this world. We are discovering that ours isn't the only brain to contain intellectual capacity.

Let's Pray:

Dear God, the longer we live on Earth, the more we learn about our neighbors here, the ones we used to call dumb animals. Help us to accept a shift in our worldview. Amen.

Today's Thought Is: **There is more to this God created world than we know.**[118]

*I*nside a windowless room in a Connecticut hospital, there once lived an old woman on a ventilator. The ventilator limited her mobility and prevented her from talking. When the reverend met Mrs. Blossom, she'd been there for three years, moving only between her bed and her chair. Using a pen and pad, she wrote that paying for her health care had cost her savings and her home. She was miserable and prayed for death.

One day, she wasn't in her bed. Was she finally at peace? At the nurses' station, the reverend asked, "Where is Mrs. Blossom?" Standing nearby was a doctor dressed in a white lab coat. Hearing Mrs. Blossom's name, he looked up and asked disinterestedly, "Who are you?"

"Her minister," said the reverend.

"Mrs. Blossom is in cardiac care. She had a heart attack. You'll be happy to know that I saved her life." The doctor looked back to his clipboard.

"WHAT!?" exclaimed the reverend. "Happy? You've condemned her to more misery! She's nearly ninety. She's bored to death! Fed up! She hates her life! In her own words, she exists but can't talk. She can't read. She never sees the sun! She has no friends, no family! Have you ever spoken to her? Why didn't you let her die? That was her hope."

Mrs. Blossom lived an additional five years. She wrote that she wished her doctors had let her die a natural death, instead of condemning her to live an unnatural life.

Let's Pray:

Dear God, if it is your will, answer the prayers of those suffering medical misery. Release them and grant them the freedom to go home to you. Amen.

Today's Thought Is: **Medically and spiritually,
quality of life matters.**

An e-mail came claiming he had found my name on the desk of his late boss, the millionaire Paul Getty. He explained that Mr. Getty had left a very large sum of money to a Mrs. Gutierrez, who had died before she could receive the funds. I was next in line. He claimed to be a London lawyer and the executor of the Getty estate. He wrote that, if I were to send thousands of dollars for processing fees to cover expenses for his financier in Canada, then I, on behalf of my unnamed Christian Organization, would inherit three million dollars for use in spreading God's message. I must act immediately. He finished, writing, "Is spending $6,000 to make $3 million worth it?"

It sounds like it would be, doesn't it?

Lawyers are highly educated men and women with a strong grasp of the English language. This man's consistent, outrageous, and obvious mistakes in spelling, sentence structure, and grammar, as well as his insistence that I act immediately, raised a red flag.

He was trying to scam me.

Honest and trusting families are taken in by this kind of fraud every day. One family lost $8,000 when they received word that a long-lost uncle in South Africa had remembered the husband in his will. Another man lost $70,000 in an attempt to gain $5 million.

The lure of easy money gets many of us. Don't be fooled

Holy God, give us wisdom and intuition to protect us from con men who would
prey on us. Protect the honest, innocent, and trusting among us. Amen.

Today's Thought Is: With the exception of God's heaven,
if it sounds too good to be true, it is.

*Y*ou've probably heard this joke:

A Sunday School teacher asks, "What's God's name?"

"Harold," a boy shouts.

"Why Harold?" teacher replies.

"Because, 'Our Father, who art in Heaven, Harold be thy name.'"

Actually, in Hebrew God has no name. Sure, when Moses asks the burning bush, "Who should I tell the people you are," God replies, "I am who I am." That's not a name. It's a cryptic self-description. You might be thinking, wait a minute, God has a name. It's Jehovah, or Yahweh. Actually, neither is correct. Jehovah is a German translation of the word Yahweh, which itself is sort of made up. In the original Hebrew the word has no vowels. In fact, it's the only word in the Bible without vowels. It's written: Y-H-W-H.

In the ancient world, if you knew a person's name, it was believed you had power over him. Think of the story of A'dam when he was naming the animals and plants. He had power over them. The idea is this: God is so far beyond concept, thought, and idea that he has no name. Using a name, the thinking goes, would be to try to domesticate God, to make God smaller, which is not possible.

This is not to say we can't experience God. We can. God is present. Right here, right now. And we can know about God through the Scriptures. We just can't control or contain God.

Let's Pray:

God, you are present. Let us feel your sweetness, even when we are unable to articulate our need for you. Amen.

Today's Thought Is: God exists beyond human language.

Swearing isn't what it used to be. In the olden days, say, back in the fourteenth century, swearing was about blasphemy. Since blasphemy was a crime, punishment could be severe—an iron collar, the stocks, tongue or lip piercing (that doesn't sound so bad these days, though), death at the stake. To avoid punishment, and just in case God was listening, folks invented euphemisms like "Gosh!" and "Darn it!" "Jeezum crow!" and "Dag nabbit!" are two I remember from when I was a kid. Recently, on T-shirts, I saw "Cod Clammit" and "To Halibut."

When people swear in my presence, they say, "Jeez, sorry, Reverend," as if I had tender, holy ears, as if God doesn't hear every word they say even when I'm not there.

Swearing is always about saying what's taboo, saying what's unacceptable. There isn't much left in our society that remains unspeakable, but as long as there are taboo words, if you must use them, please take others, and particularly young children, into consideration. My ears might not be tender, but there are many ears that are.

Let's Pray:

Dear God, whenever we speak, whatever we say, let our words be appropriate to the circumstance. Amen.

Today's Thought Is: "Must swear off from swearing. Bad habit."[119]

*O*n a moonless cloud-covered night on our wooded rural road, there is true darkness. With my eyes wide open, I see darkness. Around me, in the woods, trees creak, animals rustle dry leaves, an owl hoots, twigs snap, and the hair on my neck stands on end. My rational mind says there is nothing to fear. There are no dangerous animals here—no lions, no crocodiles, nothing that hunts humans. Even so, I click on my flashlight.

Having light is good. Genesis says so—in the beginning the first thing God made was light. It's not that darkness is bad; it's not. But darkness can be scary. Imagine a time before flashlights, before kerosene lanterns, before whale-oil lamps, before olive-oil lamps, before fire. In the time before humans controlled fire, night was dark. After the sunset, there was deep darkness, unless the moon was full. Humans weren't the only hunters. We were the hunted. In Greek mythology, among the many other technologies Prometheus stole to give to the primitive humans was the fire he stole from Zeus.

In that mythology, Prometheus' gift provides heat, light, and the ability to cook. It's the technology of fire that angers Zeus enough to torture Prometheus. Why? Because from fire, from this source of heat and light, humans learn to change everything. With fire we dispel the darkness.

Let's Pray:

Dear God, there are many kinds of darkness—the darkness of night,
the darkness of ignorance, the darkness of hate, of loneliness, of despair,
of depression, of fear. Dispel our darkness. Be our light. Give us hope.
Let us be a light to others. Amen.

Today's Thought Is: **You are the light of the world.**

𝒯've been pondering the judgment aspect of my near-death experience. After I died I was still me, only without a physical body, and I was in a place I can only describe as an infinite void. God called my name without language, without sound. I heard it in my mind. He used my soul name, the essence of my being. Hearing it, I knew I was fully known, and nothing of who I was or how I lived was hidden. I was filled to overflowing with love, beauty, joy, and truth. It was all sweetness until judgment came. Then I saw, felt, and experienced all the pain I had ever caused anyone in my entire life, from the moment of my birth until the moment of my death. I felt their intense pain. I experienced it from their perspective. It was terrifying and made worse because simultaneously I understood all my paltry reasons for causing each and every pain. My reasons were nothing compared to the suffering I had caused the people I loved—even the people I didn't love—and their pain was everything. I judged myself as sinful. Sin, it seemed to me, was the pain that I caused others. I judged myself unworthy.

Mercifully, God provided the another perspective. God's soundless voice spoke inside my mind, repeating, "I love you. I made you. You are my creature. I made you this way. It's okay. You are forgiven." At God's word I was forgiven and the sweet beauty of love returned to my soul.

Let's Pray:

Dear God, forgive us the pain we cause others. Be merciful. Amen.

Today's Thought Is: God is merciful.

*A*s a cell phone slowly sank in the water off the dock, the boy said, "Don't worry, mister. Your phone's waterproof because the little red light is still on. Oh, I guess not. The light just went out."

Months later, on a morning following a rainstorm, the replacement cell phone was finally found in the driveway where it had lain all night, after having fallen out of a jacket pocket. Three days of drying it out didn't bring it back to life.

Yet another phone was put in the pocket of a pair of dirty jeans. Then the jeans got washed. The phone came out clean, but it never worked again.

Every time his phone got wet, he was out of touch for weeks until a replacement phone came. It got to be a cycle. Get a phone, get the phone wet, spend some time out of touch, get another phone.

Similarly, my spiritual life is somewhat cyclical. Maybe yours is, too. As much as I need and want to be in touch with God all the time, circumstances seem to conspire to make me drop out of touch for a while. In touch, out of touch, in touch, round and round. The thing is, when I get back in touch, it's like being in the presence of an old and dear friend, like someone who looks you in the eyes and knows your soul without saying a word.

Let's Pray:

Dear God, sometimes we drop out of touch with you. It's not that we don't need you, we do. We miss you. Remember us, and touch our souls. Amen.

Today's Thought Is: **The cyclical nature of spiritual lives is natural.**

The pine-board bench seat in the local restaurant was narrow enough for one patron—that patron was me, and, not that it matters, but I was eating fish chowder on that rainy day. A tourist couple came in and sat by the window near the cash register. That's my favorite seat, but it accommodates two to four people, and I couldn't really take it since I was by myself that day. Because I didn't have a window to look out of, I watched that couple instead. They ordered sandwiches and coffee. After the waitress put their plates on their table, after she had walked away, they paused, held hands across the table, closed their eyes for half a moment, said a quiet prayer, and then began to eat boisterously.

It's not often these days to see anybody saying grace before eating in a public place. Maybe it's not that common in homes either? Saying grace reminds everybody just who it really is who provides the food, and, more important, it invites God to be present at the meal. It's an easy way to connect faith to real living. I don't say grace before every meal. I didn't say it that day before eating that chowder. We do try to say grace nightly at the family dinner table. "Thank you, God, for food and family," or "Thank you, God, for food and friends." It's simple. It's quick. It's a reminder.

Let's Pray:

Dear God, thanks for the food we will eat today, whether we dine alone, or with family, or in prison, or with enemies—we thank you and remember that you are present. Amen.

Today's Thought Is: It only takes a moment to remember eternity.

For eight years, Dave's driven Maine's toll road nightly. He knows its dips and bumps. He knows where "stateys" hide with their radar ready, and where the wild lupine blooms. There's a toll-booth he passes through between nine and eleven where the same woman holds out her hand to collect his coins. They've seen each other hundreds of times. Dave recognizes her. She recognizes Dave because he always asks for a receipt. The toll taker is younger than she looks. Her life hasn't been easy. She's thin, with sunken blue eyes and wrinkles covering her face. All night she watches her tiny TV as she collects state tolls and thanks the motorists with her smoky voice.

At the tollbooth one night, Dave placed his coins in the toll taker's hand. Their eyes caught and communicated deep thoughts without words. Her eyes said, "You, too? You work for a living, night after night? Crazy, ain't it, that we're both out here on this highway at this hour. But ya do what ya gotta do, right? Glad to know that I'm not the only one. It's good to see you."

They smiled like old friends. The moment was genuine and real, without pretense or masks. She was who she was, and so was Dave. It was a naked, holy moment. Nothing kept out God.[120]

Dear God, we thank you for your flashes when the world thins and we see your charming spark in the eyes of another, when we sense that we aren't alone and that we share a common humanity. Amen.

Today's Thought Is: God sparkles through human eyes.

---

*Namaste means "I recognized and honor the Divine Spark of God in you."

One night, as I fell asleep, I prayed my first prayer. God, if you are real, come to me. I fell asleep. Hours later, a pounding on the back door woke me. Funny thing, the dog didn't seem to hear the knocking.

"Go away," I shouted. "It's too late for visitors!" The pounding grew insistent. This time I got up, opened the bedroom window, and shouted, "I'm tired. I don't want you now. Come back later." The knocking grew louder. Again, I shouted from the window, "Whatever it is you want, it can wait. Go *away!*" All night long the knocking continued. I covered my head with a pillow. I stuffed my ears with earplugs. The knocking gave me a headache, but I refused to go downstairs. I was not going to answer in the middle of the night. The persistence seemed rude.

In the morning, I went downstairs. The knocker was still at the door. *Pound pound pound.* "Stop it," I shouted through the door. "Go away. I don't need you!" Finally, the knocking stopped. I cautiously opened the door. There was a business card. On it was printed, "I stand at the door and knock, open and let me in." In handwriting it said, "You called me and I came. I'll be back."

Let's Pray:

Dear God, we think we don't need you, but then in desperation we pray. Then when you show up, we don't let you in. Open our stubborn hearts. Amen.

Today's Thought Is: God is persistent, and we are stubborn. Why not just open the door?[121]

"here's God?" the unexpected guest demanded. He claimed that he had driven all the way from Manhattan in hot, bumper-to-bumper summer traffic just to ask me this question.

"No way," I said. "You couldn't have driven all the way to Maine in Friday traffic just to find God. That's crazy. Why would you do that?"

"I did," he insisted. "I heard that you could show me God. I've traveled the world looking for God. I've been to Zen monasteries in Japan and Buddhist monasteries in Thailand. I've meet with lamas, gurus, priests, nuns, mystics, ministers, rabbis, mullahs, a shaman—everybody I could think of to visit. I've read every book ever written on God. I know all the theology from every viewpoint. I can quote every verse. I have four advanced degrees from three universities. Seriously, I am seeking God. Where is God?" By the time he finished talking, he was shouting and sticking his bony finger into my chest, demanding, "Where is God?"

"Jeez, I'm sorry," I said. "God was just here a few minutes ago; you just missed him. God went to New York looking for you. He said something before he left. God said, 'That guy . . . what a frustration. Always on the move, physically and mentally, never stays still enough to enter into conversation. I'm always chasing him, and he never stops long enough to talk to me.'"

Let's Pray:

Dear God, we look everywhere for you. High and low, here and there, we look and look everywhere but where we should, which is right here, right now. Stop us. Show us yourself now, today, right where we are. Amen.

Today's Thought Is: **If God is everywhere, then God is here.**

*I*t was a beautiful outside. The sun was shining. It was warm. The church windows were open, letting a cooling breeze move through the sanctuary. Nobody wanted to be in church. The head deacon, the leader of the church, went up to the minister and said, "Please, whatever you do, don't make it complex this morning. Make it easy. Make it simple. Make it short."

When it came time for the sermon, the minister waved his four-page single-spaced manuscript in the air, saying, "I spent all week working on this sermon. I researched it. I wrote it, rewrote it, and edited it. It's a brilliant sermon. Maybe it's the best one I have ever written. I read theologians for this sermon. I researched ancient texts. I worked back and forth through the Scriptures. It has big words in it. It'll take concentration to follow it, but I promise it's worth it. That means no staring out the open windows and no listening to birds singing." He paused, then added, "I could preach this today, or quote the world's shortest sermon and pretty much say the same thing. What do you want me to do?"

As one people, as one body, the congregants shouted, "The shortest sermon!" The minister smiled, glanced out the window at the sunny day, looked back at the congregation, cleared his throat, waited a moment, and then said clearly and loudly, "Love," and promptly sat down.

Dear God, no matter what we say about you, one word sums up what you feel for us—love. Help us love like you do. Amen.

Today's Thought Is: **Love**

*I*n medieval Spain an abbot bought a bell for his monastery's tower. A scaffolding was built with a crane made of block, tackle, and rope. They planned to hoist the bell using monk muscle, and then set it into place. On the day of the bell's arrival, the monks and the abbot laid hands on the rope and hauled. One monk avoided all the work, claiming that spiritual life mattered more. He stayed in the church praying. When the bell reached the tower's top, the scaffolding collapsed. The prayerful monk emerged from the church, grabbed the bell, levitated up, and placed it. He descended and sought a reward for his spiritual prowess. The abbot banished him.

This monk, who had solved their problem with a miracle, had done so for personal praise born out of spiritual pride. He lacked humility. Humility is not being mild, or meek. Humility is not seeing oneself through one's own eyes, or through the eyes of anyone else. Spiritual humility is a gift of grace which teaches that all of us, including the greatest among us—the saints, the prophets, and our leaders—are equally human, and equally loved in the eyes of God. Pride in one's work often leads to success, but spiritual pride—pride in one's salvation, or in the superiority of one's faith—gets in God's way.

Let's Pray:

Almighty God, in our spiritual lives, in our daily lives, in the places where these two intersect, bless us with the grace to understand that, no matter where we are on our spiritual path, you are infinitely greater. Grant us true humility. Amen.

Today's Thought Is: Humility comes from dissolving into God.

*H*ere's a story that originated in the third century:

Brother John was tired of weaving baskets to make a living at the monastery. He hadn't left his family, his home, his friends, to weave baskets. He joined the monastery to pray, but little time was spent praying. He went to the abbot, saying, "Abba, I'm leaving to go into the desert to pray full time."

The abbot said, "Go pray." Three nights later, after the monks had gone to bed, there was knock on the abbot's door. "Who is it?" Abba demanded.

"It's me, Brother John. I'm hungry. Let me in."

"Brother John? Who?" Abba said. "Once I knew a Brother John—most amazing man. He left the monastery to become an angel, to live in the desert, to pray full-time. He never needed to eat, so he didn't work. Are you that angel?"

"I'm not an angel. I'm Brother John," he whined, "and I'm hungry."

"If you really are Brother John, and not an angel . . . then, I wonder, will you work to eat?"

"I'm sorry, Abba, I was wrong—to pray one must eat, to eat one must work."

The abbot opened the door, saying, "Work can be prayer." Brother John went inside and later learned to weave the most beautiful baskets.[122]

The spiritual life is not just navel-gazing in prayerful meditation. It is not just about good times with God. Work's necessary and prayerful, if we're open to God.

Let's Pray:

God grant us work, at a livable wage, with time for our lives, for our needs;
time for our families; and with hope for a better future.
Be with us at work today. Amen.

Today's Thought Is: When working keep, God in mind.

A congregation was having trouble keeping track of its money. There was never enough. Every month its trustees juggled bills, trying to decide which ones to pay and which ones not. One month the light bill would be paid while the phone bill was not. It went on like this for years. This congregation continually begged its membership for money. Pretty soon there was anger, bitterness, and harsh words sounding in the pews. Finally, a thief was discovered in their midst. He went to jail and then eventually returned to town. The pastor invited the thief back into the congregation. The membership was aghast and told the minister to throw him out. The minister ignored them. Again the people asked. Again he refused. Finally, the congregants called a meeting to demand that the thief be shown the door or they would all leave as one group.

The pastor said to the people, "You know right from wrong, do you not?"

The people agreed.

"Then you have no need to stay. You may go. This thief, however, does not know good from bad, or right from wrong. If you choose to leave, he will remain within the church, for where else will he learn such things if not in the house of God?"

The congregation was silenced. The thief repented and asked forgiveness.

Congregations aren't for perfect people. They are for imperfect people who want to draw closer to God. People who are perfect, faultless and holy have no need of church.

Let's Pray.

For persons in our midst whose imperfections cause pain to others, we pray. God grant us the power to give and accept forgiveness. Amen.

Today's Thought Is: In giving forgiveness we are forgiven.

Over a lovely lunch a man demands the answer to every question of life, God, the universe, and everything. He wants to know about creation, and Jesus' return, and which church has it right, and what Bible to read, and which words to say in prayer, and should he help the homeless, and where is heaven. We talk of quantum physics over salad, the ethics of torture during dessert, the fruitless search for peace in the Middle East, and, of course, of where God is.

I don't know what answers to give because I know what he really wants. He wants what we all want, even if we don't know it. He doesn't need an accurate idea of God, or theology, or history, or anything else. What he needs is God. I say to him that he should be like a freshwater mountain stream running irresistibly to the sea from whence it came, unable to stay still, unable to resist the attraction of the great salt ocean or the force of gravity. If I can tell him what God is like, I would say, "Irresistible love; run to it."

God is the greatest attraction, the overwhelming force, the single, the one, the holy, the only. It's what we want. It's what we need. It's why we ask such questions. If I can answer any of his questions, or perhaps the root questions of all, "Who am I? Where am I from? Is there eternal life?" I answer this: "Seek God, now, with an open heart; always now."

Let's Pray:

Answer our questions, God, but, more important, show us your love, touch us now, lead us home. Amen.

Today's Thought Is: Practice being open to God.

A collection of spiritual misfits—Catholics, Protestants, Jews, Buddhists, and Muslims—took a literature class, the Comparative Study of Mysticism East and West, at a public university. "There'll be no navel-gazing," declared the professor, a deacon in a local congregation. "This is a rigorous course for advanced students. There'll be an optional weekend of silence and meditation at St. Joseph's Abbey for those who endure."

It was a difficult course, but all the students attended the prayerful retreat. The weekend's highlight was meeting the novitiate master—Father Theophane Boyd—a gigantic, gangly old man with a protruding Adam's apple, huge hands, and shaggy gray hair, whose eyes, like blue laser beams, seemingly pierced the false masks worn by all to see the naked soul within. It was disconcerting. A conservative Jewish student from a kosher household, asked him, "What's it like to be you?"

Theophane rocked silently back and forth with his eyes shut tight, then spoke, "I used to be asleep. Now I am awake." What is it to be spiritually awake? Is it to realize that we are transients on Earth? Is it to give oneself completely to God? Is it to trust Christ so dearly that one would lose one's life to gain it? Do the sleeping know they sleep? If we sleep and we do not know it, how shall we awaken? We slowly awaken by seeking God and believing.

Let's Pray:

Awaken our souls, God, through your love and your Christ,
by your presence, and with your grace; give us eyes to see, ears to hear,
and hearts to know you. Amen.

Today's Thought Is: **Awaken me, God.**

A Vermont country woman wasn't a city driver and was way too embarrassed to admit this to her professor friend when she was visiting in the city. "I'll find a way into the city and worry about getting out when the time comes," she told herself. After spending a day on the inner-city campus, the time came to go home. It had been a relaxing, enjoyable time, but panic set in. It was getting late. She wasn't up to the task. She said a silent prayer. Unasked, her friend unexpectedly offered, "I'll show you the way out of the city."

With their good-byes said, they got into their cars. The professor went first and waited on the street in traffic just to make sure his inexperienced friend was following. The Vermonter had no idea where to go, or what turn to make. She just trusted. Secure in her journey, confident in the outcome, she relaxed and followed as her more experienced friend led the way through the convoluted one-way streets to the relative familiarity of the highway.

Following God can be like that. When we are uncertain and insecure about the road we are on or the journey ahead, we can call on God in prayer and God will say, "Follow me."

Let's Pray:

Dear God, when we're lost in the twisted turns of our lives, when we don't know which turn to make, lead us, send your guidance, and we will follow. Amen.

Today's Thought Is: When lost—pray. God will say, "Follow me."

*T*here was a time when humans believed that the sky was a solid dome that held back cosmic waters. Stars were set in the dome, giving light at night. There was a time when humans believed the Sun revolved around the Earth. Galileo proved that idea wrong, and paid the price for opposing religious views with scientific ones.

There was a time when we believed the speed of light was absolute. In recent years, scientists have shown that light can be slowed down to thirty-eight miles per hour. Other scientists have stopped light. Recently scientists have accelerated light to move faster than the speed of light; in the same experiment, they made light move backward.

It seems we are only at the beginning of understanding the mechanics of this universe. Historically, we have believed one idea about the way the world works only to discover new information that suggested things are quite different from what we thought. Science relies not on faith and belief, but on verifiable evidence. We use our God-given brains to think, to seek new information, to analyze that data. When new evidence comes to light, we readjust our thinking. A thousand years ago, who would have thought the Earth was not the center of the solar system? Fifty years ago, who would have ever imagined that light could be slowed, stopped, sped up, or moved backward? Who could have predicted it? God. God not only imagined it all, he created it all. What wonders are left to be discovered? We shall see.

Let's Pray:

Dear God, sometimes scientific discoveries frighten us because they change the way we see ourselves, our world, and you. As we learn more about your universe, let our faith increase. Amen.

Today's Thought Is: Science is complementary to faith.

ifty hamburgers were roasting over charcoal briquettes at a church barbecue. I was standing with George, a first-generation Greek American. He's tall, strong, tanned, well dressed, and smiling. An older Greek leaned toward me, whispering, "George has a big job. He's in charge of the NFL referees." The old man asked out loud, "Georgie, how was the Super Bowl?"

George said, "I took my dad and my family. Got them seats on the fifty-yard line. Before the game, I was talking with them, and Dad was so happy he was crying. Suddenly, the coin toss was over. I realized I was on the wrong side of the field. The captains were walking to their teams. I jogged out. Everybody in the stadium, the football players, and millions of viewers, and even God was watching me. The TV sports announcers were asking one another, "What's he doing on the field?" A team captain stopped and waited. Thank God. When I got to him, I said, "Make it look like I'm saying something important. I got caught on the wrong side of the field, and I'm just trying to get to the other side."

George put a good face on it, but he got caught on the wrong side of things. Anybody can make a mistake, publicly or privately. No matter who else is watching or not watching, God is always watching. The important thing is getting over to the right side by correcting the mistake.

Dear God, when we make mistakes, in big or small ways, give us a chance to make them right. Amen.

Today's Thought Is: When we step out in faith,
God takes care of the rest.

A clergy friend of mine, Lynn, led a funeral service one morning for a veteran of World War II. Several members of his honor guard had stayed up late the night before telling old stories while liberally celebrating the life of their brothers in arms. Eventually they'd gone to bed drunk, but before they went home that night, they'd decided it would be best to start off the next day back at the bar, where they'd fortify themselves with strong coffee laced with stronger drink.

Despite their commemorative condition, they were an orderly and mostly dignified detail that marched behind the flag-draped coffin as it was carried to its place above the grave. Removing themselves from the scene by several yards, they mounted a nearby knoll to prepare the twenty-one-gun salute. As they fired the first volley, they were seen suddenly rolling head over heels down the hill, having been knocked backward from the recoil of their weapons. Every mourner at the graveside was facing away from this ruckus and looking toward the Reverend Lynn, which meant only she could see the impromptu tumbling act unfolding on the hillside.

After the service Lynn was asked why she looked briefly startled during the twenty-one-gun salute. Not wanting to upset the widow, Lynn bit her tongue, closed her eyes, and shook her head.

Let's Pray:

Dear God, there are times when saying nothing is the only choice. Give us the wisdom to recognize when saying nothing is the best choice, and the willpower to bit our lips and keep our mouths closed. Amen.

Today's Thought Is: Sometimes silence is the right reply.

*T*he hours of any day seem unending to children to whom there is never any hurry. Time is endless. Young teenagers hurry their days, rushing to age sixteen, the magic number for a driver's license. Then they threaten, "When I'm eighteen . . ." Harried middle-agers ride with one foot on the brake of time, slowing down what they see coming. Old folks say, "Time moves so swiftly it feels like it's time for breakfast or time for bed every five minutes." Meanwhile clocks, analog and digital, move at a steady measurable pace.

Our experience of time is relative to our age. When we are young, there is sooooo much time; when we are old, there is so little. It's all a matter of perspective. Whether time speeds or crawls, it moves in one direction, and we are caught in its irresistible flow. Time is God's creation, and we are stuck within it. But time and creation is not all there is—thank God. There is more right here now outside of time, in eternity. It's called heaven, as Jesus described it—among us and beyond us—a timeless place of peace, love, forgiveness, consciousness, and sweetness.

We catch glimpses now and again; we see shimmers, flashes—in the twinkle in a child's eye; in the fondness of a true love's hand; in gifts exchanged between strangers. These are timeless glimpses of true eternity embraced in love. Heaven is among us. Look for it.

Dear God, whether time passes quickly or slowly, give us the time we need to do what we must, and love those we will before eternity arrives. Amen.

Today's Thought Is: Eternity is now.

*Y*ears ago Pete flew to Aspen for a retreat. Seated in a row by himself, unshaven and scruffy-looking, Pete thought it was a perfect place for meditative prayer and closed his eyes. It wasn't long before he had that creepy feeling that somebody was watching him. Pete focused on his prayer, trying to ignore the feeling, but failed. When he opened his eyes, there stood next to him in the aisle a stunning woman, smartly dressed, watching him. He was uncomfortably aware that he was the shabbiest passenger aboard.

"You're somebody, aren't you?" she said loudly.

"I'm nobody," he said, shutting his eyes again.

"No, I recognize you. My friend does, too. You are definitely somebody—a movie star. You can't fool me by the way you're dressed and with your scruffy face. What's your name?" Half the plane was now looking and listening.

Pete insisted, "I'm nobody."

"You can't fool me," she said, pointing at him, smiling, "I know you're somebody, and I'm going figure out who." She sidled off to her seat.

The more Pete insisted, the less he was believed. There was whispering and glancing in his direction for the rest of the flight. It's a strange experience to be mistaken for a "somebody" while being content as a "nobody." God never makes that mistake, because to God there are no "nobodies." To God, everybody's a "somebody." We are each loved as we are for who are.

Let's Pray

God, if we're broken, if we feel forgotten or alone, remind us that you love us and that to you we are important. Amen.

Today's Thought Is: **Everybody is a somebody to God.**

*H*ow do you get to work? Walk, ride a bike, drive a truck, fly your F/A-18A Hornet jet fighter? With six days' bidding left on eBay, one Blue Angel navy jet which had cost 28 million of our tax dollars in 1997, was going for $29 million in 2004. With just 3,793 total hours in the air, this was perfect for the traffic-hating commuter. It's the only privately owned Hornet on the planet. The owners said that they'd paint it any color for the buyer. It was in pieces, so assembly was required, but for a fee they'd reassemble it for delivery.

These are the zoom-zoom specs: 1,400 mph; climbs to 30,000 in a minute; fully loaded—bomb racks, drop tanks, ejector seat, and pylons. This blue baby has two zero-hour GE engines and one spare-parts engine. How it ended up in private hands is a mystery. Normally, used military aircraft are demilitarized, but the navy says these jets can occasionally be sold to third parties on a case-by-case basis.[123]

Sure, it'd be cool to own a Blue Angel, but doesn't spending $29 million seem a tad excessive? Besides, true cool doesn't come from what we own, or how we look, or what our wheels, or wings, cost. True cool comes from soul wings, the eternal, inner, God-given kind.

Let Pray:

Dear God, if ever we have that kind of cash, help us spend it righteously, by building a business to employ the unemployed, or feeding the hungry, or clothing the naked, or even building a yacht to employ craftsmen. Help us, in our little ways, to get started on such projects today. Amen.

Today's Thought Is: Give us wings of grace.

On a salt pond off a harbor, Mr. Vogel kept his Old Town canoe rolled over on the shore, above the tidal line, and ready for use. An autumn tropical depression blew away Mr. Vogel's green canoe. He hunted for it but didn't find it. In January, the owner of a local inn, Mr. Pilgrim, was flying his Cessna low over the salt pond when he spotted the green canoe half in the snow, tucked up in the cove amidst brambles and brush. The pilot phoned Mr. Vogel with the news. The canoeist thanked him, saying, "With our new baby, and our other two kids, I'm not going after my canoe for some time." Word got around the island that the canoe had been sighted.

A teacher, Mr. Woods, and his friend, Mr. Parsons, with nothing to do one Saturday strapped on their snowshoes, bushwhacked to that cove, found the canoe, and skidded it down the frozen shoreline, leaving it turned over and tied where Mr. Vogel could find it. Neighbors helping neighbors takes believing a good deed is its own reward.

The Rabbi told a story about a man who had been mugged and left wounded by a roadside. A stranger who happened along assisted the mugging victim unasked. Through one man helping a stranger, they became neighbors.

Let's Pray:

God, thanks for the help you've sent us in the form of folks who've given us a hand when we've most need it. If the chance arises, let me be the person who helps. Amen.

Today's Thought Is: **Helping a neighbor is an act of prayer.**

On a Wednesday after work, Kay caught a bus down Fifth Avenue from Eightieth Street, trying to get to the Meditation Center on Twenty-second. Kay needed to begin meditation classes, because Kay was stressed. Recently divorced, forced to sell her apartment, and with her job coming to a end, Kay craved God and calmness. At five-fifty she was still stuck in traffic. She'd never make it on time. Frustrated, she headed back to her apartment, where she found her temporary roommate and her roommate's guest, Simon. Kay told her story.

Her roommate said, "Oh, Simon's been meditating and praying for thirty years. He can teach you."

"It's easy," Simon jumped in, "I can have you practicing in less than an hour, and then you won't need to trek downtown. You can practice right here on your own."

"Oh, no," said Kay. "I can't do that. I need the class."

"Not really," volunteered Simon, "all you need is instruction and the discipline to practice on your own, and then God will find you."

"I lack discipline," said Kay. "I'm happier sitting an hour each way on a bus to go meditate for an hour than I am sitting alone in my apartment meditating by myself for twenty minutes."

Simon knew enough not to argue. When Kay is ready for God, she won't find excuses.

Let's Pray:

Dear God, don't let our ideas about how, and where, and when we should seek you get in the way of our seeking you. When giving us a gift, help us recognize it and accept it. Amen.

Today's Thought Is: Seek God, not where we think God lives.

*I*t's on the Lower East Side. There's no sign above the nonde-
script door. There's no crowd gathered outside. Many New
Yorkers believe that it's an urban myth and that the bar known as Milk and
Honey doesn't exist. But it does. There are house rules: no name dropping,
no hooting, no hollering; no fighting, no talking about fighting; gentlemen
will remove their hats and will not introduce themselves to ladies. Ladies
are free to start conversations with gentlemen or ask for an introduction.
If a man, a stranger, speaks to you, lift your chin slightly and ignore him.
Members are to exit the bar swiftly and silently. Admittance is by invitation,
referral, and appointment. Don't bring anybody whom you wouldn't feel
comfortable leaving alone in your own living room. They used to require a
password to get in. Just knowing the password didn't get you in—you had to
obey the house rules, too.

There's a similarity between this bar and heaven. Many people believe
heaven is a myth. I've been to the edge and back. It's not a myth. The
Teacher says that not everybody who has the password gets into heaven. To
get in, you also have to live by the house rules. What are the rules? Love your
neighbor, love yourself, and love God; do justice, love kindness, and walk
humbly; and forgive as freely as you are forgiven.[124]

Let's Pray:

God, write your password on our hearts, even if our lips never speak it;
let your word live inside our souls. Show us daily how to live love,
and then open the door for us. Amen.

Today's Thought Is: **Write your password on my heart.**

*D*avid is brilliant. His job is fixing broken cities—cities that were politically corrupt or economically marginalized. Politicians hire him because he has the unique ability to find creative solutions to complex problems. When he arrives, it's with fanfare; but when he launches into the job, stumbling stones are commonly tossed in his path. No matter how bad things are, some citizens and politicians like to cling to their pain, saying, "We like things just the way they are. We prefer the devil we know to the devil we don't know."

That's not to say those citizens and politicos don't admit that there are structural, political, or economic problems. They do. It's just that they didn't believe that fixing things meant actually changing. Being frightened of change, or feeling insecure, or lacking solutions themselves, they resort not to argument or persuasion, but to making David's job harder, sometimes even maliciously spreading gossip slandering him in an attempt to destroy him. It's a tactic found where the powerful or powerless fear change and feel threatened by competence.

The Scriptures teach us to rid ourselves of malice, guile, insincerity, envy, and slander. These caustic agents hamper spiritual growth, doing as much injury to us as to those we attack.

Let's Pray:

Dear God, when we feel the envious or malicious desire to destroy using slander or guile, touch us with insight; show us that these emotions and tools are as destructive to us as they are to those we try to harm. Amen.

Today's Thought Is: The stumbling stones we meant for others may trip us up as well.

T asked the nurse, "Where's the SCU—the Special Care Unit." She said, "The ECU?" "What's the ECU?" I asked. She said, "The Expensive Care Unit." She's got that right. Spend a month in an SCU, and suddenly we're talking an amount equivalent to the annual budget of a small town. Paying that bill is a worry for the families who sit in the waiting area for weeks, but it's nothing compared to the stress of worrying about the health of their loved one in the adjacent SCU room.

When I first made a daily habit of visiting a family who was sitting vigil in the SCU waiting room, I wondered, What do I say to these people? I asked an experienced minister. She said, "Sit with them. Cry with them. Pray with them. Keep quiet. Be helpful. Ask useful questions. Advocate for the patient. Don't fix their pain. You can't. Share it, feel it, but don't fix it."

I'm reminded of the mother who sent her daughter to the store. The girl was late returning. When asked why, the daughter said, "My friend's doll was broken. I stayed."

"Why?" her mother demanded. "You couldn't fix the doll."

"No," said the girl, "but I could cry with her."

God doesn't ask us to cure the ill, only to help heal them by showing empathy.

Let's Pray:

Dear God, bless us with compassion. Help us hold the hand that needs to be held, cry with the one who needs our tears, sit silently by the side of the one who needs our presence, and be open to your presence in our hearts. Amen.

Today's Thought Is: **When I was sick, you visited me.**[125]

*S*he doesn't have to do this. Nancy sold her real estate business for a tidy sum. She doesn't have to work. She doesn't have to do anything. She doesn't have to clean her house or mow her yard. She could just tend her flower gardens, host cocktail parties, and eat chocolates all day. She can do anything she wants to do and nothing she doesn't want. Nancy doesn't have to volunteer at the hospital as a chaplain, but she does.

Between you and me, she got shanghaied by that hospital chaplain. Reverend Judy knows one when she sees one, so she persuaded Nancy to take the six-week course. It took persuading because Nancy is no nancy pants pushover. Nancy isn't afraid of much. She never was. If a door was closed to her, she'd figure out a way to open it, or she'd find another way in. It turns out, much to the surprise of Nancy but not to Judy, that Nancy has a knack for chaplaincy. It takes fearlessness, a steady stomach, the ability to talk to anybody, and faith.

Halfway through life, when Nancy was getting ready for fun, God called her to a new job. Nancy's never felt more fulfilled. If your life is changing, and God suddenly puts a door in front of you, try opening it. You might be in for the time of your life.

Let's Pray:

Dear God, if we have time, and you have a job for us, show us what it is and give us the tools to do it. We are here for you. Amen.

Today's Thought Is: **To what adventure is God calling you?**

I once heard a great-grandmother comment about a mother I knew, "I've never seen that mother but she had a baby in arms or child on her knee. That's how happy kids are made." It turns out that research agrees. I read somewhere that babies who are frequently carried in loving arms are more at ease with life, better adjusted, happier, more trusting. They feel safer and, most important, know they are loved. Babies crave being held hugged, and comforted by loving parents.

Do not we all? On the other end of things, in nursing homes, it's pretty much the same thing. Older residents crave touch—a hand held, a gentle hug, a kiss on the cheek—to know they're loved and to feel connected. The Scriptures are full of talk about the arms of God. Embraced in the arms of God, we, the children of God, find unconditional love.

Let's Pray:

Dear God, if we need comfort, or rescue, or protection, or security, take us in your arms today; love us unconditionally. Amen.

Today's Thought Is: God's love utterly embraces us.

A guide for private investors advises: "Do not put all your eggs into one basket." We know what this means: "Do not concentrate all your prospects or resources in one thing or place, or you could lose everything." Or simply put, balance your investments. This is, of course, excellent financial advice. If all our eggs are in one basket and the basket falls, all our eggs are shattered.

But the Gospel of Matthew says that finding the kingdom of heaven is like the merchant in search of fine pearls; on finding one pearl of great value, he went and sold everything he owned and bought it. One rabbi's perspective on that passage is this: on finding a hot deal on the perfect pearl, the merchant sold his home, everything in it, and his land. He sold his car, his wife's car, and their boat. He cashed out his life insurance, his mutual funds, and his pension. He withdrew everything from their kids' college funds and their life's savings and dropped all of it, every cent, every thing he owned in the world, on this one hot pearl tip. Brokers would agree—such a move is extremely risky. In matters of finance, this is true.

But if it's God you want, if it's heaven you seek, *do* put all your eggs in one basket. Buy the one holy pearl. Ultimately, there's nothing more valuable.

Let's Pray:

Dear God, show us your great pearl that we may buy it with all we are worth. Amen.[126]

Today's Thought Is: Give God your all.

꽃

*S*he rode up to the top of the bunny slope on the chairlift so she had no choice except to ski down. It wasn't just gravity. It was a duty to her kids. It was a challenge to her. She went up because her husband convinced her she could learn to ski even in her forties. The kids ride snowboards, he skis; it's a family essential that she face her fears and learn. After he got her feet into the "pizza-slice" shape, he advised her, saying, "Looking down the steep slope causes fear; fear is the enemy; do not look down; do not look directly at the fear; look across the slope and relax. Fear creates tension; tension creates falls."

Relaxing while on skis was nearly impossible for her. Worry causes falls and frustration. Did she quit? Did she go sit inside with a hot cup of cocoa? Nope. She signed up for a lesson and with a real instructor, went to the top twice, and did not fall at all. Was she afraid? Yes. Will she go again? Yes.

Facing fears is tough, but letting them control us is worse. Believe it or not, there are people who're afraid of God. They're afraid for what they've done or said, or what they haven't done or haven't said. Rather than quitting faith because of your fear and worry about God, keep hope in our loving God and trust. If you do, you'll likely to discover God is not so frightening after all.

Let's Pray.

Dear God, be with us as we face our mountain-sized fears. We trust you, and you love us; grant us courage over our fears. Amen.

Today's Thought Is: **Courage is mastery of fear.**

*D*ark secrets are alive. We tell them to lie still, be quiet, go to sleep, but they do not. Secrets are creatures with wills of their own. We lock them in; they fight back stronger. We quiet them; they become louder. Secrets reproduce, creating new lies to protect old secrets. They permeate families passing through generations. Dark secrets are infectious to loved ones. What's hidden in the family closet? Do not say it! Do not speak it! Who knows? It's dangerous! Secrets want out. They demand a voice. They tell themselves in our dreams; they dribble from mouths of drunken people at parties who tell us too much; we tell them to strangers to keep from telling the ones who truly need to know.[127]

Keeping terrible secrets destroys intimacy, invites isolation, constructs obsessions, fuels addictions, and causes psychological destruction and spiritual withering. Secrets feed shame. Confession, we know, is good for the soul. It's good for our emotions, our minds, our relationships, and our faith.

The first ones who need to hear our confession, the admission of our secret, is ourselves. First we must own it and name with its real name. In ancient days, knowing the true name of a person gave an individual power over him. If your secret is theft, do not say borrow. If it's adultery, do not say affair. Name it truly for yourself, then talk to God. God sees right through euphemisms and falseness. Be honest with yourself. I know it's hard. Be honest with God. Seek healing. It will come.

Let's Pray

Dear God, there's something we need to tell you, something we've hidden
from ourselves and from the ones we love. Here it is, honestly said.
We confess to you that. . . . Amen.

Today's Thought Is: **Dark secrets are self-destructive.**

*H*e's a boy headed for trouble. Most say so. No child likes him, though he's never noticed that. He has no friends, but he believes every child is his best buddy. He laughs loudly at bad jokes, and he dances when he ought not to. For fun, he punches kids, meaning no harm. He has no talent at math, or reading, or science, or history, or social studies, but he loves them all. He enthusiastically volunteers wrong answers, and forever forgets to raise his hand, and apologizes when scolded. His spelling is awful, terrible, atrocious. His parents thrive on confusion. Shouting and fighting is what he sees at home. Ignorance is what hears. He's a troubled kid, but every teacher loves him. He's a smiling spark with a goofy gladness. He has no idea that he has a fine mind for mechanics, with strong hands built to fix. If he graduates high school, it will be a miracle.

Each one of us is God built, with latent talents. Not everybody sees the talents in others. It takes a keen-eyed teacher to see the possibilities in a child who will never pass a test. Teachers may see our potential when we do not. God sees our potential even if we cannot. If life is a bit of a struggle for you, or if you feel you are headed for trouble, take some time to pray to God that you will discover your purpose. Whatever God has in store for you, you can be sure it's what you're made for.

Let's Pray:

Dear God, you made us with talent and potential.
What and where is it? Amen.

Today's Thought Is: **We're God built.**

OUTSOURCING

*M*y laptop developed a software problem. Dialing an 800 number to seek expert advice, I got Pam. I recognized Pam's accent as sort of British and sort of Indian. Turns out, she works in Mumbai, India, at night for an American company, talking with people like me on the other side of the Earth whose PCs have problems. Pam asked if I had tried rebooting—yes; defragmenting—yes; repairing the software—yes; unloading then reloading the software—yes; unloading and reloading in Safe Mode—yes. "That's the extent of my PC-repair knowledge," I confessed.

She laughed. "It's okay. We can't be experts in everything. Your laptop has a complicated problem, but we can fix it," and within an hour, using my hands and her brain, we did. Trusting a trained expert to help us is what we often need to do. We outsource many aspects of our lives—car repair, the education of our children, law enforcement, and surgery, just to name a few. We can't be experts in everything.

For instance, we can outsource our relationship to God—that's right, our relationship to God. Once a week we can temporarily place our relationship to God in the hands of experts. There we can sit and listen to the local clergy help us deal with spiritual issues. It's helpful to use expert assistance. They're the ones with experience, training, and know-how. But the rest of the week it's up to us.

Let's Pray:

Dear God, thanks for your clergy, who study, learn, and work for you, and therefore make it easier for us. Amen.

Today's Thought Is: Trust the ones with know-how.

he pediatrician shouted, "We do not know what causes colic, but colicky babies have above-average intelligence." The doctor intended this as comfort, but it was hard to hear above the nonstop piercing and earsplitting infant voice. Okay, it wasn't nonstop. Occasionally, she breathed in or slept. At two A.M., only rhythmically dancing in her dad's arms to Bob Marley's reggae beat with the base line fully turned up would quiet her. "Exodus" was her favorite. If her dad stopped, the shrill wail began again. Dad discovered wonderful foam earplugs. It didn't stop him from hearing her; it stopped the feeling of her sharp vocals stabbing him in the back of the neck. This man was a good dad, and a good guy. He loved his daughter, his wife, his dog . . . and he even tolerated the cat.

It was in the middle of one night when he thought it. He and his wife were exhausted, worn-out from the near-constant screaming that had now lasted four months. The daughter awoke wailing in the next room. His sleepy thought was, "I'll just place a pillow over her mouth till she stops." That horrible idea awoke him quickly. He didn't mean to have it, and he didn't act on it. Instead, he grabbed his earplugs, picked her up, carried her downstairs, and danced. It's easy to see where stressed folks might not be able to draw the line between a bad thought and a worse action. Just because we think it doesn't mean we have to say it, or do it. We can control our actions. We have free will.

Let's Pray:

Dear God, help us understand we're responsible for our actions because of free will. Amen.

Today's Thought Is: **Free will is the freedom to choose what's right.**

he hillside, spotted with apple trees and brushy spruce, was frosted in a knee-deep snow, covered with a crust of ice. Two neighbor men took their young daughters snow sliding on saucer-shaped sleds. The girls were too little to walk up the slope, and the men were too lazy to stomp down. The dads each took rope, tied one end to a saucer, and tied a stopper knot in the rope's other end. The girls zipped down on their saucers with their dads controlling their speed, slowing them to a comfortable stop. The girls stayed aboard and were hauled hand over hand back up. It worked well. The men sat in the snow, talked, controlled, and hauled. On the final ride down there was no stopper knot at the end of the line, and the girls zipped away, down, and down, faster, and faster, with the dads running behind, shouting, "Duck the branches, lean to the left, drag your feet."

The girls were gleeful. The dads were panicked. Providentially, the girls ducked, leaned, and dragged when told. At the bottom, they were delighted; the men were breathless and frightened.

All's well that ends well, but we know that our children are not truly ours. We do the best we can, helping them, teaching them, giving instructions, and making mistakes, knowing all along that there'll come a time when the stopper knot is gone and they must ride life's quick trip on their own.

Let's Pray:

Dear God, we pray for the empty nesters whose children have grown and left home while they were talking, but who remain in their parents' hearts. Also bless the parents, who love them, miss them, and did the best they could. Amen.

Today's Thought Is: Remember to call your parents.

In the city of Antakya (the ancient Antioch), we visited a cave called Saint Peter's Grotto. This cave was a church in the time of Peter, Barnabas, and Paul. Church attendance was dangerous in those early days, and this cave had an escape tunnel behind the altar, just in case.

In Antakya, it's believed that this church is where the followers of Jesus were first called "Christians." Inside that sacred cave, our small group decided to pray and sing. Hand in hand in a circle, we each added words to our prayer.

As we prayed a group of Muslim tourists blustered into the cave. Seeing us, they quickly quieted, and politely waited until we finished our prayer and song. Afterward, a man from their group approached us, begged pardon for their interruption, and complimented us on our beautiful song and voices. We'd been in Turkey for two days during the week when the U.S.S. *Cole* was bombed by terrorists. But we'd come to understand that there's variety of faith styles and affable acceptance among the gracious Muslims we met. Civility, respect, hospitality, and tolerance were guiding forces in their lives.

Let's Pray:

Dear God, when Muslims and Christians meet on our streets, may our hearts be filled with the warmth of faith and friendship. Amen.

Today's Thought Is: **Muslims and Christians are people of faith.**

*N*o one but you needs to know the details of your personal toilette or if you still need a night-light. That stuff's private, not a deep secret. Dark secrets kill intimacy. You can't feel fully connected to somebody from whom you're keeping important information, but confession is risky. Some people, even spouses, may reject you if you claim your whole identity, if you tell them the whole truth about yourself. The one who rejects may be the very one you love the most.[128]

Love is not blind. Even if it can't put a finger precisely on the problem, it often has a sense, an intuition, that something's wrong, that some truth is being withheld and driving a wedge into a relationship. Most spouses and friends can sense when you hide things, creating latent frustration, isolation, and anger. Whether you choose to confess your dark secret to your spouse or friend, or not, is between you and God. Remember, you can't lie to yourself, not really, and you can't lie to God, not ever. We are fully known by God. It's like the Scriptures say, "Everything that's secret will eventually be brought to light" . . . in this life or the next life. Thank God, because God is merciful.

Let's Pray:

Dear God, as we struggle with our dark secrets, all of which you already know, we need to know that, should we tell, you'll be with us. Bless our relationships as we face our struggles. Amen.[129]

Today's Thought Is: **Secrets kill intimacy.**

*I*n a small Connecticut town, Cecile was standing in line at a grocery store, when a woman about her age, standing behind her, said, "Excuse me, I know you—aren't you Norm's sister from Waterbury?"

Cecile replied, "Yes. Who're you?"

"I'm Carla. My older sister, Dee, dated Norm in high school. They went to the senior prom together. She still talks about him and has their prom picture up on her fridge. After her husband passed away, she prayed she'd find Norm again. Too bad how Norm died not knowing Dee loved him."

"Dead? Norm's not dead," said Cecile. "I talked to him just yesterday on the phone. He's been divorced for nearly twenty years, with five grown kids. He lives alone in an apartment in New Hampshire."

Cecile dashed home and dialed Dee. Dee looked up Norm's number in New Hampshire and called him that night.

They began to talk on the phone once a week, then every day, and then Dee invited Norm to Florida for a winter visit—just to see. Immediately, it was like old times. Six months after their sisters' accidental meeting in the grocery line, Dee and Norm, very much in love, and to the delight of all their children and grandchildren, married in a church. They actually lived happily ever after.

Let's Pray:

Dear God, thanks for love that lasts decades, for chance meetings, and for hope and daring where love is concerned. Amen.

Today's Thought Is: "Love prays. It makes covenants with Eternal Power on behalf of this dear mate."[130]

*n Maine, on snowy days our newscasters wear heavy sweaters and turtlenecks. Awakening in a Washington, D.C., hotel to a wintry weather report on TV I noticed their button-down weatherman was jacket-free and tie-less. His weather map showed expected amounts—a quarter inch here, a half inch there. Warnings and cancellations scrolled across the screen—all schools canceled; government offices requested essential personnel only; highway driving was dangerous.

Our Maine Storm Center forecasts its snow in feet, not fractions—"Two feet at the coast, four feet in the mountains. Traffic is slow; schools are delayed."

In Maine during the summer, I hear locals complain about the unbearable heat if it hits eighty degrees, saying, "It's hotter than a boiled lobster on Independence Day." Eighty summer degrees for Washingtonians is considered a cooling trend, and they are glad for it.

It's all what you're used to. We tolerate, even celebrate, these differences, even as we kid one another about them. Overall, Americans are tolerant of weather, of one another, and of religion. While we might disagree about which day of the weekend we worship, we do agree there's room enough for all weathers . . . I mean, religions.

Let's Pray:

Dear God, we're thankful today that we live in a land where
the freedom to practice our various faiths, or not practice,
as the case may be, is secure. Amen.

Today's Thought Is: **We are free to worship.**

$\mathcal{N}$ ow boarding our elite passengers." The announcement came over the P.A. at the airline gate. The elite dashed to take their narrow cramped seats for the flight. There was polite jostling for the primary positions.

"Now boarding rows nineteen to twenty-nine."

The coach-class people dashed to crowd and cramp themselves aboard the flight. They, too, politely jockeyed for prime line positions.

"Now boarding the remaining seats." When the line came to an end a young woman stood, gathered her gear and waited. She was last to board. The man next to whom she sat, having seen her leisurely reading at the gate, asked why she boarded last.

She replied, "I do not mind being last. Why should I push my way into line? We all get aboard eventually, don't we?"

After the plane landed, the passengers snapped off their seat belts, jumped up, opened the overhead bins, and grabbed for their gear. They jostled for their cases, coats, and bags and waited until finally the door opened.

The woman never moved. She sat contentedly reading. The man, standing bent over next to his seat, asked her, "What are you waiting for?"

She said, "You're waiting, too. The door just opened. You're standing with your head uncomfortably tilted against the overhead bin because this is a small jet. I'm comfortable enough to wait. We'll all get off, won't we?" At the end, the smiling young woman got off the plane with a book of Scriptures in her hand. Among the faithful, it doesn't matter who's first or who's last, because God is generous to all.

Let's Pray:

Dear God, being last is not so bad because you treat us with equality.
Thanks. Amen.

Today's Thought Is: Practice patience.

*T*he Reverend Doctor Roy Howard wrote, "Remember the mother in Bosnia comforting her child who couldn't sleep from the sounds of bombs falling nearby? She hugged him close and said, 'It's okay to go to sleep, God is with you.'

"The child looked at his mother, saying, 'I need a God with skin on.'"[131]

Love is God with skin on. Sharing love is what we do for one another when we hold a hand or lend a hand, giving comfort as we can. Embodied love (charity, hope, kindness, sharing) is a way congregations offer a living response to any person who needs "God with skin on." We may be in need of love, or we may be able to give the love someone else needs.

Nothing else matters in the end except love. When everything fades away and you see God, not through a glass darkly but face-to-face, when you cross from this life into the next, what do you think will matter most from your mortal life? If you could, what will you carry with you?

For Dr. Howard, and for me, at the end of the day, it's love. That's all.

Let us Pray.

Dear God, let us be your skin. Let us love as you love. Let us reach out to comfort as you comfort. If we are in need of love, reach out to us that we may feel your love through those people who love you. Let your love flow through the eyes and fingers, arms and hearts of your people; let it be seen, felt, and known. Let comfort come to those in need. Amen.

Today's Thought Is: **Love embodied is God's presence.**

*I*n the musical *Oliver!*, the character Fagin comes off as a protective, lovable rogue who saves orphans from starvation by teaching them how to pick pockets.

In the novel, *Oliver Twist*, by Charles Dickens, on which the musical is based, we discover that Fagin is not so lovable. He's a monster who breaks the morals, wills, and hopes of orphans, leading them into crime by making crime into a game, and using isolation, fear, abuse, and intimidation until they are his to control.

Fagin's goal for the abused and tortured orphan Oliver is to destroy Oliver's inner moral compass. Through experience, Fagin has learned that children—depending upon a combination of a particular child's inner resources and the external forces applied—are morally or immorally moldable. Fagin succeeded so often with other children that he expects success with Oliver, too.

In the end, however, no matter the cruelty and afflictions Oliver endures, his genteel inner strength, enhanced by prayer and the occasional kindness of decent people, enables him to remain strong and resist Fagin.

In fiction, as in life, there are few children who have the inner muscle necessary to resist the monstrous pressures of vice and immorality for very long without help. It's the rare child who can resist alone. Our societal and faithful duty has always been to teach all children what's good and what's decent so that they might make the correct choices when faced with temptation.

Let's Pray:

Dear God, help us be good examples to children. In our frailty, even with the mistakes, failures, and errors in our lives, help us teach goodness by example. Amen.

Today's Thought Is: **A good tree produces good fruit.**[132]

*C*ontrary to popular belief, Jesus was a funny, entertaining guy. Okay—maybe not in a Jay Leno, showbiz kind of way, but Jesus was certainly worth stopping to watch. The man walked on water, raised the dead, healed diseases. What a way to get people's attention for God's real message.

If Jesus had only told good stories of truth, not as many people would've paid attention. His miracles weren't the message, but they sure brought in the crowds to listen. His parables and stories are wonderful pieces of common life used to explain the sacred. He used examples from farming, vineyards, merchants, and fishing. He talked about real life. He had a way with words that provoked the mind and stirred the soul. He was a master storyteller who used the absurd to point to heaven.

An example: "Why worry about a speck in your friend's eye when you have a log in your own? How can you think of saying, 'Hey, let me help you get rid of that speck in your eye,' when you can't see past your own log? First, get rid of the log from your eyes; then perhaps you'll see well enough to deal with the speck in your friend's eye."[133]

Come on. Use your imagination. That's funny. Jesus was saying, "Hey, buddy, you've got a cut, split, stove-length log stuck in front of your eyes, blocking your view, while you're delicately trying to flick a speck, out of you neighbor's eye. Imagine this on film with, say, Laurel and Hardy, or the Three Stooges.

It's funny, but it tells a truth.

Let's Pray:

Dear God, thank you for humor in our lives. Thanks for making Jesus tell the truth with a light touch. Amen.

Today's Thought Is: **God has a sense of humor.**

*T*hunder pealed distantly to the west, beyond sight, as the locals and tourists gathered around the harbor waters on that hot June afternoon in Boothbay Harbor, Maine; it was Windjammer Day. Hundreds of small boats motored and tooted, awaiting the lovely and variously rigged windjammers to come sailing grandly in. Plying the harbor were sailboats prettily under sail, adding a graceful gaiety. Onshore, the crowds of land-lubbers stood, or sat, or walked about, all enjoying this local festival. One or two windjammers had already anchored when, to the northwest, there appeared an unpredicted squall line, dark and black, billowing, roiling—growing and foreboding. Boaters and sailors had few minutes to prepare. Sails dropped, motors started, bows turned toward its approach, and people braced themselves. The great wind struck like a solid wall at what must have been fifty-seven mph or more. The sky above blackened. Lightning flashed and blazed. Thunder rolled nonstop. Bright white chop covered the harbor with a whipped-up froth.

Then came rain pellets hitting liked a sky-born flood. It was suddenly, and wickedly, dreadfully dangerous to be on the harbor where hundreds of boats were being tossed about.

Unexpected squalls can come crashing into our own lives, tossing us about, slamming us off our keels. At times like these, we scramble for safety and survival.

Let's Pray:

Dear God, when whatever squalls crash into our lives, when the unexpected catches us, help us make it through, be with us as we seek safety and survival.
Amen.

Today's Thought Is: **Keep a wary weather eye for squalls.**

*I*n early spring, after the last frost and after all the sand is cleaned off the roads, I usually pull out my in-line skates. I like to skate just before sunset around Ocean Point, which is when traffic moves slowly and everyone watches the Artist paint a pretty sky. Once in a while, if a particular sunset catches my eye, it'll slow me down. One evening, after a spectacular sunset, I sped toward home, knowing I was pushing it—skating in the near dark. Along a section of straight road, a car came toward me, headlights shining.

"Good," I thought, "I'll see everything." Then the lights got in my face, blinding me, my wheel got caught in a crack, and I took a pitch into a ditch. Unhurt, I got up and skated again. At the top of a hill a sedan came up alongside me, helping me see the road. The driver said, "I'll stay beside you for a while to help you see." It was half a mile to home. Her headlights made the difference.

When we've got faith to share, coming at a person headlong and beaming our lights into his eyes is likely to blind him and make him want to ditch us. If, instead, when sharing our faith, we come up alongside, helping out, gently illuminating the path ahead, well, that works better for everybody.

Let's Pray:

Dear God, when we uncover your lovely inner light, help us not to shine it in people's eyes in our eagerness. Help us walk beside them, lending assistance, while quietly illuminating your pathway. Amen.

Today's Thought Is: Let your little light shine, but do not blind people with it.

When Hurricane Gloria roared ashore, Reverend Fred Lyon was serving a Congregational church in the Connecticut coastal town of Stratford. He tells this story about that day:

In front of the white church, along the wide boulevard, was a line of strong trees, appropriately old and stately, well suited to the site. Gloria blew down a quarter of those trees in a day. Her winds didn't uproot them. Instead, each tree that was destroyed snapped neatly along its trunk, looking as if it had been struck by a giant's big machete. On closer inspection, each tree's breaking point revealed a lot of interior rot. Before the hurricane came, there was no way of telling that the interior damage of these trees was so enormous. On the outside they appeared perfect. Before Gloria, each tree managed to keep thriving, or seemingly so, while this unseen disease, this rot, worked its evil within, remaining hidden. We certainly can keep thriving, or seeming to thrive on the outside. Meanwhile, living within us, hidden away, are, perhaps, the deep, dark, and destructive secrets that work to cause spiritual, emotional, and psychological disease.[134]

In this condition, how well will we weather life's hurricanes?

Let's Pray:

Dear God, on the outside our lives may look terrific. We may have it all, or at least have lots of it. People may envy us. At work we may whistle happy tunes; at home we may have domestic bliss, but in the middle of the night we feel the destructive nature of our hidden secrets stewing within us. Sometimes we feel like our past is eating us on the inside, and it gets harder to hold it all together. God, we confess to you and ask for your love to heal our inner lives. Amen.

Today's Thought Is: Confession stops rot.

I stoked the shed stove where the old butcher-block table was drying, its final coat of polyurethane gleaming. My wife came out to see it, helped me stack some firewood, and we got to talking about how the nuns had used the butcher block as a cutting table for a hundred years, and how in the homeless shelter it had helped support thousands of dinners.

"Now it's just our family table. It already did God's work," I said.

She said, "Not 'just.' It's a *family* table now, for homework and conversation, and it's where we'll eat together."

That old butcher-block cutting board is now the center of our family life—our home's heart. Evenings, we sit around it, holding hands, saying our quick grace, remembering God, remembering we love one another, remembering we're family. Although the table has served God in bigger ways in the past, it serves us now. But I think about the volunteers who once stood around this piece of wood, preparing dinners at the homeless shelter—chopping, slicing, talking, and living with God living in their hearts.

Now we pray our grace around it. I like to think the prayers penetrate the wood, giving it a certain holiness, a gleam. But perhaps that's mostly a wish on my part. Instead, I guess, it's enough to know and respect its history of serving God's people. It serves us.

Let's Pray:

Dear God, let the tables in our lives where we sit to eat be places of happiness and connectedness, and may you always dine with us. Amen.

Today's Thought Is: Saying grace binds us to one another and to God.

*J*uan Monroy, a journalist in Madrid, Spain, was among those reporters selected by the Spanish government to interview the American astronaut James Irwin, who was on a European tour after his *Apollo 15* mission to the moon. Monroy asked the astronaut, "What did you feel when you stepped out of that capsule and your feet touched the surface of the moon?"

To Monroy's surprise, Irwin replied, "It was one of the most profoundly disillusioning moments of my life."

"How could standing on the moon be so disappointing?"

Irwin explained, "All of my life I have been enchanted by the romance and the mystery of the moon. I sang love songs under the moon. I read poems by moonstruck poets. I embraced my lover in the moonlight. I looked up in wonder at the lunar sphere. But that day, when I stepped from the capsule onto the lunar surface and reached down to my feet, I came up with nothing but two handfuls of gray dirt. I cannot describe the loss I felt as the romance and mystery were stripped away. There will be no more moon in my sky! When we come to the place that we think we comprehend and can explain the Almighty, there will be no more God in our heavens."[135]

Let's Pray:

Dear God, if in our arrogance we claim to fully explain you, fully understand and know you, gently put us in our place. Amen.

Today's Thought Is: **God's bigger than we think.**[136]

I want a baby with all the bells and whistles, custom-made to suit my dreams. Tall, superior intelligence, artistic, scientific, athletic, strong, sensitive, capable, empathic, practical, ambitious, loving, courageous, beautiful, spiritual, and . . . did I leave anything out? Give me the perfectly designed child with enhanced genetic qualities.

While this sounds like the stuff of science fiction, designer babies for those who can afford them is not so far-fetched. As we continue to learn, understand, manipulate, and improve the human genome, we will be able to create designer children.[137] If this happens, we will remove a God-given universal reality shared by humans for eons—the learned humility of parents accepting any child born to them and loving that child unconditionally. Parents blindly launch into parenthood, not knowing what characteristics their child will have. It's scary.

Everybody understands that, even with the best parenting, genetics play a role in children's behavior, IQ, talents, and temperament. Everyone understands that we may choose our friends, and we may choose our spouses, but we do not choose our children. Maybe there's a blessing in that. Maybe the children who are born to us have lessons to teach us.

Let's Pray:

Dear God, we thank you for humility, and we pray for the unloved children who live with parents who reject them and for the parents who face daunting tasks while child rearing. Amen.

Today's Thought Is: The children born to us are often our teachers.

ome from college for the weekend, Lissa's older brother spent Saturday teaching her how to ride her new two-wheeled bicycle. As he held her bike seat with one hand and ran behind and beside her, he repeated, "You can do it, Lissa."

Lissa was game to learn, but, like all of us on our first two-wheeler, she was frightened. "Do not let go," she warned her brother. When it was time, though, he did let go. Before she knew it, she was riding alone, believing he still supported her. After realizing he wasn't there, she shouted, "Look at me! I'm doing it on my own!"

Is that not how we all feel when we succeed at a challenge? In the moment of success, it's easy to forget that, before we balanced on our own, there was somebody, or perhaps even many people, who taught and supported us. Humility understands that we succeed because of gifts given to us and the people who supported us.[138] We can't take responsibility for those gifts. The talents we have are God-given gifts. To see them as such creates a certain humility.

Let's Pray:

Dear God, we are indebted to all who taught us, who provided for us, and sacrificed; we are indebted to you most of all, for the gifts you give us. Amen.

Today's Thought Is: Even for our breath we are indebted to God.

*T*hree thoughts on practicing faith:

In her book *Speaking of Sin,* Reverend Barbara Brown Taylor observes that one of the Hebrew words for a righteous person, whose translation suggests "one whose aim is true,"[139] gives her an image of righteousness as target practice. Whether her arrow finds its mark or falls a hundred feet away, her daily practice of a right relationship with God and with her neighbors is how she improves her aim. She knows that she will continue to sin, continue to miss—no doubt about it—but that's not her aim. Her true aim is to live as God wants her to live. Brown believes that the wish to please God does, in fact, please God.

"In the beginning, there is struggle and a lot of work for those who come near to God," said the third-century Christian mystic Amma Syncletica. "But after that, there is indescribable joy. It is just like building a fire: At first it's smoky and your eyes water, but later you get the desired result. Thus we ought to light the Divine fire within ourselves with tears and effort."

A wise spiritual guide once said, "We're as good at praying as we are at the other relationships of our lives. If you want to get better at prayer, work on the key relationships in your life."

Being in relationship to God is vertical, horizontal, and interior. Vertical means directly to God in prayer and worship. Horizontal is how you meet him in people, in the world, in nature. And lastly, interior is how God lives within our hearts. Work on all three, and the connection is strengthened.

Let's Pray.

Dear God, be with us in every way that we might be with you
every day. Amen.

Today's Thought Is: **Seek God now.**

The Shazam, at 159 feet, is among the finest luxury sailing yachts in the world. In one winter, on a new moon low tide, *The Shazam* was making for the Intercoastal Waterway in Florida at a place where the water depth on that tide was about fourteen feet; unfortunately for her captain, she draws fifteen feet. According to newspapers, she drove hard aground, struck a bridge, stopped traffic, closed the waterway to cruise ships, *and* knocked her owner and crew to the deck. Not good.

Sea captains say that you're not really a sailor 'til you've run aground. I've run hard aground myself. It happens. In the owner's eyes, the captain of *The Shazam* had committed the unthinkable and, apparently, the unforgivable with his world-class yacht, and so he was made to walk the plank.

But God is merciful and forgiving (unlike some yacht owners). Most of us slip up at our jobs sometime, and a few of us have been fired. But there's nothing we've ever done that God can't forgive.

Let's Pray:

Dear God, help us avoid running hard aground at work, or in our relationships, or with you; but if we do, help us accept our responsibility and our fate, your forgiveness, and help us learn from the experience. Amen.

Today's Thought Is: **Every skipper runs aground.**

*P*olar bears have hollow-tubed and clear-colored hair shafts that look white when they reflect light. It's perfect camouflage for living in the icy Arctic. But what's the proper camouflage for polar bears living in the lush green tropics, say at the Singapore Zoo? They turn green.

Two polar bears in Singapore, Inuka and Sheba, turned totally green, because the humid tropical weather allowed for a harmless algae to grow inside their hollow hair shafts. If Sheba and Inuka had had the inclination, opportunity, and ability to escape captivity and head into the tropical jungle, they would have easily blended into the foliage as free, and almost invisible, bears.[140]

Blending in is what many of us do in life. We move to a new place, or join a new circle of friends, and we try to adapt, fit in, look right. Years ago, when my family moved to Down East, Maine, from Buttondowntown, Connecticut, I quickly learned that a black beret, crisply pressed shirts, and snappy chinos made me unapproachable. Nobody would talk to me. Happily, it was an easy switch to jeans, flannel shirts, and a ball cap.

We may make certain accommodations so we look the part for the role we play, so we fit in, so we do not feel out of place. That's fine, as long as we stay true to our core values, our faith, and our beliefs. True faith can survive external changes because true faith lives within the grasp of God, deep inside our hearts. Sure, we change, but the deep, inexpressible love of God inside our hearts is singularly eternal.

Let's Pray:

Dear God, as we change on the outside, as fashions shift, help us remain true and steady in our hearts. Amen.

Today's Thought Is: **Green polar bears are still polar bears.**

On Goranson Farm, situated on the flood plain between the Kennebec and the Eastern rivers, maple sugar season starts in late winter by the setting of 1,300 taps at a slight upward angle, two and a half inches into trees. The farm is on flat land, so strong farmer Jan and her husband, sweet Robin, haul most of their sap the traditional, old-fashioned way—in buckets, by hand and on foot, with the *ping-ping* of the sap dripping into the tree-mounted buckets playing the overture of spring in the background. Jan loves the time of year when she stomps about in the melting snow of warm winter days, hauling buckets to their sugar shack.

Early in each season, Jan and Robin produce Light Amber Syrup by hauling twenty-five to thirty gallons of sap for one golden gallon of sweetness. Later in the season, when there's more water in the sap, it'll take forty gallons to produce a big jug of Dark Amber.

It takes heat, hard work, time, joy, and the right conditions to purify the sap into syrup. In our lives, we encounter situations that make us feel we're in the boiler, getting refined by God. It's not comfortable, it's not fun, but the results are sweetness to heaven.

Let's Pray:

Dear God, if you must, if you want, refine us, remove our excess, boil off our impurities, so that we may be sweetness to your tongue and beauty to your eye. Amen.

Today's Thought Is: A spiritual journey requires refinement for its sweetness to manifest.

*J*esus knew he was a troublemaker. He deliberately antagonized the Roman-installed religious leadership by healing the sick on no-work days, raising the dead, and generally undermining the Temple's authority in his speeches. He intentionally provoked the authorities by calling them hypocrites and blind leaders. He knew where his rabble-rousing might lead. How did he know? He was a bright man. He looked around.

Jesus saw what happened to other agitators, both religious and political. Agitators routinely ended up publicly swinging by their wrists for their crimes. Jesus wasn't the only man to recognize the threat of heinous execution by the state.

Rome regularly eliminated her problems with crucifixion—tens of thousands of times. It kept the people peaceful. Ticking off the Temple leaders in Jesus' day was like dissing the Pope during the Spanish Inquisition.

Jesus knew exactly what he was doing and where it would lead. According to the Gospels, he did it on purpose, because that was the God-given plan. To buy time before his arrest, Jesus did some fancy ducking and weaving to stay free. At one point, when Jesus knew the authorities were looking for him, he stayed outside of Jerusalem and hid in a safe house. Who's to blame for his death? Jesus made the choice himself—not Rome, not the Temple leaders. They participated, but Jesus *chose*.

Dear God, we pray for all the agitators who strive against repressive
governments. Protect them; let their voices be heard. Amen.

Today's Thought Is: Jesus picked his path. So can you.

*I*n his younger days, Dad was a wild man, much beloved and often very funny. He married well and was tamed a tad by his sweet darling. Dad, an offshore fisherman by trade, played hard—racing cars, riding four-wheelers, ice fishing, and spending time with his good kids.

Months later, in a snowstorm at night, the fisherman's son watched through a window in their home as his dad's snowmobile headlamp crossed a road near the frozen pond and headed toward home. Strangely, though, the headlight stayed small. It never got any closer. A search party went out and found a tragic accident had occurred.

Funerals and wakes are hard, but necessary, for everybody, kids included. At this funeral home, the hundreds of teary-eyed mourners, dressed in everything from pinstripes to fisherman flannels, crowded into the office, the conference room, the hallways, even the closet. In the same way that funerals make the thin veil between this life and the next real for adults, it makes it real for kids, too. It reminds us all how to live by showing us mortality.

Let's Pray:

Dear God, bless the children, widows and widowers, parents, siblings, and friends who grieve. Let them believe in the great hope of eternal life. Amen.

Today's Thought Is: **Life's brief. It's time to believe.**

※川彡

lagiarize. If you want success, that's a good first step. If writing is not your thing, you can always lie to Congress, run over revelers with your SUV, practice mail and wire fraud, or work for the mob and whack a few guys. The point is, one step toward fame and fortune is to do something bad, get caught, make the national news, then temporarily face dishonor, disgrace, and infamy.

Give interviews. Tell all. Say you're sorry—or not! Wait five minutes. Get contract offers from publishers, movie moguls, and/or the media. Find yourself quickly restored to society. Lastly—make oodles of money.[141]

In the twenty-first century, Hester Prynne, antiheroine of the novel *The Scarlet Letter*, set in 1642, wouldn't be ashamed. Instead, she'd write a tell-all bestseller. Reverend Arthur Dimmesdale, her secret lover, would immediately confess, lose his pulpit, pay child support for Pearl (their daughter), then rise to fortune and fame by founding his own church.

These days redemption is cheap, and being disgraced is not so bad. In any case, shame is unfashionable. Shame is caused by the consciousness of our guilt, by the awareness of our impropriety—this feels bad. We do not want to feel bad about ourselves, at least not for very long, especially when there's money to be made.

Remember the Prodigal Son? The son did wrong, suffered, changed his behavior, and was truly sorry. We prefer to skip the middle part and head right to the party. Who wouldn't? God wants genuine repentance, remorse, and reform, then there'll be genuine forgiveness.

Let's Pray.

Dear God, if we've done anyone wrong, we're sorry.
We won't do it again. Amen.

Today's Thought Is: Genuine forgiveness comes from genuine remorse.

*I*n the old city, with its narrow cobbled streets and its squeezed-together four-storied redbrick storefronts, in Quito, the capital of Ecuador, the gringo wandered with time to kill. Going nowhere, he turned left or right as impulse told him, enjoying the sights and street culture of that foreign land.

Around one corner he encountered, unprepared, the street of the casket makers. For the length of a city block, on either side before him, lining and almost blocking both sidewalks were stacks of black wooden caskets, piled one atop the other in front of every little shop. The bottom box of each was always big-man-sized, the next slightly smaller, and the next smaller still, until, stacked above the gringo's head, was the littlest of all. Around the caskets were playful children running, eating, or bouncing red rubber balls off the stacks in games of catch. Twenty casket craftsmen showed their wares out there while their lively children laughed and romped.

Intertwined on their sidewalks was life and death. On that street among those people, dying was openly part of life, not hidden, nor feared, or ignored.

Let's Pray:

Dear God, you made us with a limited warranty. We might not like it, but help us accept it. Help us find healthy ways to talk about death and dying. Amen.

Today's Thought Is: **Death is not alien.**

*T*his is a story told to me by a man who asserted a family relationship to the artist Norman Rockwell. A decade after landing the job as the artist for the covers of *The Saturday Evening Post*, Mr. Rockwell and his family moved to the bucolic beauty of Arlington, Vermont. In those days, the *Saturday Evening Post* was the window on America. Everybody read it. From his Vermont studio, Rockwell mailed his weekly submission to New York City. According to my friend, each time Mr. Rockwell mailed in a painting, he was a nervous wreck, convinced it would his last submission. "They'll hate it. I'll be fired," he thought.

Imagine being so successful and respected but still fearing rejection. Rockwell would fret until the check arrived relieving him until the next cover, the next week. According to the tale teller, his anxiety about losing his job was so bad that he eventually moved to Stockbridge, Massachusetts, in the Berkshire Mountains to the north of New York City, in order to shorten his weekly wait. I haven't been able to confirm this anecdote by any scholarly means, so do not take it as gospel. If this tale is true, and it could be, consider that Mr. Rockwell's insecurity may have actually driven his artistic improvement and commercial success. And if Norman Rockwell felt insecure about his obviously brilliant talent, then it is okay for us to feel insecure occasionally, too.

Let's Pray:

Dear God, at times we might feel a little shaky about our own value, and how secure we are in the world. If so, teach us to use that feeling for success. Amen.

Today's Thought Is: **Insecurity can be a useful tool.**

red Rogers, host of *Mr. Rogers' Neighborhood*, once said that most people want to know that somebody loves them, and that there is somebody to love. Love was the basis of his program. He said that the space between a viewer's television and the viewer is holy. Maybe you knew that Mr. Rogers was also an ordained Presbyterian minister who took his lead from the Teacher who was all about love.

Every child needs to know and feel that she or he is loved. To give love to a child is more than just a feeling. It means caring for and caring about the whole welfare of the child. It means meals, hugs, kisses, good-night tucking, baths, arguments, direction, scolding, teaching, and the ten thousand other things parents do. If the space between the viewer and the TV is holy, then the space between a child and a parent is even more so. That holy space begs to be filled with acts of love.

Children can't comprehend this world the way adults do; the world can be a scary place for children who are without love. What they do understand and need is love both expressed and shown. Without love, children can feel lost, lonely, and afraid.

Let's Pray:

Dear God, we long to love, and need to feel loved, not just by you, as good as that is, but by human beings, by our parents, and by those who ought to love us. Today, help us find a way to give love away, for it is in giving that we receive. Amen.

Today's Thought Is: **Share love.**

*W*hen my young son went into the ski lodge to eat, I seized the chance for a few fast runs. The stranger next to me on the double chair lamented skiing alone. All his ski buddies were busy with family. "Me, too—same thing," I said. "But today I'm with my son, who's eating in the lodge." He said, "I wish my pals were here." An hour later, with my son, we saw a boy in front of us fall on a beginner slope. We stopped to see if he was okay. He was. He followed us down and joined us in the lift line, talking about how he'd forgotten his skis and had had to rent the pair he was using.

At the peak he waited for us, then went down with us, and up and down again, talking the whole time. Obviously he needed love, or the attention of family and friends. The ease with which he joined us said "needy child." While standing under the double chair at a trail intersection, just curious, I asked him if he was with anyone.

"My stepdad's here, but he leaves me on this side and skis by himself over there on the expert trail. At the end of the day we have one race down to see who wins."

Providentially, the boy's name rang out from the chairlift above us, saying, "Stay there." His stepdad was the man with whom I had ridden up earlier, the one who had said he was alone.

Dear God, we pray for lonely, needy children who attach themselves to any stranger who shows them kindness. Bless those who could love them with the power to love fully. Amen.

Today's Thought Is: Without love, who wins?

*A*t the age of ten, his body changed. It started on a Saturday morning while he bicycled to the corner store for a half pint of chocolate milk. By the time he'd drunk the milk and had ridden the mile home, his tummy hurt badly enough to suggest a trip to the allergist. Tests at the allergist revealed lactose intolerance, allergic rhinitis, and asthma. One day the boy was healthy and fit, and the next day it was as if he had a permanent wheezing cold.

No more milk. No more ice cream. No pizza. No cheese. Medicine every four hours, day and night, shots once a month, and an inhaler. The allergist urged the end of outdoor activities in spring, summer, and fall for him. After a year of restrictions, the boy had had enough of it: no sports, no running, no biking—no fun. The boy decided he would rather suffer and have fun than suffer by not having fun.

Thirty years later, an enzyme allows this athlete to eat ice cream, and medical advances continue to manage his allergies and asthma. Here's the thing—his sickness gave him inner strength and drive. It wasn't going to beat him. It still doesn't.

Sometimes God gives us what feels like a curse—a chronic sickness, a physical deformity, or a terminal pronouncement. Sometimes, if we look hard enough, there's a gift to be found as well.

Let's Pray.

Dear God, thanks for the gifts that arise from suffering.
Let us use them. Amen.

Today's Thought Is: **Curses can be blessings.**

Humility can be the understanding that we are born with our gifts and talents. For those, we can thank God alone. Knowing this about ourselves, we should understand this about others, too.

There's a deeper humility, which is to the awe we feel when looking to the starry heavens and seeing clearly how vast this universe is, and how infinitesimally small we are in comparison. Humility comes from perspective.

Normally, we measure ourselves by making comparisons to other humans. Am I greater or lesser than she is? Am I cooler and hipper than he is? Am I smarter, faster, stronger, richer than you are? Yet the Teacher taught us not to judge, lest we be judged, for the judgment we give is the one we'll get. It's hard not to judge, or measure, or compare. To reach a deeper and truer humility, maybe we shouldn't measure ourselves horizontally, one person to the next—but vertically, as in me versus God. In that context, I'm the small one. When greeting others, if we can keep in mind the sheer greatness of God, then there'll be no room for the greatest of ourselves.

Humility, by the way, is not meekness, weakness, or cowering. Spiritual humility sees the equality of all people, of all souls, not because of a philosophical outlook, but because we are all equally nearly nothing when compared to the Creator of galaxies, stars, seas, and human beings.

Let's Pray:

Dear God, you are vast beyond words; we are small.
Teach our hearts this lesson. Amen.

Today's Thought Is: Only God is great.[142]

*D*avid said, "I kept thinking she'd be okay. It was like holding a rope in your hand and watching it run through your hands, like you do every day. By the time the rope's end flies from your fingers, you stare, disbelieving." That morning they'd thought it was stomach flu, but later that same day when Mary, David's wife, was on morphine and headed into surgery, the realization struck him that she might not live. In fact, Mary didn't survive.

Weeks later, David stopped by and talked about the suddenness of her departure, of the new motorcycle they'd bought five months before, and of the lonely rides he's taken since her death. On the bike, David feels relief because the immediate world flows by so fast and his focused attention is required to stay alive. But he also feels a sense of betrayal. Betrayal to the one lost, and to those who know him and think he ought never smile again.

David told me, "I'm afraid to laugh because they might not understand my heart's really broken. I have laughed, and smiled, and I do try to look my best, but all the color's gone out of my world. I cry a lot, and I do not know who I am anymore, except I remain an optimist."

Grief takes many forms and a long time. Express your grief.

Let's Pray:

Dear God, you love those who mourn; let us love them, too, and let us laugh and cry with them, as their needs arise. Amen.

Today's Thought Is: All will be well.

*W*hen life is good, and everything's going your way, has anyone ever said to you, "Wow, you must be living right" or "You have all the luck"?

Carrying rabbit's feet, hanging horseshoes, throwing salt over the shoulder, finding a penny and picking it up . . . all done in an effort to ensure you'll have good luck.

I've encountered Westerners in our monotheist traditions who treat God in a similar way, expecting their faith to be a lucky charm. They suppose that if they do everything right, if they follow all the rules and rituals, if they believe absolutely what they are taught to believe and never deviate or doubt, if they are perfect little do-bees, then all God's good blessings will be theirs. They'll have no difficulties. Parking spots will be easy to find. Laundry will never shrink. The sun will shine on their days off. Checks won't bounce. Fortunes will be made. Love will be found. All troubles will end!

The trouble really comes when this plan fails. God's not a good-luck charm. Superficial faith believes that God won't allow any trouble to happen—but trouble does happen. Sturdy faith understands that God promises to be with us in our times of trouble, not to prevent the troubles from occurring.

Let's Pray:

Dear God, when trouble comes, give us faith. Be next to us when we struggle; be with us as we face trouble. Thanks. Amen.

Today's Thought Is: Seek heaven, not luck.

We were on a spring skiing trip with a teacher and his students. To monitor everybody's whereabouts, we all carried those popular fourteen-channel walkie-talkies. Those small walkie-talkies are a blessing and a curse. When you hear "dad" over the airwaves, every dad on the mountain answers—all at the same time. Then nobody can hear anything because the channel jams.

That day a snowboarder in our group fell off a grinding rail in the terrain park, struck his helmetless head on ice, took a sled ride down with the ski patrol, and had an ambulance ride to the ER. He was okay, other than a minor concussion. His buddy, on seeing him fall, immediately tried alerting the teacher to the situation via radio. With so much noise on that channel, it took a little time to convey the urgent message.

Sometimes it's hard to hear what's important above life's rumpus. Even vital messages may get jammed. With all the static in life, all our busyness, all our thoughts, and all the rushing about, it can be hard to hear what's spiritually necessary, vital, urgent, and important. If we're talking all the time, listening to music all the time, or busy every single moment, then it's difficult to listen to God. What urgent message is God trying to give you?

Let's Pray.

Dear God, in moments of silence we ask to hear you. Clear our minds
and our time for several moments this day so that we might,
maybe, hear you. Amen.

Today's Thought Is: Listening for God is a spiritual practice.

"eep your shoulders back" is advice often given to horseback riders. One rider recalled riding with a horse crop propped against her back, forcing her into the correct posture. She decided to invent a comfortable and practical device to wear while riding. Designed for middle-aged woman in the riding market, her company has also heard from runners, health professionals, speech therapists, concert violinists, and chronic back-pain sufferers. Proper posture, on and off the horse, projects an image of confidence and grace, and it's better for your back.[143]

How's your spiritual posture?

Proper posture before God, similar to proper posture while in the saddle, creates a better God-servant rapport, and vice versa. It's not about a spiritually straight back. I'm talking about the posture of your heart, your openness to grace. Is your heart open to God, or closed? Is it partway open and willing, or mostly closed and slouchy?

The device invented by the woman mentioned above teaches correct posture. The body learns and remembers.

If you want to improve your spiritual posture before God, one tool that helps is sitting in a sanctuary during services, or mass. Another device that can be used anywhere is prayer. You can pray while kneeling, sitting, standing, showering, lying in bed, or even while riding your ATV. After all, prayer's about an open posture of the heart, not the position of the body.

Let's Pray:

Dear God, open our hearts to you. Amen.

Today's Thought Is: **Pray anywhere, anytime.**

*A*pril school vacation was three days away. The children were excited about taking family trips, spending time at the mall, or just having the chance to loaf. The recess bell rang. Cheerful children, all except one, dashed out the door into the school yard. The last boy approached his teacher's desk, asking, "If you're going to be in school next week working, can I come here every day and be with you? I'll clean the boards and not be any trouble."

The teacher said, "I'm sorry, but I'm going to be away. Do you not like being home?"

The boy's face twisted. Saying nothing, he turned and ran outside.

The teacher already knew that he had learning disabilities, and that, although diligent, he was never going to do well in school. She had quietly and tactfully asked questions about him. She learned he lived a tough home life—his father was prone to violence and his mom admitted to drugging and drinking while pregnant with him, which physicians believed caused his learning troubles.

By the time report cards were being prepared, she had compelling reasons to fear that, should his father see poor grades, the boy would be physically abused. The teacher couldn't bear it, so she secretly doctored his grades—just enough—hoping to spare him more violence.

It's a tough position to be in—choosing a child's safety over strict honesty. At times, we may find ourselves in difficult positions, where ethics are not as clear as right or wrong. How do we choose? What would you do?

Let's Pray:

*Dear God, when we are faced with ethical choices, guide our prayers,
guide our thinking. Help us make the most loving, highest,
and best choice. Amen.*

Today's Thought Is: Is selfless love worth the risk?

After completing his tour of duty at an air station in Maine, the southerner returned with his family to Kentucky, where he enrolled in medical school. On earning his degree and having fallen in love with Maine, this new ophthalmologist moved his family to the Downeast region and joined an existing practice. As part of the standard of care while examining patients, ophthalmologists are required to inquire about the comfort level of their patients.

In his first week of practice, this ophthalmologist asked a native Downeastner, "Are you comfortable? Is this okay?" The native replied with an intact of breathe, "Ayuh." Having never heard this Maine affirmation before, the doctor repeated his question. The native replied once more, "Ayuh." The doctor became alarmed at the gasping sound. Unable to identify it, he dashed out of the examination room, quickly found his new partner, and explained the situation, saying, "I think my patient may be chocking, or dying." With both doctors in the examining room, it was clear to the partner that the patient was merely saying yes.

"Ayuh" said with inspiration, or on an intake of breath, is a unique and colorful way of saying yes.

In Genesis, it says that, when God created humankind, he breathed life into them. The breath, or spirit, of God inspired them. A simple prayer could be saying "ayuh" to God while breathing in or out.

Saying yes to God is an open prayer of affirmation that conveys, "God, come be with me and breathe your spirit into me."

Let's Pray:

Dear God, we long to say yes to you. Inspire us with your breath, with your spirit. Amen.

Today's Thought Is: Pray "ayuh" to God.

hree months after relocating to a Downeast Maine island from New York City, their daughter was born. Within days, islanders dropped by, one by one, to see the new baby. One old woman, Arby, kept repeating, "Ain't she cunnin'."

The ex-urbanite couple had no idea what she meant.

At first they figured that cunnin' was a shortened way of saying "cunning." They couldn't figure out how Arby could possibly think that their newborn child was deceptive. They were concerned the old woman was insulting their innocent baby, but Arby's sweet way of saying "cunnin'" seemed a contradiction. It wasn't until later that the couple learned a much older definition of the word *cunnin'*: cute, pretty, or pleasing. Arby had been saying, "Isn't she cute."

People of the same country who speak the same language but come from different regions often have difficulties understanding one another because of their local dialects and accents.

When we embark on a spiritual journey, we may encounter unfamiliar language, which may leave us wondering just what is being said. Words like *grace, righteousness, transcendent, immanent, homiletics,* and *salvific* can leave us scratching our heads.

If you're starting on your spiritual path, do not worry about all the fancy language, you'll understand the new words as time passes. What matters most is opening your heart to God's charming love.

Let's Pray:

Dear God, bless our souls with your sweet touch. Amen.

Today's Thought Is: **God speaks the language of your heart.**

*S*ummer camp had been in session for weeks when the lately hired counselor arrived to finish out the season. On his way to his room to drop off his luggage, Dave saw another counselor swinging a camper around and around by holding onto the boy's ankles. Slipping from the counselor's hands the camper's head struck the ground. He lay still. Dave dashed to help. The camper wasn't breathing.

Dave palpated the limp body and checked for a pulse. Detecting a heartbeat and no indications of a spinal injury, he began mouth-to-mouth resuscitation. The headmaster arrived with the station wagon. Dave climbed in, continuing the CPR. Halfway to the hospital Dave checked the wrist pulse. Nothing. Dave said, "There's no heartbeat. I'm continuing CPR." He worked on the boy for half an hour. As they rounded the corner into the hospital parking lot, the boy vomited, indicating a beating heart and breathing body.

Dave had breathed life into that boy that day.

Take a deep breath. The air we breathe keeps us alive. We share this air. It's all around us and necessary for life.

God breathes life into us. Although we may take it for granted and can't see it, or taste it, or touch it, without God's breath of life in us, without God's spirit inspiring us and keeping us alive, we would cease to be. The spirit of God is in us, as our breath is in us.

Dear God, be our breath of life. Inspire us this day. Amen.

Today's Thought Is: **God's breath is life.**

*T*he final rehearsal for a children's theater production of *Oliver!* was at night. In the cast of 105 performers, there were three adults. On the day of the final rehearsal, the man finished his work early and expected to spend the afternoon practicing his lines. With the pressure mounting and his lines still not perfect, he had just picked up his script when he heard an odd noise emanating from his cellar.

Pulling on his mud boots, overalls, and a pair of work gloves, he ventured down to investigate. The cellar was flooded with six inches of water, threatening the water heater. The pump wasn't pumping. For the next three muddy, wet hours, with trips back and forth to the hardware store, he made several attempts at repair, encountered repeated failures, and finally experienced something like success. The strange thing was that the most important replacement part worked only when it wasn't properly connected. When it was glued in place, as it should have been, it wouldn't work. When it was unglued, wrongly, it worked perfectly. Meanwhile, the final rehearsal loomed ever nearer. Fortunately, he had time to get the cellar cleaned up; unfortunately, he didn't have time to practice his lines.

Some days it seems like God's having a grand time toying with your life. But onstage the man remembered all his lines, and when he got home, his cellar was still empty of water.

Let's Pray:

Dear God, when we're ankle deep in it, and the pressure's mounting,
and we're about to become unglued, just make sure it all works out, okay?
Amen.

Today's Thought Is: **We make plans; God changes them.**

All winter, a skilled and congenial carpentry crew, pleased with their intricate work, pounded nails, lifted lumber, cut, measured, and enjoyed themselves while constructing a finely designed new home. On a day in early spring, when the home had taken shape, the owner arrived to visit and brought with him his six-year-old granddaughter. As the owner talked and walked with the construction boss, eyeing this and that and smiling, this darling blond-haired and blue-eyed sprite of a granddaughter danced and played outside and inside.

She was the talkative, inquisitive sort who asked many questions of the workmen. "Why this?" "What's that?" One curious carpenter, a father himself, finally asked her why she was so comfortable talking to people she didn't know and to whom she had not been introduced.

She simply said, "We're all brothers in the eyes of God."

All the men stopped their work and looked at her, marveling at her words, as she twirled on tiptoe through the sawdust, smiling.

Let's Pray

Dear God, children sometimes speak your truth plainly and prettily, making grown-ups stop to ponder how we could have forgotten who we are—your children, sisters and brothers all. Amen.

Today's Thought Is: **Brothers and sisters all.**

*I*s it any wonder that nations fight when kids in the same family do not get along?

I do not recall what happened. Maybe I chucked an ice ball at my younger brother, David, or maybe I shoved him into a snowbank. Whatever it was, he ended up crying. What I do remember is my mom scolding me, saying, "You think that was fun? You think that was funny? How'd you like that to happen to you?" Whatever it was, I didn't want it done to me. Mom was pointing to the Golden Rule. Pretty much every major religion has a version of the Golden Rule. Here're five examples:

In Christianity: "In everything do to others as you would have them do to you; for this is the law of the prophets."

In Judaism: "What is hateful to you, do not do to your fellowman. This is the entire Law; all the rest is commentary."

In Islam: "None of you truly believes until he wishes for his brother that which he wishes for himself."

In Hinduism: "This is the sum of the Dharma [duty]: do naught unto others which would cause you pain if done to you."

In Buddhism: "Hurt not others in ways that you yourself would find hurtful."[144]

And still, we fight, we shove, we hurt, we war.

The Golden Rule works only if we remember it and live it day to day.

Let's Pray:

Dear God, help us see and understand that when we hurt others,
we are asking to be hurt in a similar manner. Teach us to treat everyone
we meet as we wish to be treated. Amen.

Today's Thought Is: Do to others as you would have them
do to you.

It's been predicted that by 2010 two-thirds of our payments will be cashless.

In 1999, most retail purchases were made in cash or by check. By 2003, only half were, with the other half being made with a swipe of plastic. In 2001, almost three-quarters of households paid their bills by check. That number dropped to 60 percent in 2003 as automatic payment and online banking became popular. Cash and checks now seem almost inconvenient.[145]

Like it or hate it, money is part of human life. Most of us spend the bulk of our week working for money. We need money for food, for shelter, for clothing, and for a thousand other things. At best, money's a tool that gets us what we want and need. Contrary to popular belief, money (cash, coin, plastic, or electronic) is not the root of all evil. The Scriptures say that the *love* of money is the root of all kinds of evil.[146] Money is not intrinsically bad. It becomes evil only when we worship it.

Let's Pray:

Dear God, money is old, and it pays our bills. We work for it,
but do not let it control us. If money has become our deity, help us to
understand that only you are God. Amen.

Today's Thought Is: **Money is a tool.**

*T*t's the dream of every sci-fi fan—a flying car. The creator, Dr. Moller, hopes the price will drop below $80,000 when in full production. Sound wild? Check out The Skycar™ at www.moller.com. A chief scientist at NASA Langely Research says, "The Skycar will do for our car-based society what the automobile did for the horse-based society." Its praises are sung by *Investor's Business Daily, Inc.* magazine, *Forbes FYI* magazine, the *L.A. Times,* the *Wall Street Journal,* and *World News Tonight.* The Skycar has few moving parts and redundant safety systems; it flies faster than a helicopter and is expected to alleviate traffic congestion.

A century ago it was said, "If man was meant to fly, God would have given us wings." Instead, we've discovered that God has given us something better—imagination and creativity.

Let's Pray:

Dear God, you've blessed us with imagination and inventiveness. Help us use these tools for the betterment and strengthening of our communities. Help us find solutions to truly pressing problems like hunger and housing. Amen.

Today's Thought Is: Imagination is limitless.

*F*or many families the war in Iraq is as close as a photo on the mantelpiece, an awaited e-mail, or an anticipated homecoming. You who have loved ones who are in harm's way, who live with anxiety and fear, stop a moment to read these ancient words from the Psalms:

"Even though I walk through the darkest valley; I fear no evil; for you are with me; your rod and your staff—they comfort me."[147]

"The Lord is my strength and shield; in him my heart trusts; the Lord is my light and my salvation; whom shall I fear?"[148]

"The Lord is the stronghold of my life; of whom shall I be afraid? When evildoers assail me to devour my flesh—my adversaries and foes—they shall stumble and fall. Though an army encamp against me, my heart shall not fear; though war rise up against me, yet I will be confident. One thing I asked of the Lord, that will I seek after: to live in the house of the Lord all the days of my life, to behold the beauty of the Lord, and to inquire in his temple. For he will hide me in his shelter in the day of trouble; he will conceal me under the cover of his tent; he will set me high on a rock. Now my head is lifted up above my enemies all around me, and I will offer in his tent sacrifices with shouts of joy; I will sing and make melody to the Lord.[149]

Let's Pray:

Dear God, protect and keep safe the troops and all the people we love who are in harm's way. Relieve our fears and anxieties. Help us trust in you. Amen.

Today's Thought Is: God's love is everywhere,
even in our fears.

Massachusetts state trooper pulls over a driver to the side of the highway, and asks for his license and registration.

"What's wrong, Officer?" the driver asks. "I certainly wasn't speeding, not in this traffic."

"No, you weren't," says the trooper, "but I saw you angrily give the one-finger salute as you swerved around a lady in the right lane a couple miles back. I further observed your flushed face as you shouted madly at the Lexus driver who cut you off, and how you pounded violently on your steering wheel when the traffic ground to a halt, and how you honked your horn at every car around you."

"Are those crimes, Officer?"

"No, sir, but when I saw the 'Jesus Loves You' bumper sticker on the back of this car, I figured it must be stolen."[150]

We are measured by what we do, what we say, and how we treat others—no matter where we go and regardless of whether we have bumper stickers on our cars proclaiming our faith. We sometimes think our cars make us anonymous, or even somehow separate us from the normal civility and courtesy we might show one another face-to-face. It's possible to have a bad day, get angry, and behave poorly. We have all said and done things we shouldn't have, in cars and out of them. Be that as it may, folks still judge us by our words and actions.

Let's Pray

Dear God, on a bad day help us remain calm, keep it under control, and not allow anger to rule us. If we feel like exploding, help us find civil ways of dealing with our stress. Amen.

Today's Thought Is: "One who is quick-tempered acts foolishly."[151]

*T*his is used and edited with permission from *Homiletics* journal:
A farmer purchases an old, run-down, abandoned farm with plans to turn it into a thriving enterprise. The fields are grown over with weeds, the farmhouse is falling apart, and the fences are collapsing all around. During his first day of work, the town preacher stops by to bless the man's work, saying, "May you and God work together to make this the farm of your dreams!" A few months later, the preacher stops by again to call on the farmer. Lo and behold, it's like a completely different place—the farmhouse is completely rebuilt and in excellent condition, there are plenty of cattle and other livestock happily munching on feed in well-fenced pens, and the fields are filled with crops planted in neat rows. "Amazing!" the preacher says. "Look what God and you have accomplished together!"

"Yes, Reverend," says the farmer, "but remember what the farm was like when God was working it alone!"[152]

A lot of God's will gets done on Earth because people like you do it. The only way much of God's good work gets done is when we all pitch in. We do not need to assume responsibility to fix up the whole world, we just need to work on our small part of it. By giving a little love and labor, we improve the whole.

Let's Pray:

Dear God, let our hearts love you; let our minds listen for you;
allow our hands to do your work this day. Amen.

Today's Thought Is: **Earth's a bit of a fixer-upper.**

*M*r. Stilts is a giant—not a real giant, but a wooden-legged, floor-clomping behemoth just under nine feet tall. Backstage, when his fellow child actors first met him, they were both frightened of him and delighted by him. They laughed and pointed, but they kept clear of his long stomping legs. At first, the children stayed away as he stomped, stepped, jumped, kicked, twirled, and practiced. Onstage, they feared he would fall on them, or tramp on their feet. Gradually, as rehearsals continued, their delight and fear of him lessened as they grew more familiar with him.

Off stage, they trusted him as he practiced. By opening night, while the children sat on the floor playing cards, they allowed Mr. Stilts to clomp around inches from their toes. They never looked up. Both the fear and delight had vanished. But their familiarity with Mr. Stilts bred disregard. In the dark on the stage, during their final performance, a rushing child knocked against his leg and Mr. Stilts tipped, spun, and nearly tumbled.

One can become so familiar with faith, with God, that initial delight and awe vanish. One may become so comfortable with faith that faith becomes normal, and then sometimes disregard creeps in, leading to precarious choices.

Let's Pray:

Dear God, do not let our faith grow stale; do not let us take you for granted; do not let us tumble. Amen.

Today's Thought Is: Strive for balance.

On Little League tryout day, Pete rode his green Stingray bike a mile on sidewalks to the ballpark behind his school. He went by himself with his glove dangling from the handlebars, nervous, but with big-league dreams. Pete signed up along with a couple hundred other city kids and waited. Over the loudspeaker a tinny voice eventually said, "Pete Prose, on deck."

At that point in his life the closest he'd come to playing was street ball with his sister and neighbors. The first pitch came fast. Pete swung. "Strrrriiike one!" On the next pitch, he hit. It sailed high over the second baseman's head. Pete ran. The center fielder missed the catch. Pete's hit turned into a home run. As a result, Pete got on the best team in the league that year, but that homer was the only ball he hit all season.

His coach had had this idea that Pete was some great ball player—but Pete wasn't, really. He was the worst kid on the best team. Some of the dads were vicious about Pete's playing at all. They'd shout. They'd scream. But the coach diligently taught Pete how to swing, and eventually how to hit

Let's Pray:

Dear God, do not let the little stuff ruin us. Help us to see the little stuff in life for what it is. Amen.

Today's Thought Is: God will judge us for everything we do, including every secret thing, whether good or bad.[153]

FALLING

A fire started inside the grease hood in the kitchen of a popular steakhouse. The diners got out safely. The fire station was only a half mile away, so the restaurant wasn't destroyed. A construction crew consisting of five laborers and a crane operator worked the reconstruction. Using chainsaws, the men cut large sections of the roof, wrapped them with heavy chain, and then the crane lifted each section and placed it in the parking lot.

The process was going well. As the third section was being lowered to the ground, Jerry, who was in the parking lot guiding the placement of the sections, glanced up to the roof and saw four men cutting the roof into sections. A moment later he glanced up again to see that one section and one man were gone.

Jerry dashed inside the restaurant to find the worker and the rubble from the section he had been working on had fallen two stories. The worker had landed on his back atop a bench seat between two tables. The crane operator called the ambulance. Jerry, who'd been on the National Ski Patrol, arranged the chainsaw men to create leg and head traction, to support the man's dangling body and to immobilize him until a backboard, neck brace, and immobilization straps could be secured. Their support prevented further injury.

There are times when our world falls from beneath our feet and we land in a terrifying, painful, or difficult position. It's at times like that when we need support. Maybe it's friends, maybe it's family. If you do not have family or friends nearby who can be there for you during tough times, a worship community can be. If you're alone, now might be a good time to seek a supportive community of faith, before the bottom drops out.

Let's Pray:

Dear God, you know our needs before we do. If we need a spiritual home, lead us to one soon. Amen

Today's Thought Is: **The faithful are supportive.**

*L*ong ago, she left. Her unexpected departure during her freshman year of college left behind wounded hearts in the family members, all of whom missed her and never understood why she abandoned, without a word, those who loved her.

Once a year her postcard came, with no return address. This token was both a blessing and a curse. The blessing was knowing she still lived; the curse was the ever-open wound. It was four years before her first brief return, then eight years, and after that, never again. Thirty-one years have passed since she left.

What's remembered by her family are the tears her mother shed every night as she hopelessly watched by the curtained window, staring down the dark street while praying for her daughter's return; each night her mother cried herself to sleep as her other children, in their own beds, listened.

Many families, often silently, suffer the sting of estrangement. A child, a parent, a sibling abruptly disappears, never or seldom to return. Those left behind grieve evermore.

There is the story the Teacher told about the return of a Prodigal Son, the forgiveness of his father, and the anger of his brother. The disaffected brother fell to low estate, wasted his life, and then humbly returned, begging merely for employment. With his broken heart, the father, sensing the sorrow and contrition of that wayward son, forgave and welcomed him home.[154]

Let's Pray:

Dear God, for all the broken families who suffer quietly the wounds of estrangement, we pray that humility and remorse lead the wayward to renewed and right relationship. Amen.

Today's Thought Is: God receives the contrite of heart.

A farmer advertised in our newspaper, "Nothing says spring-time to your neighbors like a pile of cow manure in your garden." We give our garden a fresh coat of manure each springtime and then turn it all over and mix it in, a pitchfork full at a time, come a sunny day. As soon as the garden's turned over, the boots'll get kicked off, and then it'll be barefoot in the humus for me.

The Latin root "hum" is the same one that shows up in both human and humus. It's similar to how in Hebrew "a'dam" means both human and soil, or of the earth. One of the Greek words for humility literally means rooted, or low to the ground. Perhaps humility means being bent down to the earth, to the soil, in the midst of God's heavenly grace.[155]

Let's Pray:

Dear God, we are mud made; our toes touch the soil, and our souls are entangled in your heaven. We are made of humus, we humans, and when we truly feel you, we unearth a holy humility. Amen.

Today's Thought Is: Humus, humans, humility.

*G*od's a dancer.

Much to the embarrassment of Saul's daughter Michal, but to the delight of God (one suspects), King David danced and leapt, and generally had a good time, celebrating in front of the Ark of the Covenant. King David, like us, was a man who regularly fell, at least once in a big way, but who got up and danced again.

What more can one do in life? When we fall, we can quit, or we can get up again. Once we are up, what next? Should we freeze and fear falling again, or should we dance?

God's there with us when we fall down, or get knocked down. We need to get up, and all the while, like King David, keep dancing for joy and for God.

Dear God, even if we can't dance, or walk, let our hearts dance for you. Amen.

Today's Thought Is: Get up; let your heart dance for God.[156]

In Massachusetts, blue laws kept stores closed on Sundays. When I was a kid, if we ran out of milk or eggs on Sunday, it was tough bananas until Monday morning. Later on, stores opened on Sundays; Sundays used to be sacrosanct, but times have changed.

Professionally, as an adult, I worked every Sunday for eighteen years. Of course, I was standing in a pulpit inside a church, so I can't complain. These days, our pluralistic society consists of Christians, Jews, Muslims, Hindus, Buddhists, and others. Friday, Saturday, and Sunday are each holy to somebody. Scheduling workers of various faiths is becoming harder and harder. Complaints of religious discrimination have risen 75 percent in the past decade. That's the hard news.[157]

The good news is that, as a nation with religious freedom, we remain a faith-oriented people. The vast majority of us believe in God, even if we disagree about the particulars.

Let's Pray

Dear God, even if we do not agree on faith, we can agree on you. Amen.

Today's Thought Is: **Take a Sabbath day.**

*R*achel announced to her parents, "I'm quitting piano. I want to play the flute." Early every morning she practiced, as if making up for lost time. The teacher, who taught band and gave private lessons, called a meeting with Rachel and her parents. He said, "Rachel, you do not have the correct mouth shape to properly play the flute. You might choose, perhaps, the clarinet." Ten-year-old Rachel looked at the teacher, and then, turning to her parents, said, "Well, I guess that means I'm getting a new flute teacher."

Nine years later, Rachel performed at New York's Carnegie Hall as her college orchestra's principal flautist. A calling had seized Rachel. Her love of flute helped her say no to the teacher and yes to her vocation.[158] A similar seizing is true of those called to pastoral leadership. They are caught by the lure of grace and God's unfailing love. Rachel submitted her self to the disciplines of her vocation. Nothing would have come of her calling, this lure of love, if she had neglected practice, education, and dedication.

It's as true in ministry as it is in music, or any other vocation. Don't quit. Stick to your calling, keep at it, and there will be blessings.

Let's Pray:

Dear God, here I am hard at work; help me keep focused and help me be dedicated as my vocational path opens before me. Amen.

Today's Thought Is: First comes the calling,
then comes the work.

*P*aul was an old hermit living in his once-prosperous home on a nice street in the middle of a harbor town. The place stank. Paul was aware of that and was apologetic. He had sold off his furniture long ago, so he slept on the floor in two thin sleeping bags with some blankets. Social Security bought his food. His house was unheated. He lost three toes to frostbite.

For decades, Dr. Paul had been a well-regarded physician and a respected church deacon. His wife, whom he loved dearly to her dying day, took seriously ill with a sickness that caused them to lose everything except their home. She drank herself to madness. He stopped practicing medicine and chose instead to stay with her, protecting her as best he could from herself. He spent their savings on her treatment. He spent his life for hers and was, in the end, at peace with himself and his decision. By the time she died, with his practice gone and his being too old to start over, he chose to live alone, to read, to think, to stay through the winter in his cold house, and to wait.

The Rabbi said, here is how to measure love: "The greatest love is shown when people lay down their lives for their friends."[159]

Let's Pray:

Dear God, you notice when we sacrifice for others. You do not judge us by our poverty, but by the riches of our hearts. Amen.

Today's Thought Is: Love is wealth unseen.

His position was precarious—twenty feet up, his left foot on the extension ladder, his right foot not secure, his left hand holding on to a ladder rung, and right hand grasping an open gallon of stain. Affixed to the gallon's handle was the wire hook of a coat hanger. As the twenty-year-old lifted up the gallon, preparing to hook it, the hook caught prematurely on a lower-than-intended rung. It happened just as the bottom of the can wedged on the top of the next rung. The result was that the can, being at belt level, tipped and began to slowly and steadily pour down the inside front of his shorts. He was stuck.

If he let go with his left hand, he'd fall. If he tugged up or down with his right hand, the gallon would dump completely. Instead, he waited helplessly as a half gallon of permanent brown stain slowly poured down his shorts and soaked his skin.

On the ground, another worker was literally breathless lying on his back on the ground, laughing at the precision of the pour.

What should one do in such an embarrassing and difficult situation? The ladder man laughed, too. His stain lasted through the summer. Sometimes you're darned if you do and darned if you don't; you can't turn left or right; you can't go up or down.

Times like that call for the Serenity Prayer: God, grant me the Serenity to accept the things I cannot change, Courage to change the things I can, and the Wisdom to know the difference.

Let's Pray:

Dear God, grant us the insight to change what should be changed, to accept what we cannot change, and the wisdom to laugh at ourselves. Amen.

Today's Thought Is: **Enjoy the moment.**

*H*is kid was going to have trouble getting through college. That made him not so different from his old man, who also had had trouble getting through college. So the old man made a deal with the boy. "If you graduate from college, I promise to God I'll dance an Irish jig on national television." It wasn't as far-fetched as it sounded. The old man was an NFL referee.

After the son graduated college, the Bengals were scheduled to play. All week the new grad told his pals, "Come see the game with me on Saturday. My dad's going to dance on the football field in the middle of the game." In a sports bar the large group of rowdy, happy grads gathered to watch.

The dad knew they were watching and he knew what they expected of him. A promise was a promise, especially when made to God. During the game, he was trying hard to figure out the least embarrassing and most plausible way to dance a jig in front of football players, a crowded stadium, and a million viewers. As one play ended, a player rolled on the ground and hit the referee's ankle. Seizing his chance, the ref danced around as if hurt, but with movements that were unmistakably an Irish jig. The sports bar erupted into cheers.

Promises can make us play the fool, but the promise matters, here and in heaven.

Dear God, sometimes it is tough keeping promises to those we love, particularly if we promise you, too. Help us keep our promises, when we can. Amen.

Today's Thought Is: Promises kept aren't always remembered, but promises broken are never forgotten.

*T*tell this dream as my friend told it to me in his words: "I dreamed I was in an infinite void. There was no end of darkness extending in every direction, yet I could see. I knew that I was dreaming and that I was asleep in my bed, but I could think in this dream as I do when I'm awake.

"A presence arrived, or always was there, I could feel it, like love, but couldn't see it. A voice without sound said inside my head, 'This is yours, my gift to you.' It was God. I can't explain it, he said. I do not understand it; I wasn't frightened. A human hand appeared. Between forefinger and thumb, it carried a small glass vial filled with sparkling gold dust. The vial of gold dust was opened and poured into my cupped hands. The soundless voice said. 'This is yours.'

"Then the voice said, 'Now give it away.' A breath of wind blew, or perhaps just a breath, and the gold dust blew, flew from my hands, not a grain was left. I awoke in my bed."

"What does this dream mean," he asked.

"I do not know," I said, "but if God gives you a gift, then you ought share it."

The Rabbi teaches that in giving we gain. He says, "Give, and it will be given to you. A good measure, pressed down, shaken together, running over, will be put into your lap; for the measure you give will be the measure you get back."

Let's Pray:

Dear God, show us where to share the gifts you've given us.
Teach us that to give is to gain. Amen.

Today's Thought Is: **A generous person will be enriched.**[160]

*C*hurch coffee hour was crowded. Kids, grandparents, young parents, retirees, and singles of all ages were sipping and chatting. Everyone was celebrating New Member's Sunday, a day when individuals join a congregation. A self-important woman, with lips compressed to a thin line across her face, approached the pastor.

"Excuse me, Reverend," she began, "out of the nine persons who joined our church this morning, one, perhaps two, were the type of persons we ought to be attracting. Only one is a member of the country club."

"I'm afraid I do not understand," replied the minister.

"I'm sure you do not, dear," she said. "Only one, perhaps two, of the new members seem to be the right sort of person, a better sort of person, the type of person *you* ought to be attracting to our church. Since your arrival here, the church is growing but you seem willing to accept anyone. I'm afraid you've lowered the standards."

"Actually," he said, "we do not accept just anyone. We do accept those who believe, and those willing to make a commitment to faith, and maybe even those who want to believe and are seeking their faith. This is neither your church, nor mine. It is God's church. Prosperous or poor, educated or semiliterate, gainfully employed or struggling, conservative or liberal, immigrant or native, sinners and seekers, all are welcome to worship in God's house."

Let's Pray:

Dear God, the doors of your houses are open to all who seek you. Keep the doors of our hearts open, too. Amen.

Today's Thought Is: The crucible is for silver, and the furnace is for gold, but the Lord tests the heart.[161]

You may have seen a TV commercial that went something like this: A man is outside his suburban home, riding his fancy lawn tractor over his perfect green grass, asking, "Do you not love my beautiful home? It's filled with beautiful furniture." Cut to the same man driving his new minivan slowly down a lovely tree-lined street, asking, "Do not you love my brand-new minivan?" Cut to the same man barbecuing in his backyard by a swimming pool, during what appears to be a crowded picnic. Smiling, he says, "Do you not love all my beautiful things? How can I afford it all? I'm in debt up to my eyeballs."

Responsible use of money is a spiritual issue. Here's a three-thousand-year-old saying from the Bible: "Some pretend to be rich, yet have nothing; others pretend to be poor, yet have great wealth."[162] Debt is hard to avoid—mortgages and car payments, for most of us, are necessary. We all need a place to live, and we need a way to get around. Reckless use of credit cards and mounting debt in order to live in the illusion of wealth is fiscally dangerous and spiritually false.

Let's Pray:

Dear God, there are so many things in life we want, and using credit is an easy and tempting way to get them. Strengthen our resolve to resist using credit cards irresponsibly. Amen.

Today's Thought Is: Some pretend to be rich,
yet have nothing.

*R*ural dwellers have likely seen bald eagles, osprey, and turkey vultures on the wing. Up close, they're all enormous and impressive flyers. One day, I heard the whir of wings. I turned and saw a huge bird I'd never seen before. It was all brown, with a basketball belly and a wingspan of forty-eight inches, and it was flying very fast, thirty feet away and ten feet up. What on Earth? My first thought was, "Is that a wild turkey?"

Wild turkeys can fly up to sixty miles per hour for up to a mile. They take a few steps, a few hops, a leap, and then they fly fast. They swim, too, by extending their necks and paddling with . . . their feet. On land, they can run up to twenty-three miles per hour.[163]

Now that wild turkey flocks are established in northern New England, I expect others will see that unexpected sight. Life is full of strange and wondrous events.

When we were traveling in Turkey, the country, everywhere we looked— on buses, buildings, cars, street signs—we'd see this word: *masha'allah*.

Curious, I asked what it means. I was told that *masha'allah* means "look at the wondrous things God has done." It was sure wondrous to see that wild turkey fly. I'd really like to see one swim, too.

Let's Pray:

Dear God, you are a God of wonder. You keep surprising us with your creations. Thanks for the joy. Amen.

Today's Thought Is: *Masha'allah!*

*W*hen Yale religious studies professor Carlos Eire visits his elderly mother, he often finds himself answering theological and pastoral questions from the small Cuban-immigrant community of her friends.

On a visit years ago, an elderly woman asked him, "Is it possible for Fidel Castro to convert on his deathbed and go to heaven?"

The professor assured her, saying, "It's possible because this is what our Christian faith is all about. Nobody is beyond redemption."

"Well, if that happens," retorted the woman, "then I do not want to go to heaven."

The great theologian Karl Barth once was asked the direct opposite of the old Cuban woman's question: "Is it true that one day we will see our loved ones again in heaven?"

"Not only our loved ones!" Professor Barth replied,[164] suggesting that we better be ready to meet there people whom we dislike here, including our enemies. Heaven is not populated only with people we like. Most of us have our own "Castros," our own enemies with whom we'd rather not share the peace of the afterlife. Heaven with them, we wrongly imagine, would feel slightly more like hell. It won't.

Let's Pray:

Dear God, it's a good thing that we aren't in charge of heaven.
It would get complicated if each of us got to choose who's in and
who's out—if that were the case, we might find ourselves on the outside.
You make it possible for those we love and for our enemies to be there
with you. Thank you for your merciful love. Amen.

Today's Thought Is: The enmity of enemies collapses in the presence of God's love.

*T*n homeless shelters across the country, people of all faiths who are down on their luck will sit together celebrating Thanksgiving with a traditional turkey-and-gravy meal, often prepared by other folks of faith who skip their own dinner. It's amazing what's said during grace in such a room.

"God, we thank you for this meal, for a warm cot, a warm room, and people to eat with. We thank you for the folks who've come here today to fix us a meal and serve us when they could be home watching football or the parade. Amen." Words such as these come from the poorest of the poor, from the folks who own the shoes on their feet and the clothes on their backs and nothing else. Imagine having nothing, being alone, being flat broke and without work, and still being able to thank God.

Maybe you don't have to imagine. Maybe you've heard or said similar graces. Such graces are said at soup kitchens by poor families who can't afford a regular dinner, let alone a Thanksgiving dinner of plenty. It's startling to realize it's the folks with nothing or little who are often most sincerely and truly grateful for their modest lives. When we sit at our tables—be it a sumptuous feast or a frozen dinner—let's say a grace and give thanks for every blessing and gift God has given, big or little.

Let's Pray:

God, thanks for everything. No matter where we are in life, we thank you for being you and for the chance, once a year, as one nation of many faiths, to remember you and thank you. Amen.

Today's Thought Is: God is the God of all people.

I wish I could sing it for you like Elvis did: "I'll have a blue Christmas without you." A blue Christmas. Plenty of people aren't into the reds and greens of Christmas. Their color of choice is blue, as in singing the blues, because Christmastime brings a heartbreaking time. A few years ago a colleague of mine started to celebrate a service of worship called a Blue Christmas.

It was for anyone in his congregation who had lost a loved one that year. It turned out that lots of people who'd lost a loved one that year, or even years earlier, wanted to be at that service.

Eventually, the Blue Christmas service ended up being held at the local funeral home. They invited everybody who'd lost somebody, as well as anyone else in town who felt the need to come. Many people came. I've been a few times, both as a celebrant and as somebody who'd lost a loved one. It's always a moving and emotionally freeing service.

Feeling the blues at Christmas is more normal than we're led to believe. It's reasonable to feel sad and heartbroken about missing somebody during the holidays. It's not just about death, either. We can miss loved ones who've moved away, estranged family members, those who are serving overseas. If you're feeling blue this time of year, you aren't alone, although it may feel like you are.

Let's Pray.

God, bless the folks who have the blues, who miss lost loved ones or loved ones who are far away. Bless especially those in the military service who are missed and loved. Keep them safe. Amen.

Today's Thought Is: **It's all right to feel the blues.**

*T*he beauty of her silk saris and lovely aristocratic face are deceptive, because Velichi's life is full of trouble and worry. Many years ago, she fled India after her traditionally arranged marriage went bad. The groom demanded a larger and larger dowry after the wedding. He locked her away in a room. Her mother-in-law treated her like a slave. She was beaten and belittled. Velichi was unwanted. Her husband decided to burn her alive and made appropriate and terrifying plans. She heard the plans being discussed, so she escaped to her father's home. Velichi's life was spared, but those months of confinement had made her a nervous wreck.

No matter how good her life became, Velichi worried about everything. She worried about finding a job. When she had a job, she worried about keeping the job. She worried about her siblings' squabbles. She worried that the husband would find her. She worried how she would pay the bills. What she would do when her visa ran out? Whether she had left the iron plugged in. Whether the stove was on. Whether the door was locked.

These are all quite reasonable worries, but her fears paralyzed her. She lives in terror.

Jesus says, "So don't worry about tomorrow. Tomorrow will bring its own worries. Today's trouble is enough for today."[165]

Easy to say, Jesus—hard to do.

Let's Pray:

God, with all the trouble we face, we do worry that tomorrow might be even worse than today. Help us understand that worrying changes nothing about the troubles that may or may not come. Help us focus on today's problems. Amen.

Today's Thought Is: "Worry is interest paid on trouble before it falls due."[166]

Holidays

*C*hristmas is over. Of that, there is no doubt. Blessings be on you, who could and did give charitably at Christmastime or Hanukkah. Your gifts—to your local food pantry, your house of worship's local charity program, the Salvation Army, Goodwill, United Way, a homeless shelter, a soup kitchen, or anyplace where there was cold or hunger—were money or assistance well given.

It's January. In many homes this is when, as the bills are opened, there are doubts about which bills gets paid and which bills do not. In many households, in order to save money on heating oil, or stove wood, or the gas bill, the heat is lowered to just bearable. In winter, for many Americans, the choice becomes between paying the holiday bills and paying the mortgage, or buying groceries or buying more oil. Now is the time of year that the need for assistance to "get by" begins.

Now is the time when the underpaid full-time hardworking employee who lives on the edge of financial disaster starts to get overdrafts. Now is when help is needed.

There is no end to the season of charity. So, if you are able, please lend a little kindness to a neighbor in need, because right about now is when food-pantry stocks start to run low, when home oil tanks runs dry, and when the meaning of a hard winter becomes reality. Charitable giving to those in need won't solve the long-term financial problems of those in want, but it will solve the real and pressing problems of today.

Let's Pray:

Dear God, it is cold outside, and your people are chilly and hungry. Help us provide help. Amen.

Today's Thought Is: **I was hungry and you gave me food.**[1]

THE DAY AFTER NEW YEAR'S DAY

What's changed since last year? Anything new? Are you new? Or are you the same old, same old? Do want to change? Did you make a resolution you won't keep? Last year, I went to get my hair trimmed. First thing I noticed was a new silver cross hanging around my barber's neck. When I'm sitting, she asks, "What's new?"

I say, "On my drive over, I was trying to figure out what to write about next. In my car, my mind latched on to that place where Jesus talks about cutting off your hand if it causes you to offend God. It's not a passage I really want to talk about while my TV viewers or readers are sipping their first cup of coffee."

"That's funny, I was just reading that last night. It's in Matthew, isn't it?"

I'm thinking, "My barber's really reading the Bible? She's sweet, but I'd never figured her for having faith, or for needing God." So I ask, "You're reading the Bible?"

"Almost every night," she says.

"When'd that start?"

"Eight months ago, when I joined a Bible study group. God's part of my life. I've really changed; I have a ways to go yet. though. If only I'd known years ago that believing in God could make life so good."

By believing in God, and making changes, she's made sustainable positive impacts in her life. Believing makes a difference.

Let's Pray.

Dear God, here it is the new year, and we want to make positive changes in our lives. Only you can really change us deep inside. So change us. Amen.

Today's Thought Is: God helps us change.

I just finished rereading an ancient book of love. It was written sometime between 950 and 750 B.C.E. It's too hot for young readers and ought to come with an NC-17 rating. It's an eight-chapter erotic love poem written in two voices—one a woman's and the other a man's.

What if I told you that one of the most famous poets in history wrote this hot love poem, and that you probably have a copy of this poem in your house, maybe even within reach. What if I told you that this provocative and flirty poem celebrating human love is in your Bible?

Today's Valentine's Day. What other day is there to talk about the Song of Songs, also called the Song of Solomon? The first line is, "The Song of Songs, which is Solomon's" meaning this is the most important song. It is the song before all songs—the song of human love. It's the story of true love. If you choose to read it, then I suggest you read it slowly and carefully, aloud, and let each word touch your ears and fill your heart. Listen not only to the words themselves. Listen with the ear of your heart. Listen so that you might hear contained and hidden within those words the voice of God speaking to you about love.

Let's Pray.

*Dear God, bless us with love; and may our love be patient and kind,
and never rude or resentful. Amen.*

Today's Thought Is: **Love is better than wine.**[2]

*A*pril Fools' Day is filled with harmless practical jokes and is celebrated around the world, but the origin of April Fools' Day is shrouded in mystery. One theory holds that in 1582, when Pope Gregory XIII ordered the Gregorian calendar to replace the Julian calendar, word of the change spread very slowly. Under the Julian calendar New Year's Day was actually an eight-day celebration starting on March 25 and ending on April 1. Some country folks didn't get the news for several years. Others, after hearing it, refused to accept it and continued to celebrate New Year's on April 1.[3] These backward-looking folks were ridiculed and labeled as fools. But there is also a religiously based theory, which states that April Fools' Day commemorates the fool's errand taken by the biblical crow who was sent out in search of land from Noah's flood-encircled ark.[4] Generally speaking, the Bible is not nice to fools. It says things like, "It's painful to be the parent of a fool," or "An employer who hires a fool is like an archer who shoots recklessly," and lastly, "Fools say in their hearts, 'There is no God.'"[5]

Let's Pray.

Dear God, bless those whose hearts are imprudent enough to exclude you.
Send them on a lifelong errand to find you, and let them find you. Amen.

Today's Thought Is: **God fits inside every heart.**[6]

THANK A VETERAN

The parade of marching veterans has dwindled over recent years. Memorial Day parades grew slowly smaller but hardly less solemn. In our small town, at least, these parades remain well attended. Whether at heart you are a patriot pacifist, a patriot warrior, or somewhere in between, it is necessary and important to stand shoulder to shoulder, side by side, as one people to honor those who sacrificed their lives at arms.

In a few years there will be more men and more women in uniformed attendance—veterans of Iraq and veterans of Afghanistan, who will march somberly. Like their veteran forebears, they march in memory of comrades lost, and they march for those still serving in war zones so far from their loved ones. Their expected presence in parades is a sober reminder that soldiers, marines, sailors, and airmen and -women are our citizens, neighbors, friends, and family. Their presence in parades reminds us that, although many have returned home, many remain abroad, at war, and some will never return. We pray and anticipate nearly everyone will come home and will march before us for years to come.

Let's Pray.

Dear God, help us keep heart, keep hope, keep strength, and keep faith. Keep safe the military volunteers. Bless the chaplains who deal with the struggles of young men and women at war; bless the medical personnel whose skills heal and save; bless those behind the scenes; bless the families of those who have lost loved ones in these wars, and in all previous wars; bless those whose hearts grieve. Bless us all with a peaceful, stable, and quick outcome. Amen.

Today's Thought Is: **Thank a veteran.**

CATHOLIC PARKING

*T*he Fourth of July is when everybody gathers on the lawn of the Catholic church that overlooks our gorgeous harbor. My friend, Reverend Charlie, met me on the church steps. After a hug hello, I asked, "How's the parking out back?" Charlie replied, "It's packed because there are plenty of empty spaces."

"Packed? Plenty of empty spaces?" I asked.

"Because," he said, "people don't understand Catholic parking."

"Oooookay?"

"Instead of having two spaces nose to nose with a driving lane behind each one, like most parking lots, this church has its parking spaces five cars deep. Each single space is long enough to accommodate an RV, an SUV, and your dinky convertible packed bumper to bumper. It means that everybody gets a parking space, and they all give up the freedom to leave until everyone else leaves. The needs of the community limit the freedom of the individual."

Whenever we gather in community—in marriage, in families, in towns, houses of worship, cities, civic groups, or as a nation—we agree to certain limitations for the benefit of the group. What we don't give up, and never should give up, are the true liberties endowed by our Creator, our God—those unalienable rights, among which are life, liberty, and the pursuit of happiness. These are rights for every day, and they don't include the right of parking.

Let's Pray:

Dear God, as one nation of many faiths and ethnic origins, let us hold as sacred those rights enshrined in our Declaration of Independence that are for all citizens of these United States. Amen.

Today's Thought Is: Liberty is an unalienable right.

THE MASK

he famed French mime, the silent Marcel Marceau, regularly performs a celebrated selection entitled "The Mask Maker." In this piece the single character onstage convincingly displays great sorrow through action and facial expression. This character then puts on a happy face mask, which, too late, is discovered to be irremovable. Struggle as he might, he cannot take it off. While his mime face is frozen in glee, his body continues to express increasing sorrow and pain. This symbolic pantomime portrays the struggles we share when we feel one way inside, but force ourselves, or are forced by others, to display a false mask upon our faces. We show the world what we think it wishes to see.

Jesus put it forcefully, "You are like whitewashed tombs—beautiful on the outside but filled on the inside with dead people's bones and all sorts of impurity." Basically, Jesus encourages us not to be false, not to be insincere, not to pretend to be one thing while hiding deceit beneath our masks. A person of faith strives for transparency. Why? Because when the light of God shines within, there is no reason to hide it beneath a mask. False masks dissolve in the light of God. So let your light shine out from your eyes, on your face, and from within your heart.

God be with us, in us, and among us. Let fall from us pretensions and
false projections. Help us in our hearts, that your light might be our goal,
our purpose, and our life; that all whom we meet might meet you in our souls.
Amen.

Today's Thought Is: "Either appear as you are,
or be as you appear."[6]

❧⫷⫸❧

*G*race is prayed with sincerity at Thanksgiving tables. Usually it's something like this: "God, we thank you for all the good gifts you've given us this year . . . for our family, for our love, for our children, for food and clothes and heat, for gathering us together, for the DVD player, for the deer I got, for our health, for teens who clean their rooms. . . ."

But here's the thing—there are plenty of people who've had a bad year and might find it hard to see anything to be thankful for. Maybe this year a job was lost, or a divorce happened, or finances are wickedly tight, or someone died. Maybe there is imprisonment, or military duty overseas, or homelessness, estrangement, abuse, or perhaps the doctor said the "C" word. Whatever the trouble, in tough circumstances it's hard to be thankful—hard, but not impossible.

God is not a puppeteer pulling our strings to make our lives easy or hard, although, admittedly, it can seem this way. The book of Job teaches that God sends rain on the just and the unjust alike, and sends sunshine on the righteous and the unrighteous. Good things happen to bad people, and bad things happen to good people. Some of it's our doing, some of it is simply life. Whatever happened this year, even if you're angry at God—take a moment to remember and give thanks that no matter what, no matter how it seems, God loves you.

Let's pray:

God, even if we feel like we have nothing to be thankful for, we're saying thanks anyway because we know you love us even when life is hard. Amen.

Today's Thought Is: **Give thanks anyway.**

*P*ictures and e-mails will be flying east and west today. Every soldier with a laptop and a digital camera, every stateside family with a desktop PC and their own camera, will be sharing Thanksgiving Day, as best as they are able, with their loved ones who are so far from home.

The media will show women and men dressed in camouflage, laughing and smiling, eating a real turkey dinner while sitting inside a large desert tent. Their plates will be heaped with turkey, gravy, mashed potatoes, cranberry sauce, and other American delights. As hard as it is to be over there in that tent, I'm wondering about those who aren't in that tent, who aren't shown on TV.

I don't want to imagine what an overly processed turkey dinner in a hermetically sealed MRE (meal, ready to eat) tastes like far from home. It can't be easy being there, eating that meal over there, knowing that the people you love are over here.

So I want to say a prayer today for all those in the armed forces, and for their children, and for their wives or husbands, girlfriends or boyfriends, moms and dads, sisters and brothers, and all those who love them, and who are loved by them.

Let's Pray:

Dear God, we're thankful this day for the many gifts you've given us, even if we wrestle with troubles in our lives. Let those who love us, and those we love, feel loved today, especially those serving overseas, no matter where they serve, or what they believe. Let them feel love now. Amen.

Today's Thought Is: **Keep them safe from harm.**

THANKSGIVING WEEK

Holy Days

*T*onight starts the annual eight-day celebration of Hanukkah, which began centuries ago with a victory of the few over the many, and the weak over the strong. Antiochus IV Epiphanes, who ruled in Israel from 175 to 163 B.C., brought Greek culture and insisted that Israeli Jews worship Greek gods. Death was the penalty for refusal.

Mattathias, a high priest of Israel, led a revolt using a small army. His son, Judah Maccabee, continued fighting for seven years. When they retook the temple in Jerusalem in 165 B.C., the rebels rededicated and purified it. Hanukkah comes from the Hebrew word for dedication. Inside the temple they found a vial containing enough oil for one night's light. Miraculously the oil lasted eight nights while Judah Maccabee searched for fresh oil. This miracle is called the Festival of Lights, and it has been celebrated in the Jewish month of Kislev ever since.

Each night in Hanukkah, a candle is lit on a menorah, an eight-branched candelabrum, and two blessings are said—one over the candles and the other in remembrance of the miracle of the oil. An extra blessing is said on the first night. There are gifts, games, meals, songs, and parties.

In this pluralistic age where we live side by side with neighbors of differing beliefs, and in this holiday season, renowned for peace and goodwill, it's right and good to know something about the People of the Book, as our Muslim neighbors would say.

Let's Pray:

You are one God with many people. In this holiday time, show us the path of goodwill and peace with our neighbors of differing faith. Amen.

Today's Thought Is: **Celebrate the Light!**

*C*hristmas wreaths are circular—you're thinking, No kidding, Reverend! Circular wreaths, you say? The unending shape of wreaths is symbolic. The circle represents eternity. Christmas wreaths are wound from evergreens. Again you're thinking, Really, Reverend, evergreens? You don't say. Evergreens symbolize life in the dead of winter. Often wreaths are left hanging all winter, reminding us of Christmas, of eternity, of life in winter. Sometimes they're left hanging simply because it's too darn cold to bother taking them down.

If you haven't hung your wreath yet, or even if you have, any time you see one this winter you might consider the wreath's symbolic and spiritual meanings of eternity and life. These symbols are all tied up in the reason for Christmas—the birth of Christ, who proclaimed eternity and new life.

Let's Pray:

Eternal God, lead us to everlasting life and remind us of yourself, of your presence in our life each time we see an evergreen wreath. Amen.

Today's Thought Is: **A Christmas wreath is more than simply something pretty.**

When I lifted the white-painted plywood well lid, ready to fill my bucket with sweet water for our drinking, what surprised me was a large living spider and her sparkling, frosted web. She reminded me of another miraculous spider—an ancient spider rumored to have saved the lives of a little family.

King Herod was afraid of the baby foretold by the three wise men. He believed only the death of every boy under the age of two would ease his nerves. So he set about their murders. Warned by God's angel, Joseph and Mary fled with their baby late one night into the desert, hoping for safety in Egypt. Fearing his disloyal subjects might love their babies more than him, Herod sent his troops into the desert to hunt babies. Mary and Joseph ran through the night, the soldiers close behind them.

Exhausted and needing rest, they found a cave, crawled inside to hide and sleep, hoping the soldiers would pass them by. A simple spider saw them enter. If spiders have a heart, then it was her heart that told her to save this baby. She spun, spun, and spun her web faster than any spider had ever spun a web before. Minutes later, soldiers arrived to search each cave. At this spider's cave, where the family hid in fear, the soldiers said, "There's a spider's web covering the entrance. Nobody's hiding in there."[1]

A fragile web woven of love and haste protected Mary and Joseph against fear and hatred. What protects us from fear and hatred?

We thank you, God, for minor miracles, for fragile beauty, and for those covered things unseen that protect us when we know it not. Amen.

Today's Thought Is: **Love is strong.**

*A*fter a recess discussion outdoors, the fifth graders asked their teacher if Christmas is about Santa Claus, or something else. Since some of the fifth graders didn't know, that means others might not know, either. So, in the interest of education, I hasten to quote the theologian Linus of the Blue Blanket:

"And it came to pass in those days, that there went out a decree from Caesar Augustus, that all the world should be enrolled. And all went to be taxed, every one into his own city. And Joseph went up from Galilee, out of the city of Nazareth, into Judaea, unto the city of David, which is called Bethlehem, to be taxed with Mary his espoused wife, being great with child. And she brought forth her firstborn son, and wrapped him in swaddling clothes, and laid him in a manger, because there was no room for them in the inn.

"And there were in the same country shepherds abiding in the field, keeping watch over their flock by night. And, lo, the angel of the Lord came upon them, and the glory of the Lord shone round about them: and they were sore afraid. And the angel said unto them, Fear not: for, behold, I bring you good tidings of great joy, which shall be to all people. For unto you is born this day in the city of David a Saviour, which is Christ the Lord. And this shall be a sign unto you: Ye shall find the babe wrapped in swaddling clothes, lying in a manger. And suddenly there was with the angel a multitude of the heavenly host praising God, and saying, Glory to God in the highest, and on earth peace, good will toward men."[2] And I add, to women.

Let's Pray:

God, thanks for curious children who ask questions, and for teachers who answer them. Amen.

Today's Thought Is: It's an ancient story that changed the world, and changes hearts.

〜⟩⟨ﻬ〜

ne day last winter I was hurrying to finish blowing the deep snow off our gravel road. I don't remember what the hurry was, but I recall working hard and fast, forward and backward, a madman with a machine—and I broke the transmission. In August, I trucked it up the River Road to a repair shop whose owner said he'd fix it in plenty of time, which he did. Five months later, with a big snowstorm threatening, I figured I'd better get that snowblower. We had to finish our prewinter chores that morning—covering the wood, putting the bikes away, nailing this, sawing that. It was already spitting flakes, making the roads slick, when we headed up to get the snowblower. It was a careful and slow drive, fueled by an internal rush of agitation as the snow mounted. We got there and retrieved the repaired machine. The next morning at five A.M., with eight inches already on the ground, I was out of bed and ready to tackle Mother Nature with my gas-powered machine. Just then we heard our faithful neighbor plowing our gravel road. It was unexpected. When I got outside to use my snowblower, there was precious little for me to do. Divine Providence had taken care of everything.

Here it is, Christmas Eve: the rush is on, and there may be a thing or two you put off, believing that you'd get round to them, but never did. All the time that's left today is to do what needs doing. Maybe you'll get it done; maybe you won't. No matter. Take it easy. Christmas will be wonderful anyway. God'll see to that.

Let's Pray:

God, on this Christmas Eve, help us relax, trust in you, slow down a bit, and remember why we celebrate this night. Amen.

Today's Thought Is: **Christmas stress isn't worth the cost of tinsel.**

*I*n my grandmother's old country, people didn't celebrate birthdays. They celebrated Name Days. Everybody with the same name celebrated on the same day. Since we didn't know on what day she was born, we picked a birthday for my grandmother—New Year's Day. Christmas is Jesus' birthday. Or is it? No one actually knows when he was born. Why this day? There are two theories. First—December 25 is borrowed from pagan celebrations. The Romans had a Saturnalia festival in late December; peoples of northern and western Europe kept holidays at similar times. Christmas, the reasoning goes, is a spin-off from, or an overlay on, pagan solstice festivals. Second—around 200 C.E. Tertullian of Carthage reported the calculation that the fourteenth of Nisan (the day of the crucifixion, according to the Gospel of John) in the year Jesus died was equivalent to March 25 in the Roman (solar) calendar. March 25 is, of course, nine months before December 25. March 25 was later recognized as the Feast of the Annunciation—the commemoration of Jesus' conception. Thus, Jesus was believed to have been conceived and crucified on the same day of the year. Exactly nine months later, Jesus was born, on December 25. This idea appears in a Christian treatise titled *On Solstices and Equinoxes,* which appears to come from fourth-century North Africa.

Let's Pray:

For whatever day he was born on, and for whatever reason we picked today,
thanks, God. Amen.

Today's Thought Is: **Merry Christmas!**

*M*erry Christmas! I can hear you saying, What's he talking about now? Christmas Day was two weeks ago. True. But today is Epiphany, January 6, which makes yesterday, January 5, customarily the last day of the Twelve Days of Christmas. Last night was "Twelfth Night," which in some places is a night of feasting. The word *epiphany* means "to show," "to make known," "to reveal," or "to manifest." In Western churches, both Protestant and Catholic, Epiphany celebrates the coming of the magi, the wise men, the three kings who brought gifts to the Christ child and who, by so doing, "revealed" or "showed" Jesus to the world as the Christ, which in Greek means "messiah." As for the three kings, in some places, they're the ones who bring gifts to good little boys and girls. Of course, we don't know that they were *kings* or that there even were *three*. We do know they were magi, or wise men of the East, perhaps of Medes, and were certainly astronomers, or maybe Zoroastrians—a sixth century B.C. religion still practiced in parts of the world—but we do continue what they started. They brought gifts that were symbols of devotion. The material gifts we give one another is a practice begun in love.[3]

Let's Pray.

Dear God, thanks for the meaningful gifts you give us, like faith, friends, and family. Reveal yourself to us. Amen.

Today's Thought Is: Celebrate Epiphany

WHY IS THIS NIGHT
DIFFERENT FROM ALL
OTHER NIGHTS?

t's believed Passover's Seder meal is celebrated for children. At the meal, the book of Exodus is read aloud, and history is celebrated in song, story, prayer, and questions. The youngest child at the table asks the questions.

Q: On all other nights, we eat all kinds of breads. Why do we eat only matzoh tonight?

A: Matzoh reminds us that when the Jews left slavery in Egypt, they had no time to bake bread. They took raw dough on their journey and baked it under the hot desert sun into hard crackers called matzoh.

Q: On all other nights, we eat many kinds of vegetables and herbs. Why do we eat bitter herbs tonight?

A: Bitter herbs remind us of the bitter and cruel way the pharaoh treated the people as slaves in Egypt.

Q: On all other nights, we do not dip one food into another. Tonight we dip the parsley in salt water and the bitter herbs into charoset. Why do we dip our foods twice tonight?

A: Dipping bitter herbs into charoset reminds us how hard the slaves worked in Egypt. The chopped apples and nuts look like the clay used to make bricks used in building the pharaoh's buildings. Parsley dipped into salt water reminds us spring is here and new life will grow. Salt water reminds us of slaves' tears.[4]

The spectacle of Seder excites the interest and the curiosity of the children.

Let's Pray:

Dear God, for all your children still living in bondage—we pray for their freedom. Amen.

Today's Thought Is: Slavery still exists in the world.

*I*n the creeds the Christ is completely human and Divine, a super soul, which places him in a rather different category than the rest of us. Palm Sunday is the Christian celebration day of when, after three years of teaching in parables, creating miracles, and ticking off the religious authorities, Jesus rides into Jerusalem on a donkey, surrounded by thousands of cheering followers. The donkey, contrary to our thinking, was not a beast of peace. It was more commonly a king's beast of war, ridden onto the battlefield because of its sure-footedness on stony ground. We can speculate that cheering crowds expected the crowning of their idealized and powerful king. What they got one week later was far from their expectations. This Christ did not follow the crowd's whim, or its desire for revolution. He followed the will and sacrificial plan of God.

For Jesus, the ideal human is not related to beauty, brawn, or brains. For Christ, the ideal is the one who follows the will of God. When we align our hearts to God through belief and prayer, trying to follow God's will, then we each become the soulful ideal human.

Let's Pray:

Dear God, so often we seek enhancement in life—better health, more wealth, smarter minds, stronger bodies. Call to us and let us hear that your ideal perfection for us is to listen and follow only you. Amen.

Today's Thought Is: **God calls. We follow.**

❧

irst, it was cosmetic surgery, and then came chemical muscular enhancement in the race for human perfection. In this series, we're talking about human perfection. But for once it's about brains, not beauty or brawn. By inserting extra copies of a memory gene into mice embryos, smart mice were created. Smart mice think better, have improved memories, and learn faster than their less-endowed siblings.[5]

Memory upgrading for humans is more complicated, but researchers are in pursuit. Ostensibly, the remedy is targeted at Alzheimer's, but the baby boom enhancement market is huge. Recently, a nurse was describing to her colleagues the supplement she takes for memory. She said, "It's, it's . . . gingko something." What middle-aged, brain-worn human wouldn't sign up for a memory upgrade? Personally, I think I could use one.

The fear surrounding the issue of genetically altered humans is that we could end up creating a two-class planet through superhumanization, or the eventual development of a superspecies and a subspecies. As always, the poor receive the short end of any economic deal, so they will not have access to genetic enhancement. Only the rich will be able to afford it. The history of capitalism shows that what were once luxuries—window glass, toothbrushes, and PCs—are now common necessities. Could necessity be the future of enhancements?[6]

Let's Pray:

Dear God, you made us who we are with our genetic flaws and our advantages.
We ask, Is it right to enhance human potential? Amen.

Today's Thought Is: **Does our DNA determine our life's course?**

hristos Anesti! That's what is said in Greek Orthodox churches on Easter. He is risen!

Humans often seek personal advantage, striving after perfection and success. We wish to improve ourselves and lives of our children. That's natural. Too often, our life's focus is this physical world, and we forget or ignore our mortality. Even if we reengineer our lives to the projected two hundred years, life will end. Christ came to prepare us for life beyond this physical world. If I understand correctly, in the Eastern Orthodox tradition, Jesus is considered the ideal human, whose life we're taught to emulate. Ultimately, to God, it's the way we live our lives that matters.

To follow Christ means believing in his resurrection, and it means seeking to live as he lived. Our bodies and brains, enhanced or otherwise, are temporary. We'll shuck them, along with their gifts and foibles, leaving us the essence of our being, with only our naked soul before God. How we lived and the love we shared is what we carry with us. These matter to God.

Christ came to show and teach us how to live and love, and to lead the way home.

Alithos Anesti! He is risen indeed!

Let's Pray:

Dear God, thank you for Christ, who lived as we should. Help us to do so; forgive us when we do not. Amen.

Today's Thought Is: Enhance your soul with love.

*R*amadan—to the Western mind this annual Islamic month of fasting is complicated. Islam follows a lunar calendar, the months of which are on average eleven days shorter than the months in the secular calendar. There are twelve Islamic lunar months, but the lunar month starts with the first sighting of the lunar crescent after the new moon. This means that Islamic months don't correspond to a particular season. Our days begin and end at midnight. Islamic lunar days begin and end at sunset.

From the shores of Maine to the shores of Hawaii, when the sun sets today the fast of Ramadan begins for America's eight million Muslims. On the opposite side of this planet, right now, the sun has already set. In those countries, Ramadan has already begun for some of the world's one billion Muslims.

Ramadan is a month of blessings shown and lived by acts of fasting, prayer, and charity. It is a time of personal inner reflection, devotion to God, and self-control. Muslims consider it an obligatory and intensive spiritual tune-up.[7]

Let's Pray:

Dear God, we all could use a spiritual tune-up now and then, because, although faith comes with belief, it also comes, like many things in life, with practice. Help us practice our faith. Amen.

Today's Thought Is: A weekly worship service and daily prayer helps keep faith tuned.

*ach morning we break our nightly fast with the morning meal we call breakfast. Not eating is part of our daily lives. Fasting is a spiritual practice many faiths encourage as a means of prayer, self-denial, and spiritual purification. During Lent, Christians fast. Hindus have several fasting rituals. In Islam, fasting during Ramadan is obligatory for almost all believers. Sick people, travelers, and women in certain conditions are temporarily exempt. During the day, abstinence is essential. At dawn abstinence begins—no food, no drink, no smoking, and no marital relations. But at night—yes, yes, yes, and yes. During Ramadan, Muslims eat a prefast meal, *suhoor,* before dawn, and a postfast meal, *iftar,* after sunset.[8] It's a month of exceptional blessings, the most important of which is learning self-control.

In churchy language, one's corporal appetites are intentionally suppressed during daylight, giving a measure of ascendancy to one's spiritual nature. Therefore, one becomes closer to God through fasting. It's a month of worship, reading the Koran, giving to charity, purifying one's behavior, and doing good deeds.

Let's Pray:

Dear God, teach us self-control. Amen.

Today's Thought Is: Fasting can bring any prayerful person closer to God.

Notes

Unless otherwise stated all biblical quotes come from the New Revised Standard Version Bible, copyright 1989, Division of Christian Education of the National Council of the Churches of Christ in the United States of America. Used by permission. All rights reserved.

EVERY DAY

1. Matthew 6:33 "But strive first for the kingdom of God and his righteousness, and all these things will be given to you as well."
2. C. S. Lewis, *Mere Christianity* (London: G. Bles, 1952).
3. Associated Press, "'Barbie Lobster' All Dolled Up Proves Easy to Pick Up," *Portland Press Herald*, December, 23, 2003, p. 3.
4. Matthew 7:15 "Beware of false prophets, who come to you in sheep's clothing but inwardly are ravenous wolves."
5. Matthew 7:7 "Ask, and it will be given to you; search, and you will find; knock, and the door will be opened for you."
6. Proverbs 22:6 GNT "Teach children how they should live, and they will remember it all their life." Scripture quotations marked GNT are from the Good News Translation in Today's English Version—Second Edition, copyright © 1992 by American Bible Society. Used by permission.
7. John Milton (1608–1674), *Comus* (Cambridge [Eng.]: Cambridge University Press, 1921), line 221. "Was I deceiv'd, or did a sable cloud turn forth her silver lining on the night?"
8. Matthew 19:24 "Again I tell you, it is easier for a camel to go through the eye of a needle than for someone who is rich to enter the kingdom of God."

9. Angelo S. Rappoport, "A Wise Lesson; or, The Dervish and the Honey Jar," *The Folklore of the Jews* (London, New York, and Bahrain: Kegan Paul, 2006).

10. Proverb 27:1 "Do not boast about tomorrow, for you do not know what a day may bring."

11. Genesis 1–11. Please read these chapters in your own Bible.

12. Leviticus 24:19–20 "Anyone who maims another shall suffer the same injury in return: fracture for fracture, eye for eye, tooth for tooth; the injury inflicted is the injury to be suffered."

13. Matthew 7:12 "In everything do to others as you would have them do to you; for this is the law and the prophets."

14. Brother Lawrence, *The Practice of the Presence of God*, revised and rewritten by Harold J. Chadwick (Gainesville, FL: Bridge-Logos Publishers, 2001).

15. Nicki Hoff-Lilavois, "Dear Diary," *The New York Times*, May 23, 2005, http://www.nytimes.com/2005/05/23/nyregion/23diary.html.

16. Thorton Wilder, *Our Town: A Play in Three Acts,* (New York: Harper Perennial Modern Classics, 2003).

17. Algernon Sidney (1622–1683), *Discourses Concerning Government*, chap. ii. sect. xxiii (Union, N.J.: Lawbook Exchange, 2002).

18. Deuteronomy 4:7 "For what other great nation has a god so near to it as the Lord our God is whenever we call to him?"

19. From the *Working Waterfront*, the monthly newspaper published by the Island Institute of Rockland, Maine.

20. Anthony de Mello, *Taking Flight* (Anand, India: Gujarat Sahitya Prakash, 1988) p. 103.

21. Courtesy of Mr. Rick Prose, West Boothbay Harbor, Maine.

22. 1 Samuel 16. Please read this chapter in your own Bible.

23. Matthew 26:39 "And going a little farther, he threw himself on the ground and prayed, 'My Father, if it is possible, let this cup pass from me; yet not what I want but what you want'"; Mark 14:36 "He said, 'Abba, Father, for you all things are possible; remove this cup from me; yet, not what I want, but what you want'"; John 19:10–11 "Pilate therefore said to him, 'Do you refuse to

speak to me? Do you not know that I have power to release you, and power to crucify you?' Jesus answered him, 'You would have no power over me unless it had been given you from above; therefore the one who handed me over to you is guilty of a greater sin'"; John 10:18 "No one takes it from me, but I lay it down of my own accord. I have power to lay it down, and I have power to take it up again. I have received this command from my Father."

24. Courtesy of the Reverend David Gaewski, conference minister, Maine Conference of the United Church of Christ, in a speech at Sugarloaf/USA, Carrabassett Valley, Maine, September 2003.

25. Compiled of material from Beliefnet.com: http://www.beliefnet.com/story/65/story_6568_1.html#contIslamiCity.com; The Five Pillars of Islam: http://www.islamicity.com/mosque/pillars.shtml#POI3; Library of Congress, Federal Research Division, Country Study: Iraq: Sunnis and the Sunni Shia Controversy; Library of Congress Call Number DS70.6 .1734 1990, http://www.loc.gov/rr/research-centers.html.

26. Michael J. Sandel, "The Case Against Perfection," *Atlantic Monthly*, April 2004, pp. 51-62.

27. Benjamin Franklin, *Poor Richard's Almanack*, "Maxims," 1734.

28. Matthew 25:39.

29. Matthew 6:21 "For where your treasure is, there your heart will be also."

30. Proverb 13:4 "The appetite of the lazy craves, and gets nothing, while the appetite of the diligent is richly supplied."

31. William Shakespeare, *The Tragedy of Hamlet* (New York: Signet Classic, 1998), act 2, scene 2, line 210.

32. Hesham A. Hassaballa, "Will the Imams Remain Silent?" Beliefnet.com, http://www.beliefnet.com/story/158/story_15872_1.html.

33. Sue Nelson, "Did Animals Have Quake Warning?" BBC News, December 31, 2004, accessed at http://news.bbc.co.uk/1/hi/world/south_asia/4136485.stm.

34. Proverbs 22:3 "The clever see danger and hide; but the simple go on, and suffer for it."

35. Mevlana Celaleddin Rumi (1207–1273), *Crazy As We Are*, trans. Dr. Nevit Ergin (Prescott, AZ: Hohm Press, 1992).

36. Sophocles, *Antigone*, trans. Nicholas Rudall (Chicago: Ivan R. Dee, 1998). Used by permission.

37. Aesop, *Aesop's Fables* (New York: Apple Paperbacks/Scholastic, 1963).

38. Ibid.

39. John 15:13 "No one has greater love than this, to lay down one's life for one's friends."

40. J. R. Minkle, "Animal Behavior: Sponge-Nose Smarty Pants," *Scientific American*, August 2005, p. 26.

41. 1 Corinthians 3:16 "Do you not know that you are God's temple and that God's Spirit dwells in you?"

42. Proverbs 29:11 "A fool gives full vent to anger, but the wise quietly holds it back."

43. Proverbs 20:7 "The righteous walk in integrity—happy are the children who follow them!"

44. Kari Lynn Dean, "Cruising at 12,666 Miles Per Gallon," *Wired*, September 2005, p. 29.

45. Luke 17:6 "The Lord replied, 'If you had faith the size of a mustard seed, you could say to this mulberry tree, "Be uprooted and planted in the sea," and it would obey you'."

46. Matthew 13:46 ". . . on finding one pearl of great value, he went and sold all that he had and bought it."

47. Mark 4:22 "For there is nothing hidden, except to be disclosed; nor is anything secret, except to come to light."

48. 1 John 3:18 "Little children, let us love, not in word or speech, but in truth and action."

49. Michael J. Sandel, "The Case Against Perfection," *Atlantic Monthly*, April 2004, pp. 51–62; 1 Corinthians 3:16 "Do you not know that you are God's temple and that God's Spirit dwells in you?" 1 Corinthians 6:19 "Or do you not know that your body is a temple of the Holy Spirit within you, which you have from God, and that you are not your own?"

50. *Beatrix Potter's Nursery Rhyme Book (World of Peter Rabbit)* (New York, Penguin Group, 2000) p. 58.

51. John 14:2 "In my Father's house there are many dwelling-places. If it were not so, would I have told you that I go to prepare a place for you?"

52. There ain't no flies on me, traditional.

53. *Homiletics*, vol. 17, no. 6 (November–December 2005), p. 66.

54. Psalm 30:2 "O Adonai, my God, I cried to you for help, and you have healed me."

55. Proverbs 4:1 "Listen, children, to a father's instruction, and be attentive, that you may gain insight."

56. Isaiah 1:17 ". . . learn to do good; seek justice, rescue the oppressed, defend the orphan, plead for the widow."

57. Astronaut Neil Armstrong. Quote available at http://www.snopes.com/quotes/onesmall.asp.

58. Proverbs 13:22 "The good leave an inheritance to their children's children, but the sinner's wealth is laid up for the righteous."

59. Proverbs 27:17 "Iron sharpens iron, and one person sharpens the wits of another."

60. Courtesy of Reverend Gary A. DeLong, executive director of the Maine Sea Coast Mission Society, Bar Harbor, Maine, http://www.seacoastmission.org.

61. David Biello, "Mice Found to Woo Mates with Song," *Scientific American*, November 2, 2005, http://www.sciam.com/article.cfm?chanID=sa003&articleID=000D1CD1-9BDA-1366-9BDA83414B7F0000.

62. Verity Murphy, "Past Pandemics That Ravaged Europe," BCC World Edition, November 7, 2005, accessed at http://newsvote.bbc.co.uk/2/hi/health/4381924.stm.

63. Paul Bloom, "Is God an Accident" *Atlantic Monthly*, December 2005, p. 106, http://www.theatlantic.com/doc/200512/god-accident12.

64. Matthew 20:1–16 "For the kingdom of heaven is like a landowner who went out early in the morning to hire laborers for his vineyard. After agreeing with the laborers for the usual daily wage, he sent them into his vineyard. When he went out about nine o'clock, he saw others standing idle in the market-place; and he said to them, 'You also go into the vineyard, and I will pay you what-

ever is right.' So they went. When he went out again about noon and about three o'clock, he did the same. And about five o'clock he went out and found others standing around; and he said to them, 'Why are you standing here idle all day?' They said to him, 'Because no one has hired us.' He said to them, 'You also go into the vineyard.' When evening came, the owner of the vineyard said to his manager, 'Call the laborers and give them their pay, beginning with the last and then going to the first.' When those hired about five o'clock came, each of them received the usual daily wage. Now when the first came, they thought they would receive more; but each of them also received the usual daily wage. And when they received it, they grumbled against the landowner, saying, 'These last worked only one hour, and you have made them equal to us who have borne the burden of the day and the scorching heat.' But he replied to one of them, 'Friend, I am doing you no wrong; did you not agree with me for the usual daily wage? Take what belongs to you and go; I choose to give to this last the same as I give to you. Am I not allowed to do what I choose with what belongs to me? Or are you envious because I am generous?' So the last will be first, and the first will be last."

65. Matthew 13:33 "He told them another parable: 'The kingdom of heaven is like yeast that a woman took and mixed in with three measures of flour until all of it was leavened.'"

66. Unnamed source, Maine Department of Health and Human Services, Augusta.

67. Luke 15:9 "When she has found it, she calls together her friends and neighbors, saying, 'Rejoice with me, for I have found the coin that I had lost.'"

68. 1 Samuel 17. Please read this chapter in your own Bible.

69. Josh Tyrangiel-Prague, "The World's Best Character Actor," *Time,* May 31, 2005.

70. 1 Samuel 16. Please read this chapter in your own Bible.

71. Ronald Reagan, "Farewell Address to the Nation," January 11, 1989, accessed at http://www.reaganfoundation.org/reagan/speeches/farewell.asp.

72. Martin Nweeia et al., "Hydrodynamic Sensor Capabilities and Structural Resilience of the Male Narwhal Tusk," Abstracts, Narwhal Tusk Discoveries, accessed at http://www.narwhal.org/index.html.

73. Ecclesiastes 3:1 "For everything there is a season, and a time for every matter under heaven." Ecclesiastes 3:11 "He has made everything suitable for its time; moreover he has put a sense of past and future into their minds, yet they cannot find out what God has done from the beginning to the end."

74. Modified from an ancient tale I once heard long ago.

75. Heifer Project International, accessed at www.heifer.org; 800-422-1311.

76. Psalm 16:11 "You show me the path of life. In your presence there is fullness of joy; in your right hand are pleasures for evermore."

77. Romans 8:28 "We know that all things work together for good for those who love God, who are called according to his purpose."

78. Psalm 111:10 NLT "Reverence for the LORD is the foundation of true wisdom. The rewards of wisdom come to all who obey him. Praise his name forever!" Scripture quotations marked NLT are taken from the Holy Bible, New Living Translation, copyright © 1996. Used by permission of Tyndale House Publishers, Inc., Wheaton, Illinois 60189. All rights reserved.

79. Henri Nouwen, *The Wounded Healer* (New York: Bantam Doubleday, 1979).

80. My Brothers' Keeper Quilt Group, http://www.reese.org/sharon/uglytalk.htm. Visit www.uglyquilts.org, or contact Flo at mbkqg@epix.net.

81. Jay Lindsay, Associated Press, Tuesday, March 16, 2004; http://www.trufresh.com/Pressreleases/Pressreleases/pressrelease26.htm.

82. Albert Schweitzer. Quote available at http://www.brainyquote.com.

83. Job 20:12 NLT "He enjoyed the taste of his wickedness, letting it melt under his tongue." Scripture quotations marked NLT are taken from the Holy Bible, New Living Translation, copyright © 1996. Used by permission of Tyndale House Publishers, Inc., Wheaton, Illinois 60189. All rights reserved.

84. Proverbs 15:4 NLT "Gentle words bring life and health; a deceitful tongue crushes the spirit." Scripture quotations marked (NLT) are taken from the Holy Bible, New Living Translation, copyright © 1996. Used by permission of Tyndale House Publishers, Inc., Wheaton, Illinois 60189. All rights reserved.

85. Matthew 7:7-8 "Ask, and it will be given to you; search, and you will find; knock, and the door will be opened for you. For everyone who asks receives, and everyone who searches finds, and for everyone who knocks, the door will be opened"; Revelation 3:20 "Listen! I am standing at the door, knocking; if you hear my voice and open the door, I will come in to you and eat with you, and you with me."

86. 1 Kings 19. Please read this chapter in your own Bible.

87. Kathleen Norris, *Amazing Grace: A Vocabulary of Faith* (New York: Riverhead Books, 1998).

88. Proverbs 10:23 "Doing wrong is like sport to a fool, but wise conduct is pleasure to a person of understanding."

89. Matthew 19:14 ". . . but Jesus said, 'Let the little children come to me, and do not stop them; for it is to such as these that the kingdom of heaven belongs.'"

90. Proverbs 21:25 "The craving of the lazy person is fatal, for lazy hands refuse to labor."

91. 1 Corinthians 3:16 "Do you not know that you are God's temple and that God's Spirit dwells in you?"

92. Exodus 20:15 "You shall not steal."

93. Matthew 18:12 "What do you think? If a shepherd has a hundred sheep, and one of them has gone astray, does he not leave the ninety-nine on the mountains and go in search of the one that went astray?"

94. This is an interpretation of the poem "The Guest House" by Rumi.

95. John 7:38 ". . . and let the one who believes in me drink. As the Scripture has said, 'Out of the believer's heart shall flow rivers of living water.'"

96. Matthew 6:19-20 "Do not store up for yourselves treasures on earth, where moth and rust consume and where thieves break in and steal; but store up for yourselves treasures in heaven, where neither moth nor rust consumes and where thieves do not break in and steal."

97. 1 Corinthians 3:19 "Be God's fool—that's the path to true wisdom."

98. Mark 9:42 "If any of you put a stumbling block before one of these little ones who believe in me, it would be better for you if a great millstone were hung around your neck and you were thrown into the sea."

99. Genesis 18:20–33 "Then the Lord said, 'How great is the outcry against Sodom and Gomorrah and how very grave their sin! I must go down and see whether they have done altogether according to the outcry that has come to me; and if not, I will know.' So the men turned from there, and went towards Sodom, while Abraham remained standing before the Lord. Then Abraham came near and said, 'Will you indeed sweep away the righteous with the wicked? Suppose there are fifty righteous within the city; will you then sweep away the place and not forgive it for the fifty righteous who are in it? Far be it from you to do such a thing, to slay the righteous with the wicked, so that the righteous fare as the wicked! Far be that from you! Shall not the Judge of all the earth do what is just?' And the Lord said, 'If I find at Sodom fifty righteous in the city, I will forgive the whole place for their sake.' Abraham answered, 'Let me take it upon myself to speak to the Lord, I who am but dust and ashes. Suppose five of the fifty righteous are lacking? Will you destroy the whole city for lack of five?' And he said, 'I will not destroy it if I find forty-five there.' Again he spoke to him, 'Suppose forty are found there.' He answered, 'For the sake of forty I will not do it.' Then he said, 'Oh do not let the Lord be angry if I speak. Suppose thirty are found there.' He answered, 'I will not do it, if I find thirty there.' He said, 'Let me take it upon myself to speak to the Lord. Suppose twenty are found there.' He answered, 'For the sake of twenty I will not destroy it.' Then he said, 'Oh do not let the Lord be angry if I speak just once more. Suppose ten are found there.' He answered, 'For the sake of ten I will not destroy it.' And the Lord went his way, when he had finished speaking to Abraham; and Abraham returned to his place."

100. Matthew 25:40 "And the king will answer them, 'Truly I tell you, just as you did it to one of the least of these who are members of my family, you did it to me.'"

101. Matthew 6:14 "For if you forgive others their trespasses, your heavenly Father will also forgive you . . ."

102. Luke 9:25 "What does it profit them if they gain the whole world, but lose or forfeit themselves?"; Luke 17:33 "Those who try to make their life secure will lose it, but those who lose their life will keep it."

103. Luke 18:1–8 "Then Jesus told them a parable about their need to pray always and not to lose heart. He said, 'In a certain city there was a judge who neither feared God nor had respect for people. In that city there was a widow who kept coming to him and saying, "Grant me justice against my opponent." For a while he refused; but later he said to himself, "Though I have no fear of God and no respect for anyone, yet because this widow keeps bothering me, I will grant her justice, so that she may not wear me out by continually coming." And the Lord said, 'Listen to what the unjust judge says. And will not God grant justice to his chosen ones who cry to him day and night? Will he delay long in helping them? I tell you, he will quickly grant justice to them. And yet, when the Son of Man comes, will he find faith on earth?'"

104. Michael J. Sandel, "The Case Against Perfection," *Atlantic Monthly*, April 2004, pp. 51–62.

105. C. S. Lewis, *The Lion, the Witch, and the Wardrobe* copyright © C.S. Lewis Pte. Ltd., 1950.

106. 1 Thessalonians 1:4 "For we know, brothers and sisters beloved by God, that he has chosen you . . ."

107. Courtesy of BBC News, "Muslim Leaders Join Condemnation," July 7, 2005, http://news.bbc.co.uk/1/hi/uk/4660411.stm.

108. Deuteronomy 32:35 "Vengeance is mine, and recompense, for the time when their foot shall slip; because the day of their calamity is at hand, their doom comes swiftly."

109. Luke 6:27 ". . . do good to those who hate you . . ."

110. Mark 4:40 "He said to them, 'Why are you afraid? Have you still no faith?'"

111. John 10:7 "So again Jesus said to them, 'Very truly, I tell you, I am the gate for the sheep.'"

112. Although popularly attributed to Pierre Teilhard de Chardin, de Chardin scholars believe this quote is not his. Scholars have not found the quotation among his works. The source is unknown.

113. Luke 7:36–50. Please read these verses in your own Bible.

114. Courtesy of Reverend Dick Wydell, Maine Conference, United Church of Christ.

115. James 5:16 "Therefore confess your sins to one another, and pray for one another, so that you may be healed. The prayer of the righteous is powerful and effective."

116. Luke 6:38 ". . . give, and it will be given to you. A good measure, pressed down, shaken together, running over, will be put into your lap; for the measure you give will be the measure you get back."

117. Courtesy of BBC News, "Dolphins 'Have Their Own Names,'" http://news.bbc.co.uk/2/hi/uk_news/scotland/edinburgh_and_east/4750471.stm.

118. Genesis 2:18–20 "Then the Lord God said, 'It is not good that the man should be alone; I will make him a helper as his partner.' So out of the ground the Lord God formed every animal of the field and every bird of the air, and brought them to the man to see what he would call them; and whatever the man called each living creature, that was its name. The man gave names to all cattle, and to the birds of the air, and to every animal of the field; but for the man there was not found a helper as his partner."

119. Rutherford Birchard Hayes, *Diary and Letters of Rutherford Birchard Hayes*, vol. 2, ed. Charles Richard Williams (Columbus: Ohio State Archaeological and Historical Society, 1922–1926), p. 272. Also available at http://www.bartleby.com/66/63/27363.html.

120. Courtesy of Reverend David Gaewski, conference minister, Maine Conference, United Church of Christ.

121. Luke 18:1–7 "Then Jesus told them a parable about their need to pray always and not to lose heart. He said, 'In a certain city there was a judge who neither feared God nor had respect for people. In that city there was a widow who kept coming to him and saying, "Grant me justice against my opponent." For a while he refused; but later he said to himself, "Though I have no fear of God and no respect for anyone, yet because this widow keeps bothering me, I will grant her justice, so that she may not wear me out by continually coming." And the Lord said, 'Listen to what the unjust judge says. And will not God grant justice to his chosen ones who cry to him day and night? Will he delay long in helping them?'"; Revelation 3:20 "Listen! I am standing at the door, knocking; if

you hear my voice and open the door, I will come in to you and eat with you, and you with me."

122. Yushi Nomura, *Desert Wisdom: Sayings from the Desert Fathers* (Maryknoll, NY: Orbis Books, 2001).

123. Nicole Lozare, "Blue Angel for Sale," *Pensacola News Journal,* February 12, 2004.

124. Micah 6:8 "He has told you, O mortal, what is good; and what does the Lord require of you but to do justice, and to love kindness, and to walk humbly with your God?"; Colossians 3:13 "Bear with one another and, if anyone has a complaint against another, forgive each other; just as the Lord has forgiven you, so you also must forgive"; Matthew 22:37 "He said to him, 'You shall love the Lord your God with all your heart, and with all your soul, and with all your mind'"; Jeremiah 31:33 "But this is the covenant that I will make with the house of Israel after those days, says the Lord: I will put my law within them, and I will write it on their hearts; and I will be their God, and they shall be my people."

125. Matthew 25:36–40 "'I was naked and you gave me clothing, I was sick and you took care of me, I was in prison and you visited me.' Then the righteous will answer him, 'Lord, when was it that we saw you hungry and gave you food, or thirsty and gave you something to drink? And when was it that we saw you a stranger and welcomed you, or naked and gave you clothing? And when was it that we saw you sick or in prison and visited you?' And the king will answer them, 'Truly I tell you, just as you did it to one of the least of these who are members of my family, you did it to me.'"

126. Matthew 13:45–46 "Again, the kingdom of heaven is like a merchant in search of fine pearls; on finding one pearl of great value, he went and sold all that he had and bought it."

127. Martha Beck, "True Confessions," *O, The Oprah Magazine,* June 2002, p. 183f.

128. Ibid.

129. Mark 4:22 "For there is nothing hidden, except to be disclosed; nor is anything secret, except to come to light."

130. Ralph Waldo Emerson's "Love," in *Essays and Poems,* (London: Phoenix/Orion Publishing, 1995), p. 91.

131. Courtesy of Reverend Dr. Roy Howard, from his sermon "When Everything Fades Away" (I Corinthians 13), Saint Mark's Presbyterian Church, Rockville, Maryland, http://www.saintmarkpresby.org/. I have modified this passage.

132. Matthew 12:33 "Either make the tree good, and its fruit good; or make the tree bad; for the tree is known by its fruit."

133. Matthew 7:3–5 "Why do you see the speck in your neighbor's eye, but do not notice the log in your own eye? Or how can you say to your neighbor, 'Let me take the speck out of your eye,' while the log is in your own eye? You hypocrite, first take the log out of your own eye, and then you will see clearly to take the speck out of your neighbor's eye."

134. Courtesy of Reverend Fred Lyon, Lewisville, Virginia, a Presbyterian minister who is pursuing his Ph.D. at Union Theological Seminary and Presbyterian School of Education.

135. Dr. Lynn Anderson, excerpt from his upcoming book *Dancing on the Rim*, to be published by Howard Books in February 2008.

136. Isaiah 55:8–9 "For my thoughts are not your thoughts, nor are your ways my ways, says the Lord. For as the heavens are higher than the earth, so are my ways higher than your ways and my thoughts than your thoughts."

137. Michael J. Sandel, "The Case Against Perfection," *Atlantic Monthly*, April 2004, pp. 51–62.

138. Ibid.

139. Reverend Barbara Brown Taylor, *Speaking of Sin: The Lost Language of Salvation* (Cambridge: Cowley Publications, 2001).

140. CNN, "Science and Space," Wednesday, February 25, 2003, http://www.cnn.com/2004/TECH/science/02/25/singapore.green.bears.ap/index.html.

141. "The Upside of Downside," *Homiletics*, vol. 16, no. 1 (January–February, 2004), p. 57–59; Maria Puente, "Disgrace, Dishonor, Infamy: They're Not So Bad Anymore," *USA Today*, May 22, 2003, 1D–2D.

142. John 8:15 "You judge by human standards; I judge no one"; Matthew 7:2 "For with the judgment you make you will be judged, and the measure you give will be the measure you get."

143. "Alexandra Cherubini '99 Stays Shoulders Above the Rest," Faces at Bates Archive, http://bates.edu/x57590.xml; ShouldersBack, About Us, Burns, Winter 2004, p. 51. http://www.shouldersback.net/ and http://www.equifit.net/aboutus.asp.

144. Christianity—Matthew 7:12 "In everything do to others as you would have them do to you; for this is the law and the prophets"; Judaism—Babylonian Talmud, trans. Michael L. Rodkinson, Book 1 (Vols. I and II), 1903, Tract Sabbath, Chapter II: Regulations Concerning the Sabbath and Hanukah Light p. 50, http://www.come-and-hear.com/shabbath/shabbath_31.html; Islam—Imam An-Nawawi, "Number 13," *Forty Hadith: An Anthology of the Sayings of the Prophet Muhammad*, trans. Denys Johnson-Davies, and Ezzeddin Ibrahim (Cambridge, Eng.: ITS 1997); Hinduism—*The Mahabharata of Krishna-Dwaipayana Vyasa*, "Mahabharata 5:1517," trans. Kisari Mohan Ganguli (published between 1883 and 1896). The Ganguli English translation of the Mahabharata is the only complete one in the public domain. Books 1–4 were proofed at Distributed Proofing (Juliet Sutherland, Project Manager), from page images scanned at sacred-texts.com. Books 5–7 and 12–15 were scanned and proofed at sacred-texts.com by John Bruno Hare. Books 8–11 and 16–18 were scanned and proofed by Mantra Caitanya; Buddhism—W. Woodville Rockhill, "Udana-Varga 5:18" (London: Trubner & Co., 1883).

145. Roy Davies and Glyn Davies, "A Comparative Chronology of Money: Monetary History from Ancient Times to the Present Day, 9,000–1 B.C.," (1996 and 1999), a timeline based on Glyn Davies's *A History of Money from Ancient Times to the Present Day*, 3rd ed. (Cardiff: University of Wales Press, 2002); Rebecca Harper, "The New Currency: Kiss Your Cash Goodbye," *Wired*, April 2004, p. 59. Mary Bellis, "The History of Major Credit Cards," http://inventors.about.com/library/inventors/blmoney.htm.

146. 1 Timothy 6:10 "For the love of money is a root of all kinds of evil, and in their eagerness to be rich some have wandered away from the faith and pierced themselves with many pains"; Hebrews 13:5 "Keep your lives free from the love of money, and be content with what you have; for he has said, 'I will never leave you or forsake you.'"

147. Psalm 23: 4 "Even though I walk through the darkest valley, I fear no evil; for you are with me; your rod and staff—they comfort me."

148. Psalm 28:7 "The Lord is my strength and my shield; in him my heart trusts; so I am helped, and my heart exults, and with my song I give thanks to him."

149. Psalm 27:1–6 "The Lord is my light and my salvation; whom shall I fear? The Lord is the stronghold of my life; of whom shall I be afraid? When evildoers assail me to devour my flesh—my adversaries and foes—they shall stumble and fall. Though an army encamp against me, my heart shall not fear; though war rise up against me, yet I will be confident. One thing I asked of the Lord, that will I seek after: to live in the house of the Lord all the days of my life, to behold the beauty of the Lord, and to inquire in his temple. For he will hide me in his shelter in the day of trouble; he will conceal me under the cover of his tent; he will set me high on a rock. Now my head is lifted up above my enemies all around me, and I will offer in his tent sacrifices with shouts of joy; I will sing and make melody to the Lord."

150. "The Art of Communication Through Preaching and Worship," *Homiletics*, vol. 16, no. 3 (May–June 2004), p. 26.

151. Proverbs 14:17a "One who is quick-tempered acts foolishly."

152. "The Art of Communication Through Preaching and Worship," *Homiletics*, vol. 16, no. 3 (May–June 2004), p. 24.

153. Ecclesiastes 12:14 "For God will bring every deed into judgment, including every secret thing, whether good or evil."

154. Luke 15:11f. Please read this parable in your own Bible.

155. From Lewis Thomas's essay "The Corner of the Eye" in *Late Night Thoughts on Listening to Mahler's Ninth Symphony* (New York: Penguin Group, 1995). Courtesy of Reverend Fred Lyon, Lewisville, Virginia, a Presbyterian minister who is pursuing his Ph.D. at Union Theological Seminary and Presbyterian School of Education.

156. Taken from "Lord of the Dance" by Sydney Carter. © 1963 Stainer & Bell, Ltd. Admin. by Hope Publishing Co., Carol Stream, IL 60188. All rights reserved. Used by permission.

157. Neal Learner, "Employers Attempt to Balance Work and Religion: Complaints Alleging Religious Discrimination Have Risen 75 Percent in the Past Decade," *The Christian Science Monitor,* April 12, 2004, http://www.csmonitor.com/2004/0412/p14s01-wmgn.html.

158. Courtesy of Reverend Dr. Roy Howard, Saint Mark's Presbyterian Church, Rockville, Maryland, http://www.saintmarkpresby.org/. I have modified this passage.

159. John 15:13 "No one has greater love than this, to lay down one's life for one's friends."

160. Proverbs 11:25 "A generous person will be enriched, and one who gives water will get water."

161. Proverbs 17:3 "The crucible is for silver, and the furnace is for gold, but the Lord tests the heart."

162. Proverbs 13:7 "Some pretend to be rich, yet have nothing; others pretend to be poor, yet have great wealth"; Proverbs 22:7 "The rich rules over the poor, and the borrower is the slave of the lender."

163. Stephen W. Eaton. "Wild Turkey (*Meleagris gallopavo*," in *The Birds of North America,* vol. 22, ed. A. Poole, P. Stettenhein, and F. Gill (Philadelphia: The Academy of Natural Sciences; Washington, D.C.: The American Ornithologists' Union, 1992).

164. Miroslav Volf, "Love Your Heavenly Enemy," *Christianity Today,* October 23, 2000, http://www.christianitytoday.com/ct/2000/012/7.94.html.

165. Mark 6:34 "As he went ashore, he saw a great crowd; and he had compassion for them, because they were like sheep without a shepherd; and he began to teach them many things."

166. William Ralph Inge (1860–1954), British dean of Saint Paul's, London. *London Observer,* February 14, 1932.

HOLIDAYS

1. Matthew 25:35-40 "'. . . for I was hungry and you gave me food, I was thirsty and you gave me something to drink, I was a stranger and you welcomed me, I was naked and you gave me clothing, I was sick and you took care of me, I was in prison and you visited me.' Then the righ-

teous will answer him, 'Lord, when was it that we saw you hungry and gave you food, or thirsty and gave you something to drink? And when was it that we saw you a stranger and welcomed you, or naked and gave you clothing? And when was it that we saw you sick or in prison and visited you?' And the king will answer them, 'Truly I tell you, just as you did it to one of the least of these who are members of my family, you did it to me.'"

2. Song of Solomon 1:1–2 "The Song of Songs, which is Solomon's. Let him kiss me with the kisses of his mouth! For your love is better than wine . . ."; 1 Corinthians 13:4 "Love is patient; love is kind; love is not envious or boastful or arrogant . . ."

3. http://www.infoplease.com/spot/aprilfools1.html and http://wilstar.com/holidays/aprilfool.htm.

4. http://www.snopes.com/holidays/aprilfools/origins.asp.

5. Proverbs 17:21 "The one who begets a fool gets trouble; the parent of a fool has no joy"; Proverbs 26:10 "Like an archer who wounds everybody is one who hires a passing fool or drunkard"; Psalm 14:1 "Fools say in their hearts, 'There is no God.' They are corrupt, they do abominable deeds; there is no one who does good."

6. Mevlana Celaleddin Rumi (1207–1273), *Crazy As We Are*, trans. Dr. Nevit Ergin, (Prescott, AZ: Hohm Press, 1992).

HOLY DAYS

1. An ancient legend.
2. Luke 2:1–14, King James Version.
3. http://www.cresourcei.org/cyepiph.html.
4. Holidays on the Net: Your Source for Holiday Celebrations, "Why Is This Night Different from All Other Nights?" http://www.holidays.net/passover/question.html.
5. Joe Z. Tsien, "Building a Brainier Mouse," *Scientific American*, April 2000, pp. 62–68.
6. Michael J. Sandel, "The Case Against Perfection," *Atlantic Monthly*, April 2004, pp. 51–62.

7. Colorado State University, Islamic Holidays and Observances, "Ramadan, the Month of Fasting," www.colostate.edu/Orgs/MSA/events/Ramadan .html; Holly Hartman, "Ramadan, the Month of Fasting," www.factmonster .com/spot/ramadan1.html; Tajuddin B. Shu`aib, Da`awah "Essentials of Ramadan, The Fasting Month," www.usc.edu/dept/MSA/fundamentals/ pillars/fasting/tajuddin/fast_1.html. USC Department of Education, "What is Ramadan?," www.usc.edu/dept/MSA/fundamentals/pillars/ fasting/tajuddin/fast_12.html#HEADING11; Colorado State University, Islamic Holidays and Observances, "Ramadan, the Month of Fasting," www.colostate.edu/Orgs/MSA/events/Ramadan.html.

8. U.S. Naval Observatory, Astronomical Applications Department, "Crescent Moon Visibility and the Islamic Calendar," http://aa.usno.navy.mil/ faq/docs/islamic.html.

Acknowledgments

I thank my teachers who believed in me—especially my seventh-grade remedial reading teacher, who taught me to read. Thanks to the English Department at the University of Massachusetts and its professors, Harold T. McCarthy, Vincent DiMarco, and Charles Moran. Thanks to those at the Divinity School at Yale University, particularly Reverend Joan Forsberg, Professor Gaylord Noyse, Professor William Meile. And to the best street-corner teacher, preacher, and storyteller anywhere, thank you, Brother Blue (aka Reverend Dr. Hugh Morgan Hill), because I know you made all the difference. Father Theophane Boyd, you gave me grounding when my soul took flight.

Heartfelt thanks go to my father and mother, Peter and Janet Panagore, for use of their Cape Cod home to finish this book, but mostly for encouraging me since the day I was born to follow my dreams and never, ever quit, and to Michelle Miclette, my totally tolerant wife, who painstakingly edited my sermons for years, and to Lex and Andy (two lights in my heart) for putting up with me.

Without the help of my dear friends, colleagues, mentors, and neighbors who held my hand, kicked me in the keister, provided opportunity, assistance, encouragement, or insight through—I could not have thrived. I am grateful to Donald Scott, Reverend Bryan Breault, Reverend Henry Brinton, Bob Jones, Otis Maxfield, Rabbi Harry Skye, Steve Thaxton, Deborah Sample, Linda Ford, Kurt Kruger and the Board of Trustees of the First Radio Parish Church of America.

I am obliged to Meredith Hays, my literary agent at Imprint Agency, who believed in my work from the moment she read it and who is the best agent in all of New York City; and to my editors at Touchstone Fireside, an imprint of Simon & Schuster, Nancy Hancock, who bought my book and gave me a chance; Cherise Davis, who helped me along, and Meghan Stevenson, whose cheerful talent and professional vision honed my writing.

But most of all, thanks to God, the Nameless Divine who gives grace and who lives in my heart like starlight.